Charles S. Robinson

From Samuel to Solomon

Charles S. Robinson

From Samuel to Solomon

ISBN/EAN: 9783337318505

Printed in Europe, USA, Canada, Australia, Japan

Cover: Foto ©Lupo / pixelio.de

More available books at **www.hansebooks.com**

From

Samuel to Solomon.

BY

CHARLES S. ROBINSON, D. D.

AMERICAN TRACT SOCIETY,
150 NASSAU STREET, NEW YORK.

CONTENTS.

I. CONSCIENTIOUS ROUTINE FOR CHILDREN 7
"Now Samuel did not yet know the Lord, neither was the word of the Lord yet revealed unto him." 1 SAM. 3:7.

II. AWAKENED RESTLESSNESS IN CHILDREN..... 17
"And Eli perceived that the Lord had called the child." 1 SAM. 3:8.

III. SPIRITUAL SURRENDER FOR CHILDREN 27
"And it shall be, if he call thee, that thou shalt say, Speak, Lord; for thy servant heareth." 1 SAM. 3:9.

IV. ELI'S FAMILY GOVERNMENT..................... 37
"For I have told him that I will judge his house for ever for the iniquity which he knoweth; because his sons made themselves vile, and he restrained them not." 1 SAM. 3:13.

V. AN OLD TESTAMENT REVIVAL 46
"Then Samuel took a stone, and set it between Mizpeh and Shen, and called the name of it Ebenezer, saying, Hitherto hath the Lord helped us." 1 SAM. 7:12.

VI. "VOX POPULI, VOX DEI" 55
"And the Lord said to Samuel, Hearken unto their voice, and make them a king." 1 SAM. 8:22.

VII. PRAYER ANSWERED UNDER PROTEST.......... 66
"Now therefore hearken unto their voice: howbeit yet protest solemnly unto them, and show them the manner of the king that shall reign over them." 1 SAM. 8:9.

VIII. SAMUEL'S FAREWELL ADDRESS................. 76
"Only fear the Lord, and serve him in truth with all your heart: for consider how great things he hath done for you." 1 SAM. 12:24.

IX. ONE SIN TOO MANY.............................. 85
"And Samuel said unto Saul, I will not return with thee: for thou hast rejected the word of the Lord, and the Lord hath rejected thee from being king over Israel." 1 SAM. 15:26.

X. GOD'S ESTIMATE OF HUMAN AVAILABILITY ... 95
"But the Lord said unto Samuel, Look not on his countenance, or on the height of his stature; because I have refused him." 1 SAM. 16:7.

XI. GOD'S ESTIMATE OF HUMAN CHARACTER 107
"The Lord seeth not as man seeth; for man looketh on the outward appearance, but the Lord looketh on the heart." 1 SAM. 16:7.

XII. DAVID AND GOLIATH 117
"And all this assembly shall know that the Lord saveth not with sword and spear: for the battle is the Lord's, and he will give you into our hands." 1 SAM. 17:47.

XIII. REAL FRIENDSHIP 128
"And Jonathan said to David, Go in peace, forasmuch as we have sworn both of us in the name of the Lord, saying, The Lord be between me and thee, and between my seed and thy seed for ever. And he arose and departed: and Jonathan went into the city." 1 SAM. 20:42.

XIV. FORGIVENESS AS A FORCE 139
"Then David arose, and cut off the skirt of Saul's robe privily." 1 SAM. 24:4.

XV. THE DEAD MARCH OF SAUL 147
"So Saul died, and his three sons, and his armor-bearer, and all his men, that same day together." 1 SAM. 31:6.

XVI. GREATNESS BY GENTLENESS 155
"And David went on, and grew great, and the Lord God of hosts was with him." 2 SAM. 5:10.

XVII. SEEKING THE ARK OF THE COVENANT 166
"And David arose, and went with all the people that were with him from Baale of Judah, to bring up from thence the ark of God." 2 SAM. 6:2.

XVIII. PROSPECT AND RETROSPECT 177
"Who am I, O Lord God? and what is my house, that thou hast brought me hitherto? And this was yet a small thing in thy sight, O Lord God: but thou hast spoken also of thy servant's house for a great while to come." 2 SAM. 7:18, 19.

XIX. DAVID'S SIN AND NATHAN'S PARABLE 186

"And Nathan said to David, Thou art the man." 2 SAM. 12:7.

XX. DAVID'S PENITENTIAL PSALM 198

"Wash me, and I shall be whiter than snow." PSA. 51:7.

XXI. DAVID'S PSALM OF PARDON 209

"Blessed is he whose transgression is forgiven, whose sin is covered." PSA. 32:1.

XXII. THE REBELLION OF ABSALOM 220

"And there came a messenger to David, saying, The hearts of the men of Israel are after Absalom." 2 SAM. 15:13.

XXIII. MOURNING FOR ABSALOM 234

"And the king was much moved, and went up to the chamber over the gate, and wept: and as he went, thus he said, O my son Absalom, my son, my son Absalom! would God I had died for thee, O Absalom, my son, my son!" 2 SAM. 18:33.

XXIV. THE VOICE OF A ROCK 245

"The Rock of Israel spake to me." 2 SAM. 23:3.

XXV. THE CORONATION OF A LIFE 255

"Be thou strong therefore, and show thyself a man." 1 KINGS 2:2.

XXVI. THE FIRST THING TO DO 266

"In Gibeon the Lord appeared to Solomon in a dream by night: and God said, Ask what I shall give thee." 1 KINGS 3:5.

XXVII. THE DEDICATION OF THE TEMPLE 277

"But will God indeed dwell on the earth? behold the heaven and heaven of heavens cannot contain thee; how much less this house that I have builded?" 1 KINGS 8:27.

XXVIII. THE QUEEN OF SHEBA'S VISIT 289

"And when the queen of Sheba heard of the fame of Solomon concerning the name of the Lord, she came to prove him with hard questions." 1 KINGS 10:1.

XXIX. SOLOMON'S FALL 300

"And Solomon did evil in the sight of the Lord, and went not fully after the Lord, as did David his father." 1 KINGS 11:6.

PREFACE.

WHENEVER a New Testament truth is found incarnated in an Old Testament biography, the analysis of each chapter of this will be sure to yield instruction. Four histories—Samuel's and Saul's, David's and Solomon's—cross the highest lines of Israel's splendor as a kingdom. Whoever understands those men will have attained a knowledge of human nature which will prove valuable to him as a citizen and a Christian.

It is easy to call the contents of this volume lectures; but the fairer thing to say would be that they have all done their duty in the pulpit just the same as if they had been sermons. I am pleased to detect in them repetitions and reiterations now and then; for it shows a fearless desire to press the expository lessons as they came from the four teachers whose lives were so individual and yet in many respects so alike.

More and more am I convinced, as years move on, that the true secret of a pastor's influence and success is found in the one counsel: "Preach the word; be instant in season, out of season; reprove, rebuke, exhort with all long-suffering and doctrine."

CHARLES SEYMOUR ROBINSON.

57 East Fifty-fourth Street, New York,
FEBRUARY 25, 1889.

FROM
SAMUEL TO SOLOMON.

I.

CONSCIENTIOUS ROUTINE FOR CHILDREN.

"Now Samuel did not yet know the Lord, neither was the word of the Lord yet revealed unto him."—1 *Sam.* 3:7.

It would be difficult to find another scene in the whole Bible so full of dramatic interest as the account of Samuel's early call to the ministry of leadership in the Israelitish nation and the office of priest and prophet in the Old Testament church. That night-spectacle grows fairly weird and beautiful as we attempt to reproduce it in our imagination. The lamps of the seven-branched candlestick are mentioned here for the last time in history; the whole narrative suggests change; a new order for the people is soon to be brought out of the confusion.

Shadows lie heavily within that sacred inclosure; the embroidered folds of the Tabernacle curtains are thin, so that a summons might easily be heard through the partitions; the steps fall noiselessly upon the floor. The young child sleeps with the unconscious fearlessness of youth, but a mysterious Voice awakes him just before daybreak. Unsuspicious and unalarmed, he supposes that Eli has wanted him for a momentary service of waiting. The old man is unaccountably dull, probably in his turn judging that his ward has been dreaming, and Samuel goes back and drops down into instant drowsiness once more. Again comes the sound of the Voice, and without a murmur of petulant feeling that amiable child reports for commonplace duty. Thus the night wears away, and the dialogue continues till at last even Eli's curiosity becomes thoughtful; the mature priest consents to be taught by his young servitor; out of the mouth of this babe is ordained strength; God's tones are recognized, and the soul of Samuel bends in acquiescent humility before Jehovah.

Here are represented three phases of religious experience in children. A study of this story will show parents and teachers much which ought to be supremely helpful in their dealings with those young persons who come under their care. Our present space in speaking we shall have to distribute over these phases in turn, taking up one at a time as the chapter invites us. We simply enumerate them beforehand for the sake of order: first, conscientious routine; then awakened restlessness; and lastly, spiritual surrender to the full service of God.

There is, first, the period of conscientious routine. For a while every child born of Christian parents, and trained as Samuel was, will follow the traditions his father and mother have passed on down to him in course of education. It is needful now that we become familiar with the facts. One of the more scholarly of our modern commentators tells us that the earlier verses, as rendered in our common English Bibles, give no very clear idea of the real meaning, as they make Eli's dimness of eyes, his being laid down in his place, and his not being able to see, all mark the moment of Samuel's being laid down to sleep, and leave indefinite the meaning of the lamp going out in the temple, besides grammatically putting the call of Samuel as occurring *before* he had laid down to sleep. But common sense will keep the English reader straight. Eli's eyes were dim by reason of age; he was lying in his place at night, the lamp was not yet out for the night, and Samuel was lying down. Eli's "place" is explained by some of the ancient commentators as "in the inner part of the court, near to the tabernacle;" and Samuel is supposed (after the Eastern fashion) to be asleep quite near, perhaps just outside the door, ready to answer Eli's call at any time, and be eyes to the blind man. Hence it will be better for us to read over the narrative as we find it in the new Revision. Some few changes in the phraseology will have to be noticed in passing:

"And the child Samuel ministered unto the Lord before Eli. And the word of the Lord was precious in those days; there was no open vision. And it came to pass at that time, when Eli was laid down in his place (now his eyes had begun to wax dim, that he could not see), and the lamp of God was not yet gone out, and Samuel was laid down to sleep, in the temple of the Lord, where the ark of God was, that the Lord called Samuel: and he said, Here am I. And he ran unto Eli and said, Here am I; for thou calledst me. And he said, I called not; lie down again. And he went and lay down. And the Lord called yet again, Samuel. And Samuel arose and went to Eli, and said, Here am I; for thou calledst me. And he answered, I called not, my son; lie down again. Now Samuel did not yet know the Lord, neither was the word of the Lord yet revealed unto him."

Here, then, is disclosed to us the exact historic point in the experience of this young lad indicated by the term we have employed. He was living along quietly, engaged in the services of a conscientious routine with Eli.

A very pathetic picture is presented of the little fellow in one of the previous chapters of this book: "But Samuel ministered before the Lord, being a child, girded with a linen ephod. Moreover, his mother made him a little coat, and brought it to him from year to year, when she came up with her husband to offer the yearly sacrifice."

This young lad's mother brought him each year new clothing, such as he would need for all ordinary wear; but Eli seems to have put him into priest's dress at once, although he was not a priest at all. He wore an "ephod," so the story says. That means a decent linen garment of two parts, front and back, and joined at the shoulders, a sort of double apron of white cloth. And our minds are arrested by the sight of this quiet and industrious boy doing his tasks there among the folds of the Tabernacle.

But now it is just as well to settle at once that it was not the showiness of Samuel's position, nor the shining of his cleanly robe, nor even the place where his mother put him, which gave him favor in the sight of God; for the sons of Eli had all this in similar kind, but they behaved awfully and were punished in a way afterwards that made the nation's ears tingle. It was Samuel's fidelity to duty, and his reverence for God's house and God's people, his care, his watchfulness, and his serious, sedate demeanor while about it, that made his work every day acceptable to Eli and to Jehovah, the great and holy God whom he ministered unto.

Then, too, we ought to remember that the word "minister" means only "a servant." It is not a name of office, but of work. It should never render any man proud, but always keep him humble.

Does any one ask what it was which Samuel found to do in the Tabernacle? We do not know exactly: but we can guess somewhere in the region of the truth. I think we might quote the words of the very wise and quaint commentator, Matthew Henry, on this head:

"He did well, indeed, for he ministered to the Lord according as his capacity was. He learned his catechism, and was doubtless constant to his devotions, soon learned to read, and took his pleasure in the law of God. He ministered before Eli: that is, he served under his inspection and as he ordered him; but not before Eli's sons, for all parties were agreed that they were unfit to be his tutors. Perhaps he attended immediately on Eli's person, was ready to him to fetch and bring as he had occasion; and that is in the verse called 'ministering to the Lord.' Some little services perhaps he was employed in about the altar, though much under the age appointed by the law for the Levites' ministration. He could light a candle or hold a dish, or run on an errand or shut an open door; and because he did this with a pious disposition or temper of mind, it is called 'ministering to the Lord,' and great notice is taken of it. After a while he did his work so well that Eli appointed that he should minister as the priests did, because he saw that God was accepting the boy and was with him."

What is it possible for any child now to do, as a follower of the Lord Jesus Christ, under the family rule? The very quietness of such a question shows how unnecessary it will be to try to give it an exhaustive answer. Young people can be taught to pray, to take the care of some practical schemes of usefulness, to study the Word of God diligently, to contribute money to religious causes, to become interested in the poor, to speak words of counsel and encouragement and warning to such as need direction or assistance. The grand old moralities are always within their reach: fidelities at school, courtesies to the aged, consideration for the weak, keeping the Sabbath, aiding in household cares, and full obedience to all God's commands.

How far is this truly religious? That is a singularly profound question; it cannot always be answered. Children differ extremely. Some of them become spiritual Christians quite early; some never know the date of any experience that might be considered a regeneration; some are alert, imaginative, poetic, sensitive; others are slow, heavy, and run to rigid moralities with supreme delight and conscientious satisfaction. It is always right to do right, and God loves a virtuous, correct life. Of this we can be comfortably certain.

As to the spiritual condition of Samuel at this period of his career, there is found one verse in the record which has given some trouble: "Now Samuel did not yet know the Lord, neither was the word of the Lord yet revealed unto him." Even our venerable translators tried twice upon it; for the margin says: "Thus did Samuel before he knew the Lord, and before the word of the Lord was revealed unto him." Evidently there passed a vivid and permanent change over this boy's heart and history in that night's experience: God called him. The scene is solemn and impressive as we watch that unsuspicious lad going backwards and forwards, trying to find out whose was the voice he heard and to learn what it wished him to do. Twice he heard, and made the mistake of supposing that Eli, his natural monitor, was the one who wanted him for some real purpose. But Eli was as blind as the boy in his unconscious ignorance, and seems to have supposed Samuel was awakened by a dream.

Here then we may as well arrest our present exposition. In this first phase of childish experience we see that Samuel was moral and dutiful, obedient, and to a certain extent religiously inclined. God was dealing with him, but neither the lad nor his counsellor knew it.

A single question arises now which may profitably claim a notice. Is there in modern times anything that answers to this description of a child's religion? Much, indeed: and yet I choose to answer the inquiry with only one illustration. It may be of the best interest for me to relate here, almost in the words of his autobiography, the fascinating story of Goethe, the great German poet and philosopher, as he penned it in his mature years for the world to read.

The young Wolfgang had gone no farther, at this period of his precocious boyhood, so he says, than to keep his convictions along on the plane of the article of simple belief in an overruling Power. He tells us he cherished an unbroken confidence that the God who stands in immediate connection with nature, and owns it and loves it as his work, seemed to him in those days the proper Supreme Being, who might be brought into closer relationship with man, as with everything else, and who would take care of him, as of the motion of the stars, the days and seasons, the animals and plants. There were texts of the Gospels which explicitly stated this. The lad could ascribe no form to this

Being; he therefore sought him in his works, and would, in the good Old Testament fashion, build him an altar. Nature's productions were set forth as images of the world, over which a flame was to burn, signifying the aspirations of man's heart towards his Maker. He therefore brought out of the collection of natural objects which he possessed, and which had been increased as chance directed, the best ores and other specimens of earths and rocks.

But the prime difficulty was as to how they should be arranged and raised into a pile. His father possessed a beautiful red-lacquered music-stand, ornamented with gilt flowers, in the form of a four-sided pyramid with different elevations, which had been found convenient for a quartet, but lately was not much in use. He laid hands on this, and built up his representatives of nature one above the other in steps, so that it all looked quite pretty and at the same time sufficiently significant.

On an early sunrise his first worship of God was to be celebrated; but the young priest had not yet settled how to produce a flame which should at the same time emit an agreeable odor. At last it occurred to him to combine the two, as he possessed a few fumigating pastiles which diffused a pleasant fragrance with a glimmer, if not with a flame. Nay, this soft burning and exhalation seemed a better representation of what passes in the heart than an open flame. The sun had already risen, but the neighboring houses concealed the east. At last it glittered above the roofs; a burning-glass was at once taken up and applied to the pastiles, which were fixed on the summit of the pile in a fine porcelain saucer. Everything succeeded according to the wish, and the service was complete.

The altar remained as a peculiar ornament of the room which had been assigned to him in the new house. Every one regarded it only as a well-arranged collection of natural curiosities. The lad knew better, but concealed his knowledge. He longed for a repetition of the solemnity. But unfortunately, just as the most opportune sun arose, the porcelain saucer was not at hand; he placed the pastiles directly on the upper surface of the stand; they were kindled, and so great was the devotion of the young priest that he did not observe, until it was too late, the mischief his sacrifice was doing. The pastiles had burned mercilessly into the red lacquer and beautiful gold flowers, and, as if some evil spirit had disappeared, had left their black, ineffaceable mark.

Thus ended Goethe's juvenile experiment in natural religion. The mischief could be covered up with the largest pieces of his show-materials; but the spirit for any new offerings was gone.

"The accident might almost be considered a hint and a warning," so remarks this singular man in a closing comment upon his own story, "in wishing to approach the Deity in such a way."

II.

AWAKENED RESTLESSNESS IN CHILDREN.

"AND ELI PERCEIVED THAT THE LORD HAD CALLED THE CHILD."
1 *Sam.* 3:8.

It is possible that such a case as that of the poet Goethe, which has already been noticed, may be considered as unusual and extreme. And sure we are that the young Wolfgang was a singularly imaginative child, and in the end the development of his infant piety was never of the most exemplary sort.

Really, a much better illustration for our present use could be found almost anywhere among our own Christian households. I should like to be permitted to perpetuate here one incident that occurred under my own observation in a parish of which I was for a while the pastor; and this for the sake of recalling the pathetic memory of one of my little friends. A young lad, four or five years old, used to hold a religious service regularly upon the Sabbath in his father's parlor. He was accustomed to summon the other children, and conduct the ordinary exercises of public worship after his own fashion. He would give out the hymn and all would sing it with their quaint music. They would repeat the Lord's Prayer in unison. Then an older member of the audience would read the brief lesson from the Word, and at the proper moment this juvenile evangelist would mount an ottoman for his pulpit and deliver his sermon with a reverent solemnity which older preachers might well emulate. Of course, a contribution invariably was taken at the close of the meeting.

Was there any good in this? It would be difficult to pronounce upon the undertaking. We cannot say what these home-promptings of religiously-directed feeling amount to anyway. One touching recollection comes to my mind now. There was brought to me, after a lengthened series of assemblies one winter, the sum of fifty-three cents for a grand result in money; and this was added (receipt being given with my own hand) to our church subscription of many thousands of dollars to erect a building for the Mission School.

That boy is now beyond childish years in strength and zeal; the sweet girl, who sang her part and passed the plate, has gone away into a higher service in heaven; the home continues yet, as it always was, a centre of life and love in the gospel; and this small record is dismissed to its end as an instance of conscientious routine, with a pastor's proud gladness as he thinks affectionately of the group which he remembers through the years.

But we move forward in our patient exposition. The matter for consideration on the present occasion is the second in order of the three phases of child-life: namely, the awakened restlessness of children under the repeated call of God. "And the Lord called Samuel again the third time. And he arose and went to Eli, and said, Here am I; for thou calledst me. And Eli perceived that the Lord had called the child. Therefore Eli said unto Samuel, Go, lie down; and it shall be, if he call thee, that thou shalt say, Speak, Lord; for thy servant heareth."

The young lad lay down quietly as he was bidden. If he slept, his heart still kept awake; for he was waiting to hear what the God who called him twice before had now to speak in the ear of his soul. When God calls a child twice, it may be expected that he will soon call him a third time. The Lord often speaks to a child directly, when his parent, his teacher, or his pastor is dull of apprehension. Eli was not ready to admit that, in all likelihood. Many a man of God since that day has told a youthful inquirer to go and lie down again, because he himself was not familiar enough with the divine voice to recognize it when it came. But there must be discrimination even in our surprise over Eli as well as in our censure. For God often is exceedingly direct, and of necessity individual or actually exclusive, in talking with children. Samuel could hear what the Lord said to Samuel better than Eli could hear what the Lord said to Samuel. At any rate, God did in this one instance make his voice heard by a child when an older and wiser person heard nothing at all.

But at last the call was recognized. When the third summons came, even this old man perceived that God was speaking to his ward among the shadows of the Tabernacle in the night. It is much to Eli's credit that he found out his own mistake and swiftly corrected it. His example ought to serve as a caution to other religious teachers to beware of bidding any child to lie down when the almighty God is arousing his conscience with a celestial call.

All this is legitimate instruction, and it comes easily from the Old Testament story. But we shall be wiser to press at once into our household experience.

There is a period in the history of almost every one who, reared in a Christian land, has been more or less directly under the pressure of the truth, in which he really faces the great question of his relation to God. And the effort is often an earnest one and is directed towards a positive decision concerning a religious life.

This period you may recognize in yourself, or detect in others, almost always by certain unmistakable signs. There will be outward manifestations of solicitude which will show how seriously the soul contemplates its own experience. Skill, however, and especially patience, will be needed to understand these revelations of inward struggle. They often partake of the nature of strategy, and press their advance in the line of a precise contradiction. Then they will have to be read, like Hebrew syllables, from right to left.

For example, you see a young man inquisitive and impetuous, ready to speak about his religious feelings, but eminently heterodox in every expression he makes. Old creeds are too narrow for him, and old forms of thought are discarded with an appearance of malevolence or spite. He dares to doubt what all education has been trying to impress upon his heart as absolutely sacred. He is in a mood of mind alarming to most of those who converse with him. Authority is lightly esteemed. Dogmatic utterances of doctrine are irreverently rejected. He now ventures to cherish views of his own. Put on his manhood to defend them, he takes an evidently malicious delight in observing how shocked are the minds of those who listen to his bold and mischievous speculations. Opinionated and headstrong, he seems to be moved with a restless spirit of contradiction or dissent, and grows more and more defiant.

You see a young woman, less demonstrative somewhat, because less argumentative, but very much in the same temper, or distemper, of mind. She is impatient of all attempt at control, and imperiously self-willed under any form of expostulation. She affects gayeties she does not enjoy, and clamors for pleasures for which in reality she has no taste. With a high profession of contempt for the opinions of those whom she understands now to be painfully on the watch for her, she seems to court the half-mournful, half-indignant censures bestowed justly on her caprice and perversity. Proud and wilful, she will not hear one word of remonstrance she can by any ingenuity avoid. She will curl her lip against any appeal, replying to it in a strain of wildest remark, and casting oftentimes most unreasonable sneers at everything she would be supposed traditionally to hallow. And the more pointed her wit and the more hateful the sarcasm, the more satisfied in her wicked spirit she appears to be. The spectacle seems pitiful, and would in the outset seem hopeless if it were not that these persons, as we daily associate with them, appear conscientious, and certainly do remain moral in behavior and in spirit measurably devout.

Such demonstrations are often seriously alarming to an affectionate circle around who are watching for better things. During the winter that I had charge of the Bible-class last we enjoyed what we considered a season of special outpouring of the Spirit of God. It was at that time I found a letter upon the question-wire which perhaps it is better that I should reproduce here.

"I am constrained to seek your advice and help under a sense of embarrassment and actual fear. You know my children, my son and my daughter. It has grieved me for years to see them growing up so unconcerned for themselves. They are now just entering society; and my heart is exceedingly anxious to have them truly converted. There can be no safety for them unless they are experimentally grounded by saving faith upon the Lord Jesus Christ before they are exposed to the world. Especially at this time, when others are going into the kingdom, I have been looking for their immediate change.

"But to my surprise, they both seem farther off than ever. They grow ribald about the meetings. My daughter is actually spiteful at times, and says the wildest sorts of things. And her brother encourages her, though he admits that she is acting strangely. I think they confirm and countenance each other in their rebelliousness and sin. They reject exhortations. They go to church, but come home declaring they do not believe what you say from the pulpit. Every day they are becoming more and more violent. They introduce the subject of religion themselves in my presence, for no other reason (as I conjecture) than to break out with some ridicule or reproach.

"I confess I am frightened. I do not know what to do in such straits. Counsel me and pray for me. It seems to me I cannot bear that these children of the covenant should become skeptics."

Thus the sad epistle concludes with the name. There can be no doubt concerning this as a living experience; it could be paralleled over and over again even now. The first thing needed in treating it, or even in treating of it, is to gain, if possible, a true and sufficient explanation of the exhibition which is made. What is it that causes these alarming demonstrations which startle friends and strangers so?

It is very easy for parents and Christian friends to be mistaken here in all such cases. This point once reached by any young man, his history becomes involved and measurably intricate. And sooner or later it is reached. Every individual of us, in these communities lit with truth, comes one day to see that his path to heaven is unlike that of any other person, and henceforth he must journey on alone. That thought is revolutionary. Every intrusion of another's experience upon his seems like a new offer of marriage to a bride pressed upon her wedding morning. The soul gets offended by an impertinent profession of interest while it is preparing to put on the white garments of its espousal to Christ. But the thing to be remembered is this: "And Eli perceived that the Lord had called the child." Men and women may forget this, and grow as sorrowfully "amazed" as was Mary when she rebuked Jesus for not paying more attention to her feelings. They ought to recollect those calm words: "Wist ye not that I must be about my Father's business?"

For really this is the explanation of the perverse disclosure thus made. Instead of becoming unbelievers, many of these persons are more nearly believers than ever before. They are at any rate roused out of the dead rut of indifference. And in so far their posture of mind is hopeful. Remember that it is not the delirious *words* of one in a fever, horrible as they may sound on our startled ears, that are his peril; *cure the fever* and the tongue will do its duty better. There is in this experience much that is worthy of truest sympathy. And so far from bitter or hasty rebuke being just the thing to meet it, nothing could be more ill-advised and dangerous.

The value of the crisis is what should render it so inexpressibly welcome. Oh, is it true that God is now calling my child? Did Hannah dream that night what was going on up at the Tabernacle? Would that she as well as Eli had been on the bended knees of their souls before the covenant-keeping God! Who can regret that the hour has arrived when the soul of his child must deal unhindered and solitary with the Spirit of grace? Better for us then to wrestle the more mightily in prayer, and leave the conflict to go on under the leadings of Omnipotent Grace, till the turbidness grows clear.

Let us understand that men and women are often in the throes of deepest conviction of sin when they seem most careless or even most belligerent. A secret misgiving is in their minds. A frightened sense of insecurity causes them to put on a face of bold bravado. The truth is, however, they are entering the long wrestle with the unknown Angel of the Covenant. When they gain the victory, as by the grace and mercy of God they frequently do, they will discover that they have not been contending with old creeds they have disputed nor with the formulas of instruction they have spurned, but with the Almighty himself, who in the moment of their first persistency has revealed to them that the fight was to be one of life and death.

Every man who is truly a man is conscious of a year and a day when the burden of his great secret of life came upon him. First dawned the perception of a purpose in his creation, then came his relationship of subjection to God, the lower to the higher, the sinful to the Sinless. No matter how it came.

It is the Spirit of grace, directly, that brings this thought to some while they rest in the careless enjoyments of closing childhood. It comes out of the dark like the voice to young Samuel in the temple. Oh, how sober is the meditation that falls into the heart when under the monitions of the family altar or the pulpit we earliest learn these vague, half-understood yearnings of our souls to have been echoes waked by the gracious whisper of Jehovah! Then it is that the inexperienced child needs sympathy and help from the guidance that is nearest it. Untried before, startled now, it looks up at the nameless and indescribable endeavors of earthly existence.

It matters little where this impression took its origin. The occasions vary, as personal histories vary; and few men have exactly the same story to tell. But such hours there are, and very precious they ought to be. They mould the soul for the future, fill it with yearning, kindle it with worthy impulse, and gird it with might. Let no one despise his religious convictions. Let no one neglect the times when God's Spirit seems speaking to him. These are the critical points of our being. They shape our whole after-career. They give the color to all our final destiny.

Now there are two things for all of us to remember in such a crisis. One of them is this: the issues in every case are delicate beyond conception. We are therefore in danger of doing too much or too little.

The other is this: if we do not help, we hinder. Eli had to say something at least when Samuel came to him. Tell the child God is calling him; tell him to answer: "Speak, Lord; for thy servant heareth." Eli told Samuel the wrong thing twice; the right, once.

III.

SPIRITUAL SURRENDER FOR CHILDREN.

"AND IT SHALL BE, IF HE CALL THEE, THAT THOU SHALT SAY, SPEAK, LORD; FOR THY SERVANT HEARETH."—1 *Sam.* 3:9.

THE continued exposition of this passage has led us along till we have reached the third phase of child-life, the period of spiritual surrender: "Therefore Eli said unto Samuel, Go, lie down; and it shall be, if he call thee, that thou shalt say, Speak, Lord; for thy servant heareth. So Samuel went and lay down in his place. And the Lord came, and stood, and called as at other times, Samuel, Samuel. Then Samuel answered, Speak; for thy servant heareth." The force of the whole narrative centres in the one reply Eli told Samuel to make, and which the docile lad repeated: "Speak, Lord; for thy servant heareth." To this we devote our attention, for every word in the sentence contains a lesson for use.

1. To begin with, there is indicated here, as a part of this boy's experience, *the exercise of unquestioning obedience.* If Samuel had been an unamiable child, he would have been fretted by these frequent interruptions in his sleep. But now we see how patiently he goes back to his couch.

God always loves to talk with good children; and an obedient and teachable disposition is the very best kind of preparation for the converse. It is wise for any one to keep steady in attendance upon the house of God, even when no wonderful "vision" is to be expected; sometimes one receives a message which is far more valuable than any spectacle. A child who does not know God's name may easily learn to know God's voice; and it comforts and helps us all, young or old, more to hear messages from heaven with our hearts than with our ears only.

If anybody asks just here whether this same Jehovah who spoke to Samuel ever speaks to human beings now, I should have to quote an Old Testament passage and then compare the words of it with those of a passage in the New, in order that my reply might be plain and clear. "Wisdom crieth without; she uttereth her voice in the streets. Whoso hearkeneth unto me shall dwell safely, and shall be quiet from fear of evil."

When I was in the East some years ago, I visited one of the noblest edifices in Constantinople, called the Mosque of Santa Sophia. It used to be a Christian church; but as the Saracens came into possession of the city they converted this fine building into a place for the ordinary Mohammedan service. Still it was suffered to retain its old name. "Sophia" is a Greek word, meaning *wisdom:* "Santa Sophia" means *holy wisdom.* And this edifice was consecrated by a Christian emperor, Constantine, for the worship of our Saviour Jesus Christ, under an Old Testament name. You know we were talking, two years ago, about "the Logos," as we found it in the first chapter of John. Now, what *Logos* signifies in the masculine gender, *Sophia* signifies in the feminine—God coming down from heaven to men so as to talk to them.

When Solomon, in the book of Proverbs, pictures "Wisdom" as speaking to us, "crying without in the streets," we have no reason to be surprised to find in the New Testament, in two places, that very word applied to God's only-begotten Son by Jesus himself.

He says once (Luke 7:35), "But Wisdom is justified of all her children," and he tells us again (Luke 11: 49), "Therefore also said the Wisdom of God." In both of these verses the plain reference is to Jesus Christ. So that I think we shall be very safe in asserting that whatever the Old Testament declares "Wisdom" says, the New Testament would have us understand Jesus himself says.

It seems to me we have something very wonderful in these verses for real use and help. God might have left us a most weary work to do, looking up Wisdom, and trying to find out what she wanted to say. But here we learn that all we need has started out for us. Wisdom is actually close at our doors. It is as if a beautiful angel from heaven had just arrived, bringing a direct message from God. It is as if she were standing out in the highway now, trying to get somebody to listen to her words. And these words are exactly what some of you have been wanting for a long time to hear. She seeks to lead you to come to a new life. She calls you to begin to serve your Maker with your whole heart. That is what many of you have declared you wished to do. And the chance, I should suppose, is now very opportune and very welcome.

Hunters tells us that they sometimes search for water in an autumn forest by carrying a hazel-branch over the spot where the spring is conjectured to be concealed. They soberly assert that, no matter how deep underground the cool fountain may be flowing, the instinct of life in the twig will enable it to detect the desired current beneath the fallen leaves. Suddenly it will droop in the hand, bending straight towards the moisture. Then, if he digs, he will discover the stream. You see, the green hazel has need of the water; it must have it, or it must shrivel and die.

Such a text as ours to-day makes me think of that superstition of these woodsmen. What a soul wants really it is very apt to go after by some subtle instinct of its own, which in certain cases it can hardly understand for itself. I take in my imagination, now, this announcement about Wisdom somewhat as men take the hazel-twig, and I pass it around among you. I say, the Lord Jesus has come from heaven for you—Wisdom is standing out in the street—Christ is calling to you to hear him! And so it seems certain to me that before long I shall notice that one or another conscience, or one heart, or one mind, here or there, is going to stir up the hidden currents of its life to recognize an invitation so welcome, to come and talk with God close at hand.

2. But now we move forward a step. In the experience of Samuel we observe, in the second

place, there was *the attitude of listening.* He lay down again, as he was bidden, but with a far different feeling. He was quite awake; he was expectant, and on the alert to hear.

My fear is that the young people whom I am addressing will not understand just how the call of God comes and just what his heavenly wisdom wants. Of course, Jesus Christ is not now here in bodily form. But he comes and he speaks none the less openly for all that. I think I can make you admit that he has come to you a great many times already.

One way in which he shows himself is by his Word. This Bible of ours is nothing more nor less than a series of letters to us from God. Often does a text, which we have read a hundred or more times without being impressed by it, suddenly appear to surprise us with a great meaning. It reaches our consciences and arouses our minds. It will always do so if we study it well.

So, again, Wisdom comes by God's people. That is, Christians are messengers to us from Christ. They say, as Martha said: "The Master is come and calleth for thee." Preachers in the pulpit, teachers in the classes, parents at their homes, zealous friends who speak to us by the way—all these are sent for our good. They were charged to do that long and long ago: "Let him that heareth say, Come." We must treat them as if they had God's message, not their own; for, indeed, it is not their own.

Then, also, Wisdom comes by the Holy Spirit.

Sometimes we find ourselves led into serious thought, we hardly know how. In an hour of quiet meditation we feel compelled to consider those greatest of all questions that concern the future well-being of our souls. We cannot tell what is coming by-and-by. Events appear like huge dark ships out in the offing; we scan them with a half-curious, half-anxious eye, for we cannot know what they have on board in store for any one. If life grows real it makes one uneasy. And now and then this feeling stretches far beyond and over the life we are at present living. I am sure I could reach your own experience if I were to press the question closely; do you never have a deep and undefinable consciousness of something yet to be accomplished, something yet to be attained, before you can feel quietly at rest? These inward monitions of conscience, these solemn reflections that will not allow themselves ever to be hushed, these imaginations of the soul looking forward, these yearnings of your nature for peace and rest and hope, these aspirations of your unsatisfied minds after what is more substantial and secure, these impatient impulses of reform when all alone it seems to come to you that you ought to be better, these cravings after the good and the manly and the pure and the true—these are just the dealing of Almighty God with every one he is determining to help and save; these are the patient strivings of the Holy Ghost within your soul. They are the cry of Wisdom to you, the voice of Jesus Christ.

3. Then next in the experience of Samuel we

observe there is *a spirit of reverence*. In the wonderful name "Lord," which Eli uses, but the boy drops, we know resided the recognition of the eternal Jehovah in person. The young heart seems to shrink back from the utterance of a word which would assume familiarity. An awful solemnity holds back his speech.

Canon Liddon said long ago in one of his thoughtful essays: "Religion consists fundamentally in the practical recognition of a constraining bond between the inward life of man and an unseen Person." We all recognize the truth of this statement. But are we ready to assert that children have any such notion? Do the young entertain any solemn and intelligent sense of the Supreme Being they are taught to reverence as God?

To this the answer is not difficult. An appeal to the memory and conscience of almost all mature people, who have been brought up under circumstances of training similar to those of Samuel, would receive a series of most interesting responses. These would vary as temperaments and personal characteristics vary; but it is a fact that children construct systems of faith even in their earliest years. They feel the stirrings of an awakened conscience, and they find themselves oppressed with the necessity of being at peace with the Being who created them. De Quincey, in some references he was making to the memories of his boyhood, says: "I felt resting upon me always too deep and gloomy a sense of obscure duties attached to life that I never should be able to fulfil; a burden which I could not carry, and yet which I did not know how to throw off." It is likely that very many mature persons can look back across the lapse of time and respond to this feeling and instance a similar experience.

When Samuel reached that name of "Jehovah," a certain awe-struck devotion must have seized his mind and shaken his voice as it broke the silence of the shadows lying in the folds of the Tabernacle curtains and he felt himself talking in the midnight all alone with Jehovah. Such moments are not rare with some who are older than Samuel. They do not hear a voice in the air, but they have the awe and the outcry in the recesses of their hearts.

4. But now let us move forward a new step. To the attitude of listening and the feeling of reverence add another particular, suggested in a word also. There is the *apprehension of obligation.* Samuel from this time forward till his death becomes the servant of the Highest. "Speak, Lord; thy servant heareth."

Certainly we now stand on sure ground. To every child there belongs an instinct of dutiful subordination to God. Even in untrained and uninstructed minds there is the voice of conscience calling for an answer. But when the New Testament speaks, and the Son of God comes into recognition, the soul feels the presence of its Master at once. This is the mysterious power of the gospel revealing an incarnation of the Godhead.

There is much force in the exclamation of the ancient father, Irenæus: "Christ made himself an infant to infants that he might sanctify them; he made himself a child to children, giving holiness to those of that age, to the end he might afford them in his person an example of piety, sanctity, and subjection; he made himself a young man to young men, giving them a pattern and sanctifying them for the service of our Lord."

So whenever Christ comes by his Spirit into contact with a young life there is the bending of the will into desire for service. Eli startled no prejudice and awaked no opposition in the son of the Lord's handmaid Hannah. This lad could have said at once, like the unknown author of the hundred and sixteenth psalm: "O Lord, truly I am thy servant; I am thy servant and the son of thy handmaid: thou hast loosed my bonds. I will offer to thee the sacrifice of thanksgiving and will call upon the name of the Lord. I will pay my vows unto the Lord now in the presence of all his people, in the courts of the Lord's house, in the midst of thee, O Jerusalem. Praise ye the Lord."

5. Thus we reach the final step in the greeting of Samuel to his Master and Maker: "Speak, Lord; thy servant heareth." There is the *temper of submission.* The entire surrender of the soul is reached in that word "heareth."

The scene, as it now rises upon our imagination, is singularly pathetic. This young child was offering himself most unconsciously to a duty immediate and pressing, but indescribably hard. And the worst of it was that the long life of public service was lying out darkly before him. From this time forward there was to be no rest, no release, for the boy, no retreat for the man. A little boy sat in front of his father and held the reins which controlled a restive horse. Unknown to the boy, the reins passed around him and were also in his father's hands. He saw occasion to pull them. With artless simplicity the child looked around, saying, "Father, I thought I was driving, but I am not, am I?" Thus it is often with men, who think that they are shaping a destiny which a higher hand than theirs is really fashioning. They do their own will, but they also do the will of God. A stronger hand guides them, a mightier power holds the helm of their vessel and saves from rock and wreck. Happy are they who quietly yield to the guidance of an almighty hand.

Observe carefully the language employed here at the close of the narrative. When the Lord called this fearless boy the fourth time, He "came and stood." So the two faced each other while this small ambassador took the message which was to make Eli's ears tingle. He was directly in the majestic presence of Jehovah for the first time. We retreat from the spectacle, ourselves abashed and dazzled, whispering to our hearts the words of Jean Paul Richter: "Surely, the smallest are nearest God, as the smallest planets are nearest the sun!"

IV.

ELI'S FAMILY GOVERNMENT.

"For I have told him that I will judge his house for ever for the iniquity which he knoweth; because his sons made themselves vile, and he restrained them not.—1 *Sam.* 3:13.

One of the greatest skeptics France has ever produced was once heard to say to the devout Pascal, "If I had your principles I would be a better man." He received this for a reply, "Begin with being a better man, and you will soon have my principles." Herein lies the great secret of success in the rearing of children. There is no mechanical system of rules which can be promulgated for all and then reposed upon in every case. Family government resides in the governor, whoever he may be at the moment. Sometimes the children govern the parents, and sometimes parents govern the children: and whichever it is, we may be sure the thing is done not by theoretic principles, but by a subtle personal power producing personal subjection.

In securing the lessons taught us to-day, the entire history of Eli's household will have to come into the discussion. The tragedy of the old man's death, and the miserable end of the sons, will better serve as an illustration of the sure results of mistakes committed through a lengthened course of years. So now a mere grouping together of a few observations will help us in our analysis.

1. In disorderly families it is likely that both parents and children will have to divide the blame. If affection does not lie at the base of all the associations under the home roof, then each in turn will feel the want and will show it.

Classic fable relates that Vulcan constructed as his first work at the forge a throne of gold, which he declared was for his mother Juno to sit upon; the moment she placed herself in it, however, she found herself unable to move. The gods tried to set her at liberty by breaking the chains that held her to the seat; but they failed, for the hard-hearted son alone had power to unloose the links. Then he explained his conduct; he said his reverence was like her care, for his cold mother had never loved him, and he had never known affection in his obedience.

2. When children grow up into vicious courses, it is wise for parents to try to change the temptations which injured them. That will perhaps keep others from a like ruin. "Tell me," once said a gentleman to a drunkard, as he urged him to reform, "tell me where it was you took your earliest steps in this terrible career." And the man replied, "At my father's table. Before I had left home to become a clerk I had learned to love drink for its own sake; the first drop I ever tasted was handed me by my mother, who calls me now a sot and calls herself a martyr."

3. When God sends a warning, it will not do

just to settle down into a discouraged apathy and consider it resignation.

The young Samuel must have had many misgivings in his heart before he could transmit to Eli the awful message with which he had been charged: "And the Lord said to Samuel, Behold, I will do a thing in Israel at which both the ears of every one that heareth it shall tingle. In that day I will perform against Eli all things which I have spoken concerning his house: when I begin, I will also make an end. For I have told him that I will judge his house for ever for the iniquity which he knoweth; because his sons made themselves vile, and he restrained them not. And therefore I have sworn unto the house of Eli that the iniquity of Eli's house shall not be purged with sacrifice nor offering for ever." But the child did his duty, and the old man settled back into what some would consider a very exemplary state of mind. "And Samuel told him every whit, and hid nothing from him. And he said, It is the Lord: let him do what seemeth him good." Not an effort to ward off judgment; not a deprecation, not a prayer! Why, even the heathen king of Nineveh did better than that (Jonah 3:6–10). Christian parents, when they discover peril close ahead, should rise with most energetic means of interposition in behalf of those whom they profess to love.

4. In considering the matter of home government, we must remember that the children have some rights. No one principle is lodged in a boy's mind by nature more deeply than that of a strict

and irrevocable justice. He wants the chance of time or opportunity to be heard, in any case of trouble; he feels that he has the inalienable right to make his righteousness appear if it can be done. Hence the need of quiet and reflection and calmness in all kinds of discipline. That is what renders parental government trustworthy. "How doth the destiny of families," exclaims the old Æschylus, in his "Agamemnon," "directing their ways according to justice, always produce good children! But ancient insolence is wont to generate new insolence, to the mischief of mortals some time or another, whenever the appointed day comes."

A lady once consulted the moralist Johnson upon the degree of wickedness to be attached to her son's having stolen some apples out of a neighbor's orchard. "Madam," said he, with rather more of his ponderous solemnity than usual, "it depends a good deal upon the weight of the boy. My school-fellow David Garrick, who was always of small size, robbed a dozen trees with impunity; but the first time I climbed up into the midst of the apples, for I was a very heavy boy, the bough broke with me, and that was called a judgment. I have always supposed since that this must have been one of the reasons why Justice was represented as holding a huge pair of scales." It is likely that the old gentleman, with deep sympathy for childhood, was doing a little something to mitigate the expected retribution, and was trying to suggest that boys were not all exactly alike.

5. Ideas are yet influential in the training of even

the stubbornest of children and even the vainest. There is a power in family instruction, and parents are to teach their children what is right and honest and decent and of good report. It is folly to think that young people are without reflection; no being on this footstool is more logical than a child in rushing out its notions into execution. One of the greatest instructors England ever knew left this published sentiment behind him when he died: "Acts grow out of thoughts. If a man's thinking be confined to trifling objects, his acts will correspond. So of religious belief. If a Christian's faith be strong and ardent, a vitality will be imparted to all he does. Pure doctrine, honestly held, begets a pure life; looseness in doctrine is followed by looseness in living, the world over."

Perhaps the time will come in which people will cease foolishly to object that the hearts and habits of children ought to be allowed, especially in religious matters, to grow up unbiassed. But that time has not arrived yet; and we must just keep on repeating Coleridge's familiar story in his "Table-Talk." He says that Thelwall declared it to be unfair to influence a young mind by inculcating opinions before it came to such years of discretion as to be able to judge for itself. A while afterwards, he showed him his little dooryard, and told him it was his "botanical garden" which he considered very precious. "Why, how so?" inquired his friend; 'it is all covered with weeds." With that quiet preaching-manner of his the philosopher answered, "Oh, it is because the land has not yet come to years of discretion and choice. I thought it unfair to prejudice the garden towards roses and strawberries, but the weeds took the liberty to grow."

6. A proper measure of permissions should be mingled with the restrictions which the family sovereignty imposes. That is, when the old child-notion of perfect liberty, which is very near to perfect license, is disturbed by the necessities of social and domestic order, then a fresh notion should be constructed in its place.

Some of us in our New England childhood used to wonder why among the "forbiddings" and the "requirings" of a Catechism so venerable as ours, "the next thing to inspiration," there had not been introduced a few, just a few, "permittings," so as to afford an outlet for animal spirits in rustic surroundings where noise did no special injury. It helped this questioning disposition when some one gave us "Quarles' Emblems," and we heard the dry old teacher saying at the foot of a picture, "If thy son be given to lavish company, endeavor to stave him off with lawful recreations; the discretion of a father often prevents the destruction of a child."

Those who are familiar with the autobiography of Goethe will perhaps recollect with what energy he exclaims, after recounting some painful frettings of parental discipline he himself endured, "If elderly persons wish to play the pedagogue properly, they should neither prohibit nor render disagreeable to a young man anything which gives him an innocent pleasure, of whatever kind it may be, unless at the same time they have something else to put in its place or can contrive a substitute."

7. The time for making impressions upon the minds and the hearts of children comes much earlier than many parents seem to suppose. Children notice the habits of those who care for them before they notice anything else whatsoever.

The principle of authority is the first to be recognized. When we were children it was publicly proclaimed that horses had to be "broken" before they could be driven with safety. Along came a man by the name of Rarey—let all respectable horses praise his memory! He taught and proved that the thing to be done was to instruct the animal, and show him kindly that he was simply mistaken in imagining he was to have his own way or remain his own master. But even Jean Paul Richter asserts, "Either the will must be broken in childhood or the heart in old age." Let the will be guided and controlled, not broken at all, and the heart will thereafter be safe, under the guidance of God.

8. When a direct conflict of authority is reached there can be no compromise. The story that Gambetta poked out one of his own eyes when a child, because his father would not permit him to do as he pleased, is perfectly true. What is not so generally known is that the elder Gambetta remained inflexible even after this appalling display of wilfulness. The boy was being educated at the Lycée of Cahors; and conceiving a dislike to the institution, asked to be removed from it. His

father refused again and again. At last Léon said, "I will put out one of my eyes if you send me back to the Lycée." It was holiday-time. "As you please," said the father, to whom it seems never to have occurred that his boy might have inherited his own strength of purpose. The same day Léon took, not a pen-knife, as the popular tradition has it, but an inkstand, which he dashed with such violence against the eye as to destroy it. Shocked as was the elder Gambetta, he would not give in; and Léon returned to the Lycée.

There could have been no other decision with such a lad. Better the loss of an eye than the victorious defiance of law. In this story of Eli he is blamed for not restraining his sons when they made themselves vile.

9. Prayer for help every instant is the one necessity for all success in family government. The devil of misrule is one of those evil spirits which cannot be cast out otherwise.

The story of the mythical king often comes to use. He had employed his people to weave for him, and supplied the silks and patterns with which they were to work, and at the same time bade them if ever in trouble concerning the labor, to come to him without fear. Among the many busy at their looms was a little child who worked on cheerfully although often alone. One day when all the rest were distressed at the sight of the terrible tangles into which their silks had been drawn, they gathered around the child and asked, "How is it that you are so happy at your work? It is not so with us; our difficulties are more than we can bear." "Then why do you not tell the king?" inquired the frail weaver; "he has told us to, and that he would help us." "We do, at night and morning." "Ah!" said the child; "I send directly whenever I find I have a tangle."

The truth is, the explosions of our own temper tangle more than anything else. The infinite calmness of even one moment of genuine supplication, when real prayer has become habitual, will do a vast work in controlling a turbulent outbreak. Only we are to remember that the opportunity passes swiftly, and the need of help is the signal for instant resort to the Source of it.

The point of consideration in every case is concerning our purpose in training children at all. One of our noted evangelists has told us a story somewhat like this: A mother lay dying, some time ago, and she requested her children to be brought to her bedside. The eldest one came in first, and putting her loving hands on his head, she gave him a mother's parting message. Then came another, and then another. To all of them she gave her parting message, until the last—the seventh one, an infant—was brought in. She was so young she could not understand the message of love; so the mother gave it to her husband for her, and then she took the child to her bosom and caressed it until her time was almost up. Then, turning to her husband, she said: "I charge you to bring all these children home to heaven with you."

V.

AN OLD TESTAMENT REVIVAL.

"Then Samuel took a stone, and set it between Mizpeh and Shen, and called the name of it Ebenezer, saying, Hitherto hath the Lord helped us."—1 *Sam.* 7:12.

Thirty years ago there used to be more said about revivals of religion than there is now. Some excellent Christians there are who think that the old system of things was better than the modern. They improve every opportunity offered in discussions to talk about it. For they really believe that the times of Nettleton, Finney, and Kirk were very like the "times of visitation" and the "times of refreshing" foretold by the prophets. They are accustomed to pronounce those historic periods to have been the most prosperous ever vouchsafed to the American churches. So they will enjoy the study of this chapter to-day.

I. In the beginning, a sermon was preached: "And Samuel spake unto all the house of Israel, saying, If ye do return unto the Lord with all your hearts, then put away the strange gods and Ashtaroth from among you, and prepare your hearts unto the Lord and serve him only; and he will deliver you out of the hand of the Philistines." It is evident here that Samuel made a most admirable improvement of the occasion. A crisis had been reached; and in his searching and solemn discourse he seems to have sought to make these four points, which certainly are worthy of employment always:

1. Those people must admit the necessity of a new departure in their conduct and life immediately; they must "return unto the Lord with all their hearts."

2. They must put away every sign and vestige of a bad past; "strange gods" would have to be entirely relinquished, groves and images, forests and feastings, everything which came between them and Jehovah's worship.

3. They must instantly enter upon a fresh spiritual consecration: they would have to "prepare their hearts unto the Lord and serve him only."

4. Then they must trust wholly to the ancient promises God had made to their fathers and to them; for he had covenanted to "deliver them out of the hands of" their foes.

II. Then followed an exemplary response from the nation: "Then the children of Israel did put away Baalim and Ashtaroth, and served the Lord only."

This sudden and thorough cleansing of themselves from forms of idolatry reminds us of what in Britain used to be called "a reformation of manners." The public conscience was moved, and certain external improvements in conduct were perceptible at once. The people were frightened and felt their need of divine help. It was comparatively, easy to start such a general uprising in behalf of what was decent and devotional.

III. Next, their leader summoned a great assemblage for a religious service of prayer: "And Samuel said, Gather all Israel to Mizpeh, and I will pray for you unto the Lord." Samuel understood that something more and something much deeper in experience would be disclosed the moment those fickle multitudes came into practical communion with Jehovah. When he began to acknowledge their sins for them, and rehearse the long, sad catalogue of their disobediences, they would either have to admit his honesty or show the hardness of their hearts by denying his impeachments.

There is a dreadful responsibility always laid upon ministers of the gospel when they propose to act as mediators and spokesmen between God and their people. How well Samuel did his duty that day we may learn from the record of him as an intercessor; for he is mentioned with Moses and Aaron as notable (Psa. 99 : 6): "Moses and Aaron among his priests, and Samuel among them that call upon his name; they called upon the Lord, and he answered them."

IV. Now comes what might be called a protracted meeting: "And they gathered together to Mizpeh, and drew water, and poured it out before the Lord, and fasted on that day, and said there, We have sinned against the Lord. And Samuel judged the children of Israel in Mizpeh."

There is always a point at which human mediation in behalf of sinners must cease; then the sinners must take up the duty of supplication for themselves, or be lost. This was true of even such a prophet-priest as Samuel (Jer. 15:1): "Then said the Lord unto me, Though Moses and Samuel stood before me, yet my mind could not be towards this people: cast them out of my sight and let them go forth."

God respects the individual free-will of each man in the reckoning of accountability; his friends and neighbors must stand aside for him to come and seek his own salvation: "None of them can by any means redeem his brother, nor give to God a ransom for him." In this case the people were intelligent enough to undertake at least these four duties which are mentioned.

1. They came to a direct posture of humiliation; they "fasted on that day." That was in those times the symbol of penitent prostration and self-denial. If there be any Christians who think that fasting is not given as a salutary ordinance for the church in New Testament times, it remains only to be said that the spirit and temper which the abstinence from food signified are certainly prescribed (Jas. 4: 8–10): "Draw nigh to God, and he will draw nigh to you. Cleanse your hands, ye sinners, and purify your hearts, ye double-minded. Be afflicted and mourn and weep; let your laughter be turned to mourning and your joy to heaviness. Humble yourselves in the sight of the Lord, and he shall lift you up." The members are to be mortified, and the heart is to be bowed under the sense of guilt.

2. Then these people made confessions of sin: they "said there, We have sinned against the

Lord." There is a mysterious power in the sound of one's voice when he is on his knees before the Almighty. Those who are entirely unmoved, even stubborn in their resistance to the Spirit of grace, have been known to break forth into tears of shame and contrition as soon as they have begun to speak for themselves. It is folly to think that one can be penitent and yet be too proud to tell the Lord so; the heart may believe, but the mouth must do the confession (Rom. 10:10).

3. Next, these repenting people soberly renewed their covenant: "They drew water, and poured it out before the Lord." It is interesting to notice the explanations made by the various commentators on this significant action. One says: "They poured out water in confirmation of the vow they were about to make, which was declared as irrevocable as the spilling of water upon the ground" (2 Sam. 14:14). One of the Targums renders the clause thus: "And they poured out their hearts in penitence as waters before the Lord." Gill says: "This signified that they thoroughly renounced idolatry, that nothing of it should remain, as when water is poured out of a cask there remains no smell, as there does when other liquors are poured out." Whatever their action did positively mean, as they understood it, so much as this is certainly true: they gave their promises of obedience once more, with this for a solemn ratification as by an oath; they pledged themselves anew unto Jehovah as their God.

4. They put themselves into condition for fresh

activity in devotion. The best explanation of that statement, "Samuel judged the children of Israel in Mizpeh," seems to be that he reorganized the people afresh, for military service and for civil order and for religious worship; he took the charge of the new plans for future obedience; assuming that they were now going to turn completely unto God, he fashioned their life for them on a permanent basis.

V. Then there came the descent of blessing in fulfilment of the Lord's covenant. It is profitable, as an exhibition of human nature, to notice this mingling of strength with weakness on the part of those people: they were so scared, and yet continued so trustful: "And when the Philistines heard that the children of Israel were gathered together to Mizpeh, the lords of the Philistines went up against Israel. And when the children of Israel heard it they were afraid of the Philistines."

1. Real consecration of Christians generally evokes new opposition from foes. Satan watches for the moment of deepest piety in order to make his most savage attack.

2. Importunate prayer is the condition of all success: "And the children of Israel said to Samuel, Cease not to cry unto the Lord our God for us, that he will save us out of the hands of the Philistines." The people plead with Samuel now, and he persists.

3. The full consecration of one's soul must recognize the sacrifice for sins: "And Samuel took a sucking lamb, and offered it for a burnt offering

wholly unto the Lord: and Samuel cried unto the Lord for Israel; and the Lord heard him." This lamb was the suggestion of atonement made by a Redeemer.

4. God is faithful to the instant in his interposition: "And as Samuel was offering up the burnt offering, the Philistines drew near to battle against Israel: but the Lord thundered with a great thunder on that day upon the Philistines, and discomfited them; and they were smitten before Israel. And the men of Israel went out of Mizpeh, and pursued the Philistines, and smote them, until they came under Bethcar." While Samuel was at the altar the need came, and the help followed the need "while he was speaking," just as it did in the prayer of Daniel (Dan. 9: 20, 21).

VI. There remained now nothing more than to erect a memorial of the transaction: "Then Samuel took a stone, and set it between Mizpeh and Shen, and called the name of it Ebenezer, saying, Hitherto hath the Lord helped us." And we might as well turn the whole force of the story at once upon ourselves, and assert that each interposition of God in our behalf, temporal or spiritual, ought to have a grateful recognition in our lives.

1. All glory and honor of the achievement should be distinctly ascribed to God: "The Lord hath helped us." Once there was made a plain enunciation of this principle (Judg. 7:2): "And the Lord said unto Gideon, The people that are with thee are too many for me to give the Midianites into their hands, lest Israel vaunt themselves

against me, saying, Mine own hand hath saved me." And once there was a denunciatory warning given (Isa. 10:12, 13): "Wherefore it shall come to pass that when the Lord hath performed his whole work upon Mt. Zion and on Jerusalem, I will punish the fruit of the stout heart of the king of Assyria and the glory of his high looks. For he saith, By the strength of my hand I have done it, and by my wisdom; for I am prudent; and I have removed the bounds of the people, and have robbed their treasures, and I have put down the inhabitants like a valiant man."

2. We should make our acknowledgment as permanent as possible. Samuel chose stone; so did Jacob (Gen. 28:18). Some of us might keep an anniversary of peculiar providences, or inscribe the family record in the Bible, or give a new name to a child, or even plant a memorial tree; and then sing the song:

> "Here I'll raise my Ebenezer,
> Hither by thy help I'm come;
> And I hope, by thy good pleasure,
> Safely to arrive at home."

3. We should take pains to group our memorials so that one shall strengthen the other. Samuel set up his pillar between Mizpeh, where this deliverance was vouchsafed, and Shen, where another had been vouchsafed in the victory gained over the Philistines twenty years before. Thus he linked the histories together, like pearls in a necklace. After a while one might be able to read famous Hebrew annals of rescue all over Canaan.

4. Each successive deliverance by a gracious God should deepen our trust and quicken our expectation; for we sing again:

> "His love in times past forbids me to think
> He'll leave me at last in trouble to sink;
> Each kind Ebenezer I have in review
> Confirms his good pleasure to help me quite through."

The careful investigation of such an incident as this has given us certain conclusions which might well be stated at the close of our study now.

1. A revival of religion is located in the church, and assumes a previous state of sad and guilty backsliding.

2. The conversion of sinners is not a revival; it is the gracious result that follows one which is genuine.

3. Any "measures" are allowable, provided they are decent and orderly, that will lead believers to penitence and duty.

4. Blessed is the congregation whose spirituality is lifted and whose life is saved by a day of God's visitation.

5. More blessed still is that church which never had a revival in all its history, and never needed one.

VI.

"VOX POPULI, VOX DEI."

"AND THE LORD SAID TO SAMUEL, HEARKEN UNTO THEIR VOICE, AND MAKE THEM A KING."—1 *Sam.* 8:22.

PERHAPS there is no proverb which is more familiar, as it is certain there is none more faulty, than this: "The voice of the people is the voice of God." We enter to-day upon the study of a fragment of history which furnishes a most decided proof of its untruth. And since the motto is Latin, it might as well go now with a comment upon it from one of the greatest of the old Roman philosophers, even Cicero himself, who says in his treatise Concerning Laws: "It is most absurd to suppose that all the things are just which are found in the enactments and institutions of a State. There is no such power in the sentence and command of fools as that by their vote the nature of things can be reversed. The law did not begin when first written, but when it first had existence; that is, when the divine mind first had existence."

In entering upon the study of Saul's biography we choose to use the Scripture record as the foundation of remark just as it meets the ordinary reader of the Bible. We can expound or illustrate as appears to promise most profit. We can take up the verses one by one, and the religious lessons will come out naturally as we read along together.

1. The story gives us the date to start with, and connects present histories with those of a great and honored past. Samuel is still at the nation's head, but failing: "And it came to pass, when Samuel was old, that he made his sons judges over Israel."

Our first practical reflection here is commonplace, but it ought to be of help in moderating the notions of a great many people: *grace is not always hereditary.* It was not in the case of Eli, and it is not here in the case of Samuel. Johnson's Dictionary defines the word gentleman, "one of good extraction, but not noble." On that basis there are more gentlemen in society perhaps than might be suspected. Piety cannot be transmitted according to physical laws, however; and yet it seems as if we might insist upon the signal benefits of being born of good stock rather than of corrupt. And on the whole, it is most likely we shall all be found quoting the familiar inferences of Thomas Fuller, from his "Good Thoughts in Bad Times," as our most contented conclusions: "Lord, I find the genealogy of my Saviour strangely checkered with four remarkable changes in four immediate generations: first, Roboam begat Abia, a bad father begat a bad son; second, Abia begat Asa, a bad father begat a good son; third, Josaphat begat Joram, a good father a bad son. I see, Lord, from hence, that my father's piety cannot be entailed; that is bad news for me; but I see, also, that actual impiety is not hereditary; that is good news for my son."

2. Who were these sons of Samuel? Unfortunately there is no account of them that gives any

satisfaction. Samuel's name has been our very spell to conjure with for three thousand years in the educational training of our children. He evidently did what he could to bring all the help possible to his boys from holy associations. He followed the custom of the times in dedicating them to God and giving the memorial of their religious responsibility: "Now the name of his first-born was Joel; and the name of his second, Abiah: they were judges in Beersheba."

The lesson we learn here is worth pressing a little: *noble names do not change bad hearts* nor make wicked men fit to hold high office. Samuel probably hoped a great deal for those sons of his when he fixed upon them such names as these in the reverent regard for the old faith of Israel. "Joel" signifies *Jehovah is God;* and "Abiah" means *Jehovah is my Father.* We have no evidence that these children cared for their fine names while they were little, as Samuel did for his when he moved reverently around in the ministrations of the Tabernacle, a devout lad, obedient to God and to Eli. And we have very sad evidence that, after they had grown up, these sons of the old priest-judge strayed far away from any recognition of the Lord's service. It must have sounded like a sarcasm and a mockery to call such creatures by such names as those.

We use now what we call among ourselves "our Christian names;" a significance ought to be attached to that fact. It does not follow in every case that they were bestowed by our parents with any direct pertinency of meaning as words, for that is not our modern custom. Still there is often in one's name a suggestion which might as well be heeded. We surely might expect that a maiden called "Sophia" ought not to be a fool, for her name means *wisdom*. And just so "Gertrude" suggests a character of *all-truth*. And "Alfred" becomes a pledge of *all-peace*. And "Leonard" must not be a coward as long as he is called *lion-like*. "Francis" is to be *frank*, and "Anna" is to be *gracious*, or intelligent people will laugh when their names are called out in the room. Surely Nathanael, Theodore, Elnathan, and Dorothy ought to bear in mind every day and hour that their names all alike signify *the gift of God*.

But it would never be fair to flaunt old and honored family designations in our faces, and claim reverence for any man or woman whose life is a shame to them. It is unbecoming to ask genteel-minded citizens to pay the old respect to sunken habits and low tastes, when some men and women come forward into conspicuousness quite unworthy of honored ancestral memories. There lived once a vice-president of the United States who had no more right to be called "Burr" than he had to be called "Aaron;" he had lost the character that fitted either name.

3. The illustration of all this grows more and more vivid as the story moves on; the next verse reads: "And his sons walked not in his ways, but turned aside after lucre, and took bribes and perverted judgment."

The lesson we learn from this is explanatory as

well as full of admonition: *covetousness is idolatry.* These young men prostituted the position which their father's name gave them; they actually sold place and influence at a price. In a word, they were bribe-takers. A curious word is this here rendered "lucre;" it is precisely that which Moses employed when he was defining the duties and character of a judge: "Moreover, thou shalt provide out of all the people able men, such as fear God, men of truth, hating covetousness; and place such over them to be rulers of thousands and rulers of hundreds, rulers of fifties and rulers of tens: and let them judge the people at all seasons: and it shall be that every great matter they shall bring unto thee, but every small matter they shall judge: so shall it be easier for thyself, and they shall bear the burden with thee." That word "covetousness" is the same as the word "lucre" in this verse before us. The old Hebrew Targum translates it, "the mammon of falsehood." It is interesting to observe how carefully the language is selected so as to show that these sons of Samuel were exactly what their office demanded they should not be. The command of the Law was direct and unmistakable: "Thou shalt not pervert judgment, and thou shalt not take a bribe." And here this verse of description asserts: they "took bribes and perverted judgment." Their covetousness became irreligion.

Men are agreed at last that the love of money is the root of all evil. But some may not have understood the meaning of the apostle who considered the greed for gain a breach of the first commandment in the Decalogue. But before we leave this part of the history we shall discover that through the system of bribe-taking these younger men did much to turn the whole nation from God's reign. Such a perversion of official trust into personal enrichment is an old, contemptible sin, with not even the small grace of originality in it; it would be better to be sold as a chattel than as a villain; the one is a free-slave, the other a bond-serf of Satan.

4. At this point the Scripture narrative begins to indicate the effect of all this disastrous corruption in Samuel's own family. Some of the influential men of the nation suddenly advance to the front and propose to interfere in governmental affairs. They think a revolution would be a very proper thing to make just now; but they coolly suggest that Samuel should vacate his place as the first condition of good. A brave attack could be started against the old man; but it seems not to have occurred to them that it would have been more to the point to suppress the bribe-givers and the bribe-takers at once, give them both an equal retribution and relieve the land, than just to push out of position the old man who had served them for unreckoned years, and stood a hundred storms in their behalf, with simple majesty of fidelity to the work God himself had set him to do: "Then all the elders of Israel gathered themselves together, and came to Samuel unto Ramah."

Croakers always find easy companionship: that is our lesson now. Ravens are said to detect afar off birds of the same black feather and the same lugubrious voice. These "elders of Israel" in the story might surely have been about better business than ministering to popular discontent. They were living under a theocracy, and God was overhead; they could have interfered before for the suppression of these corrupt judges, and in a wiser way. It was a remark of Lord Beaconsfield that "it is much easier to be critical than to be correct." Many a man can grow melancholy and even boisterous over the sins of the age who never has contributed in any cheerful degree to its purity. Failures of good men are sometimes made apologies for bad men encouraging sins. Dissatisfaction finds it entertaining to breed distrust, and at such a hint from "elders" men begin to clamor merely for a party change. And thoughful citizens wonder whether anything is going to be gained by putting in a fresh set of ungorged bribe-takers. Joel and Abiah were bad enough; we wonder if the monarchists liked the atmosphere better when Saul came into power.

The plan proceeds plausibly. Good and even venerable men are at times very unwise and much mistaken. Though numbers increase, the intelligence does not grow, when it is all folly from the beginning. It is fashionable to prate about the voice of the people: *vox populi, vox Dei:* here the voice of the people is directly against the voice of God on a great moral and political issue. A thousand votes for a wrong is not enough to make it right: once nothing is nothing, twice nothing is nothing, ten times nothing is nothing, a thousand times nothing is nothing: how many Israelite elders would be necessary so to multiply nothing as to make it foot up something at last? Just as many, we reply, as at any time it would take of wrong-headed men to make wrong right.

5. But now let us bear in mind that when a mean thing has to get itself done somehow, it requires a vast amount of meaningless talk for its advancement into recognition and success. These elders came up in a body to Samuel on the hill at Ramah, "and said unto him, Behold, thou art old, and thy sons walk not in thy ways: now make us a king to judge us like all the nations."

Our practical lesson from this part of the story is this: *graceful language is sometimes used to conceal thought, and not express it.* Diplomacy has a certain strong flavor of antiquity about it. Just notice how these crafty elders plead their hypocritical arguments for an overthrow of the government, and shake the conscientious scruples of the faithful old man by the humiliating and cruel arraignment of his sons. Those were not the real reasons why they wanted a king. Lord Bacon declares that "in all wise human governments they that sit at the helm do more happily bring their purposes about, and insinuate more easily into the minds of the people, by pretext and oblique courses than by direct methods; so that all sceptres and maces of authority ought in very deed to be crooked in the upper end." There has hardly ever been a sin so heinous as that plausible reasons of State could not be urged by elastic consciences in favor of it. It was an old saying of Pascal that the world is satisfied with words, and few care to dive beneath the surface of them.

Logic has very little to do with the utterances of a bad heart when politicians begin to reason; and there is truth in the sarcasm of one of the wittiest of Frenchmen: "When the major of an argument is an error, and the minor a passion, it is to be feared that the conclusion will be a crime, for this is a syllogism of self-love." These "elders" wanted the show and glitter of royalty "like all the nations;" what had that to do with Samuel's sons? Why did they not suppress the sons and cling to God?

6. It becomes evident that we cannot finish the exposition of so extensive a chapter in a single discourse; let us group the suggestive instructions of the passage into one for our closing to-day: we become more and more sure as we read on that *majorities are not to be trusted among even the wisest of men.* "The thing displeased Samuel when they said, Give us a king to judge us;" and in the end we shall see that it displeased the Lord and brought on the people his heavy retributions.

It has long been a maxim in this republic of ours that the openly expressed will of each majority ought to be accepted and sustained. There never was a falser or more destructive sentiment. Why, this assertion assumes that the new earth has already been created wherein is to dwell righteousness. The majority of this world is against God; so, of course, the majority would be against right and truth and godliness. The great pioneer work of righteousness has always been done by minorities and generally by martyrs. Gibbon records in his history that in the Roman Senate, at a full meeting, the emperor once proposed, according to the forms of the republic, the important question whether the worship of Jupiter or that of Christ should be the religion of the Romans. On a regular division of the senators, Jupiter was condemned by a large majority and the Christian religion was approved. What did a majority like that mean? It was a simple mockery and a lie. Jesus of Nazareth never became the deity of the Roman Empire. The liberty that the ruler allowed, the freedom of suffrages which he affected to grant to the people, was destroyed by the hopes and fears which his personal presence inspired. The senate imagined that he wished the change, and they felt it would be dangerous to oppose him. Majorities can be gotten on almost every occasion for the right or for the wrong indiscriminately, according to the popular epidemic of enthusiasm at the time.

What is wanted in our day is the virtue of an individual courage and of a personal conviction. We need voters with a conscience that impels them to stand by the right measures and support the righteous men for administering them. It ought to go without the saying that a city like this of ours should rise in its majesty against party and against trickery of placemen, and put at least common decency in the lead. Is it possible that we Christians are worse than the heathen? And yet it is true that the Koran of Mohammed says: "A ruler who appoints any man to an office, when there is in his dominion another man better qualified for its duties, sins against God and sins against the State." But how is the ruler that appoints an unworthy man any worse than the citizen that votes for such a man? And if a party joins to do it, is not that a conspiracy? And if a community tolerates it, is not that a sin and a shame? And if God is against sin, what becomes of the sinner?

It seems to me, my friends, that the hour has at last arrived in all the walks of our ordinary life when one must take his stand for an unwavering decision. In business, in politics, in theology, in Christian activity, in morals, every true believer must choose the right as God gives it to him, and be satisfied to cling to it if need be alone. To go with the multitude is easy; to go, with a surrender of our entire life, with God and the truth is sometimes hard. But the end is not yet for this history of ours. All the elders in Israel banded together in the conclave at Ramah could not make that single wrong to be right.

Once in the old times Daniel was perplexed, and there came a celestial visitant who strengthened him; what he said to him was this: "I will show thee that which is noted in the Scripture of truth; there is none that holdeth with me in these things but Michael your prince." None but Michael! but Michael was the Messiah, and the Messiah was Jesus the Christ. We can afford to be satisfied, be strong, be stubborn even, when we know that he who holdeth with us is Christ our Prince.

VII.

PRAYER ANSWERED UNDER PROTEST.

"Now therefore hearken unto their voice: howbeit yet protest solemnly unto them and show them the manner of the king that shall reign over them."—1 *Sam.* 8:9.

PRAYER is certainly a most salutary exercise whenever one is agitated beyond his strength. When the elders of Israel came to Samuel, deliberately proposing that he should give up the reins of government and set about the task of finding a successor for himself to whom they might give the power and title of a king, his mind was filled with irrepressible foreboding and alarm: "But the thing displeased Samuel, when they said, Give us a king to judge us: and Samuel prayed unto the Lord." It would not be fair to assert that Samuel was vexed to lose the patronage of the government offices out of the family, nor that he was hurt because these people intimated that he was becoming superannuated: we have no suggestion in all his history that he was either jealous or corrupt. But he discovered that the complication was now too deep for an old man like him to deal with; and so he went in prayer to God.

In the end we shall learn that the petition of these malcontents was granted, but with the answer came retribution and ultimate dismay. If we go patiently through with the particulars of the story, we shall discover that in it there is given one of the best illustrations to be found in all the Bible of just this proposition: Prayers are sometimes answered under protest. Let us, then, move on at once in our search.

I. We shall have to begin with a fair and detailed exposition of the narrative as it meets us. The old judge brought his whole case in his supplication before the Lord he had unfalteringly trusted so long. "And the Lord said unto Samuel, Hearken unto the voice of the people in all that they say unto thee: for they have not rejected thee, but they have rejected me, that I should not reign over them."

1. This verse, besides its bearing upon our main point, contains a valuable lesson of its own: *Rejecting divine providence is rejecting divine government and forfeiting divine favor.* There is no sense in a declaration that we accept God's law in general, but reserve the right to practical freedom in reference to particulars. Men seem to imagine in these times of ours that one voids his individual responsibility if he is acting in a public capacity. These people had the same absurdity in their notions of what it was their privilege to do then. Samuel was of no special account; his sons indeed were decidedly in their way when what they wanted to do was to keep up appearances, and make a parade of royalty "like all the nations." But Samuel was a providential fact; he had been put there to represent an idea; he was the announced vicegerent of God. To reject him therefore was to reject God himself.

"The end of all civil government," says an ancient thinker, writing for our times as wisely as for his own, "is to live well according to the divine pleasure." The Almighty One had been ruling over Israel and prosperously caring for the nation many years. To ask for a human king was in effect to wish to dethrone Jehovah. It was of no use just to cry out, "Oh, we mean to obey God always, only we want to take this government into our own hands!" In times farther down in the history there were those who saw all this wickedness and subterfuge of national vanity in its proper light. The prophet Hosea was inspired to tell his generation precisely the lesson to be learned from this old crime: "O Israel, thou hast destroyed thyself; but in me is thy help. I will be thy King; where is any other that may save thee in all thy cities? and thy judges of whom thou saidst, Give me a king and princes? I gave thee a king in mine anger, and took him away in my wrath."

What makes this thought of more practical value to ourselves now is the fact that in such a way only can we commit the sin or merit the judgment of those Israelites. We can say with a New Testament meaning in our language that we will not have Christ to reign over us. But a perverse mind is always ready to add that it means to be obedient as a rule to all the general commandments of the Supreme Being; only people must keep up appearances, you know, and so they have to accept the social maxims and worldly behavior of those who are around. We are surely Christians, but in general, you know; not quite so particular as we might be, possibly, but with a decided respect for religion always.

Now this will not do; Jesus Christ is everything to a man, or he is nothing. In all human history there has never been a fitter leader to command our loyalty or to win our love. We have been told that the ancient Persian kings used to elect, for the education and training of their princes, the four best men in the kingdom—the justest man, the wisest man, the bravest man, and the most temperate man—so that each new sovereign might have the highest advantages, and come to the regal throne best fitted to rule over the people. Christ is the Prince of a kingdom that is supreme in the universe; and it hath pleased the Father that in him all fulness should dwell. When the providences of God summon us to follow Jesus as our Lord, to reject him is also to reject the Lord that made us, and defy him when he is most our friend.

2. You must bear in mind, also, as this narrative proceeds, that *wilful disobedience, continuously repeated, becomes settled rebellion.* "According to all the works which they have done since the day that I brought them up out of Egypt even unto this day, wherewith they have forsaken me and served other gods, so do they also unto thee."

The reply which Samuel received reminded him that this was not a new case of sudden refusal of the divine sovereignty. That nation had actually got into the habit of it. They had never shown anything more commendable since they came up out of the land of Pharaoh; they proved an awkward and ungainly people when Moses was trying to manage them in the wilderness. Men may sin almost unconsciously till they forget how terribly lawless they are, how undermined and honey-combed with perilous corruption they have grown; and then they crash down suddenly into irretrievable crime. When one throws off God's beneficent restraints, it is surprising to see how awfully wicked he can be as in a moment of rapid demoralization. Things apparently innocent are made the baleful occasion, sometimes even the instrument, of violent outbreak in vice.

It is one of the intense severities of Montaigne to say of these atheistic people that "they infect innocent matter with their own venom." Some skeptics like to do this in their reckless arguments. They force natural science, always loyal and reverent to the Creator of the universe, to speak a lie and bring false testimony against God. In an unruly time like this of ours we ought to be able to perceive this impious tendency in debate. It is the deliberate counting out of divine government which puts this universe in such a false position. When an ingenious and ribald infidel begins to assume the right to construct a system of things to suit himself, and leave God out of his own throne, there need be no surprise if confusion follows thrice confounded. The little things go in to make up the large; and little things are what a petulant mind always seizes upon first; and by-and-by one's temper becomes irritable and his mood is defiant. He grows habituated inevitably to carping at everything that happens; and this is the same rebellious spirit in our day as that which in Samuel's day was called openly by its true name, "following after other gods." The man is then practically an idolater. He has rejected Jehovah, and is virtually in insurrection against the government of heaven. And now he wanders into stillness and shame and tries to satisfy himself with falseness: "Ephraim feedeth on wind and followeth after the east wind: he daily increaseth lies and desolation: Ephraim compasseth me about with lies, and the house of Israel with deceit: but Judah yet ruleth with God and is faithful with the saints." The only effective manner in which to deal with such a dangerous experience is found in letting it have its own way until it shall be weary and worn with its follies and be ready to return penitently to God.

3. So now we come to the point that we started to reach. In the story is found the exact expression: "Now therefore hearken unto their voice: howbeit, yet protest solemnly unto them, and show them the manner of the king that shall reign over them." *Human prayers are sometimes granted with a divine protest.* Solemn moment is that in which God gives to any man or nation in judgment what was asked of him in petulance and pride! He here tells Samuel to waste no time in expostulation; take the steps immediately to give these elders the leader they desired. He however adds the task of making them understand what sort of a monarch they will get in the end, and what a wretched con-

dition they will be in before they are through with him.

The aged prophet did his duty: "And Samuel told all the words of the Lord unto the people that asked of him a king." It may be wise for us to read over his words together just here, for a ground of congratulation, if for nothing else, that we, in this republican land, are free from the burden of any such form of endurance. A sad sort of picture is that he furnishes of a monarchical government: "This will be the manner of the king that shall reign over you: he will take your sons and appoint them unto him, for his chariots and to be his horsemen; and they shall run before his chariots: and he will appoint them unto him for captains of thousands and captains of fifties; and he will set some to plough his ground and to reap his harvest, and to make his instruments of war and the instruments of his chariots. And he will take your daughters to be confectionaries, and to be cooks, and to be bakers. And he will take your fields, and your vineyards, and your oliveyards, even the best of them, and give them to his servants. And he will take the tenth of your seed and of your vineyards, and give to his officers and to his servants. And he will take your menservants and your maidservants, and your goodliest young men, and your asses, and put them to his work. He will take the tenth of your flocks: and ye shall be his servants. And ye shall cry out in that day because of your king which ye shall have chosen you: and the Lord will not answer you in that day."

Now let us understand that *circumstances may erect a forcordained fact into a responsible sin*, for which those who are the actors are to be held accountable in the end. The Lord said these malcontents in Israel might have their wish, and yet he charges on them the guilt the transaction involved. Furthermore, this very demand of the people had been foreseen and publicly predicted three hundred years before. But a single safeguard had been thrown around it, and so it was permitted: "When thou art come unto the land which the Lord thy God giveth thee, and shalt possess it, and shalt dwell therein, and shalt say, I will set a king over me, like as all the nations that are about me; thou shalt in any wise set him king over thee whom the Lord thy God shall choose: one from among thy brethren shalt thou set king over thee: thou mayest not set a stranger over thee, which is not thy brother." Indeed, a king had been promised for that nation whenever, in the wisdom of the omniscient God, it should seem advantageous for such people to have one. And yet this whole proceeding was now wrong; it was premature and hasty, and it was conducted without reference to the overruling will of Jehovah. God's providence does not constrain any man's iniquity. Foreordination has nothing to do with free-will. Those elders were doing their own behest, not God's; and they suffered for it.

II. We turn now, in the second place, from this story to the one principle it so vividly illustrates. It is worth our while to press a valuable admonition like that which is given here. We are told to let our hearts go forth in prayer continually unto God, and God will grant us our desires. But here we learn that not even the answers we obtain are to be trusted always. What does this mean in real experience?

1. For one thing, it means that all petitions are to be offered, and all desires are to be pressed, according to the Lord's will before our will. If we thrust ourselves forward, divine Providence will frequently hedge up the way. If now we urge on, sometimes the barrier is seen to move quietly away; then we can have our request if we continue to press it. But is this safe or wise? that is the sober question. It is the creature erecting itself against the supreme judgment of its Creator and taking its case into its own hands. When a man is intelligent, and his conscience tells him that God is not exactly granting, but only permitting, his prayer, is it best for him to persevere in it in the confident hope that courage will carry him through into safety? "Shall the axe boast itself against him that heweth therewith? or shall the saw magnify itself against him that shaketh it? as if the rod should shake itself against them that lift it up, or as if the staff should lift up itself as if it were no wood. Therefore shall the Lord, the Lord of hosts, send among his fat ones leanness; and under his glory he shall kindle a burning like the burning of a fire."

2. And for another thing, this declaration means that when under protest God grants a Christian's prayer, the answer will be a positive discipline

rather than a blessing. You remember the story of Israel: "They soon forgat his works, they waited not for his counsel: but lusted exceedingly in the wilderness, and tempted God in the desert. And he gave them their request, but sent leanness into their soul." See how this bears upon every-day life. A father was once praying beside the sick-bed of his child; what he said was this: "Let him become what he will, only let him live, and I will be satisfied." At the moment the boy's face paled; he shuddered, and the physician exclaimed, "He is dying now!" The father fell on his knees and prayed again audibly, uttering his petition before all: "Let him become what he will, only let him live, and I will be satisfied." Then his son recovered. Years passed, and he was a criminal, tried, condemned; and on the walk to execution he turned airily to his father and said, "Will you please see me to the gallows?" It is well to have the right of petition; but it is not wise ever to press prayers against the divine protest.

VIII.

SAMUEL'S FAREWELL ADDRESS.

"Only fear the Lord, and serve him in truth with all your heart: for consider how great things he hath done for you."—1 *Sam.* 12:24.

A FEELING of pensive regret comes into our experience as we study the words of Samuel upon his retiring from the head of the nation. A few malcontents, influenced by their own vanity and desire to figure, tell him that he must vanish from his place, and he cheerfully acquiesces, foreseeing the worse times on which they are going to run speedily.

In the "Personal Memoirs of General Grant" there is found a very suggestive illustration which might aid us much in our thought. He says: "On the evening of the first day out from Goliad we heard the most unearthly howling of wolves directly in our front. The prairie grass was tall and we could not see the beasts, but the sound indicated that they were near. To my ear it appeared that there must have been enough of them to devour our party, horses and all, at a single meal.... But Benjamin did not propose turning back. When he did speak it was to ask, 'Grant, how many wolves do you think are in that pack?' Suspecting that he thought I would overestimate the number, I determined to show my acquaintance with the animal by putting the estimate below what possibly could be correct, and answered, ' Oh, about twenty,' very indifferently. He smiled and rode on. In a minute we were close upon them and before they saw us. There were just *two* of them. Seated upon their haunches with their mouths close together, they had made all the noise we had been hearing for the past ten minutes. I have often thought of this incident since when I have heard the noise of a few disappointed politicians who had deserted their associates. *There are always more of them before they are counted.*"

But we desire to use this incident as a religious illustration rather than as a political. In its deepest and best elements real religious experience is the same the world over, the same in the Old Testament as in the New. Amid all changes of circumstances and education there is enough of agreement in essential points of evangelical delineation to arouse our sympathy, arrest our minds, and instruct our intelligence, whenever any one begins to talk about those "great things" which the Lord has done for his chosen children.

I. Let us turn our attention, in the first place, to the history just as it stands. There is much in the posture of affairs at the time when Samuel delivered his parting address, as well as in the subject-matter of the address itself, which will give help to the lessons we shall learn concerning Christian experience, as they will come before us afterwards.

1. This famous leader of God's people does not retire out of sight under any sense of ignominious

failure. No one can peruse this account of his surrender of the government into the hands of Saul without feeling that the full dignity of the eminent and good old man is preserved. He seems to have gathered a vast assemblage of people at Gilgal, just after the coronation of their new king, and sought a hearing from their minds and their consciences with more directness than ever before, at the same time demanding a verdict upon some personal particulars which concerned his reputation in office: "And now, behold, the king walketh before you: and I am old and gray-headed; and, behold, my sons are with you: and I have walked before you from my childhood unto this day. Behold, here I am: witness against me before the Lord, and before his anointed: whose ox have I taken? or whose ass have I taken? or whom have I defrauded? whom have I oppressed? or of whose hand have I received any bribe to blind mine eyes therewith? and I will restore it you. And they said, Thou hast not defrauded us nor oppressed us, neither hast thou taken aught of any man's hand."

2. He receives the public and emphatic approval of the entire political career which he now closes. It would not be easy in all history to find a more sublime appeal than that which he addresses to those who had known him so well. Evidently he does not look upon himself as shoved out of position impertinently, but simply as retired from it by the God of heaven whom it was his highest honor to obey. There can be nothing nobler for any public man than this testimony to his perfect

integrity as he disappears to make room for another to come into the lead: "And he said unto them, The Lord is witness against you, and his anointed is witness this day, that ye have not found aught in my hand. And they answered, He is witness."

3. He now works a miracle to show that his power is still undiminished : "Now therefore stand and see this great thing which the Lord will do before your eyes. Is it not wheat harvest to-day? I will call unto the Lord, and he shall send thunder and rain; that ye may perceive and see that your wickedness is great, which ye have done in the sight of the Lord, in asking you a king. So Samuel called unto the Lord; and the Lord sent thunder and rain that day; and all the people greatly feared the Lord and Samuel." This is no foolish prompting of vanity; he does not appear to have desired to make an impression, just for its own sake, that his communion with Jehovah and his ability to wield the forces of omnipotence are as yet unimpaired. He has one supreme lesson to administer, and this undoubted miracle is wrought in order to give it intensity. His hold is perpetuated upon their consciences from this time forward; he is the old man for counsel, and Saul the young man for war. Indeed, he becomes the power which is behind the throne.

4. Then he rebukes the whole people for their sin in thus dethroning God from the supreme place: "Now, therefore, behold the king whom ye have chosen and whom ye have desired! and, behold, the Lord hath set a king over you. And all the

people said unto Samuel, Pray for thy servants unto the Lord thy God, that we die not: for we have added unto all our sins this evil, to ask us a king." We cannot withhold our exalted admiration of this aged man as he stands there on the coronation day, and in the presence of the monarch who has just received the crown, denouncing the guilt of those who have turned aside from the counsels of their fathers' God. He is plain and earnest and brave. The rain falls over them as he speaks, the thunder is in the sky above their heads; it is like the voice of Jehovah upon the waters: "The voice of the Lord is upon the waters: the God of glory thundereth; the Lord is upon many waters."

5. He holds out before them the hope of retrieval of their wrong: "And Samuel said unto the people, Fear not: ye have done all this wickedness: yet turn not aside from following the Lord, but serve the Lord with all your heart; and turn ye not aside: for then should ye go after vain things, which cannot profit nor deliver; for they are vain." They shall yet have another chance, if they will penitently return to devout service of God. Let them give their hearts to him as before, and he will not forsake the people he has loved so long. And this patient, good, forgiving old man says that he will continue to pray in their behalf, and will try to teach them "the good and right way" still.

6. So at last he counsels them to go over their history again, and consider what the Lord had done in the days gone by for their comfort and peace: "Moreover, as for me, God forbid that I should sin

against the Lord in ceasing to pray for you: but I will teach you the good and the right way: only fear the Lord, and serve him in truth with all your heart: for consider how great things he hath done for you." He exhorts in terms of humblest pleading that they will remember that, whenever they have been faithful, God has been good and patient.

II. Now it is this last sentiment, which indeed is the influential one of this whole speech, that has been given us to-day as a golden text for committal to memory. Upon it turns at once the lesson for present Christian experience. What Jehovah had done for Israel in fact he has done for every believer in figure; so that it becomes a most animating exercise for us, in the second place, to seek from Samuel's address the particulars of divine dealing with that nation which illustrate spiritually his dealings with Christian hearts everywhere.

1. Samuel told his hearers that they ought to remember how God had found the children of Israel in Egyptian bondage and had stirred them up to long for deliverance.

One of the chief things, as indeed it is the earliest of all, that God does for each believer under the New Testament is to show him the deep depravity of his whole nature while he is in bondage to sin. It is not everybody who wants to see the sad state of his own heart, but he can never be saved without a glimpse of it; for he would never long for redeeming grace.

2. Then this great leader told the people to recall how generously God had provided for Israel the

means of deliverance. He had sent to them his servants Moses and Aaron.

It would be a sad, hard thing to do, just to show a sinner his wickedness, and then leave him there in hopeless ruin. The least pity would prompt that he might be left to die in painless ignorance. Our Father in heaven has provided an atonement for sin, and actually despatched his only-begotten Son to bring the tidings of quick rescue to lost souls. Thus he has opened a way of escape through the gospel to all who will come and accept his grace.

3. Next, Samuel tells his hearers that Jehovah had himself been their sole deliverer. Moses tried it once; but, alone, neither he nor Aaron could move that frightened, stubborn people to take a step in their own behalf. For simple safety Moses had to flee out of Egypt, as one sometimes has to flee in self-defence from the flames out of which he is trying to lead dumb cattle. God came in person; he sent his pillar of cloud and of fire to show them the way out of their perils.

What the divine Presence was under the old dispensation, the divine Spirit is under the new. No man would ever enter a handsbreadth upon the path of peace with God's law unless some sort of constraining influence came to aid him, as the angels came to seize Lot's hand to pull him away out of burning Sodom. The Lord has not only shown the sinner his need, and provided a full supply to meet it, but has also given his Spirit to lead each soul into the way and help it along to the very end.

4. Samuel tells these people also that Jehovah

had removed from them the punishments they had incurred by their own obstinate disobedience. It would have availed but a little, only giving a brief respite from deserved doom, if the Lord had delivered Israel from the Philistines and the Moabites, and then reserved them to be rejected and condemned and punished by himself. But his mercy had followed them with pardon.

Here, again, we must remember how patiently and forbearingly the Almighty has removed from sinful men the consequences of their transgressions. He gives his Holy Spirit to work out an entire renovation of one's whole nature, so that the man may be rescued from all danger of ultimate ruin.

5. Then this address of the prophet-leader points out how Jehovah had bestowed upon Israel peculiar joys; it had pleased him to make them his people: "For the Lord will not forsake his people for his great name's sake: because it hath pleased the Lord to make you his people." No expression could have been more suggestive than this to those who heard him that day. Through the wilderness journey, on over the Jordan, many a weary, hard mile had he led those tribes; and yet every day and hour he had given them honey out of the rock and water in the midst of the desert, fine high inspirations of hope concerning the land of promise, comfort and expectation until now.

Surely God has given the Christian peculiar joys, and in the fair sweet future held out before each true believer great and exhilarating hopes. Peace in believing, communion with Jesus, fellowship with the redeemed, ultimate freedom from indwelling sin, progress in knowledge, eternal security at the last—these are among the joys and hopes bestowed on the pardoned ones he loves.

III. Thus we reach the orderly mention of those plain and practical admonitions which such a rehearsal is likely to give.

1. Christian reminiscence is a duty and a pleasure. All of us should diligently go over our whole history now and then, considering "how great things God hath done" for us.

2. Gratitude for the past is a chief incentive to carefulness in the future. "Look unto the rock whence ye are hewn, and to the hole of the pit whence ye are digged."

3. What aggregates of mercy and hope and peace and joy do after a while gather around an aged Christian! The Almighty once told his people that if they were faithful to him he would make their days "as the days of heaven upon earth."

4. There is need of an audible open expression of our acknowledgment of divine mercy. It is well to sing over and over again such hymns as "Jesus sought me when a stranger." It is well to speak out: "The Lord hath done great things."

5. The gratitude of believers is an argument with the impenitent and unthankful (Deut. 10:21). Let all Christians say with the Psalmist: "Come and hear, all ye that fear God, and I will declare what he hath done for my soul."

IX.

ONE SIN TOO MANY.

"AND SAMUEL SAID UNTO SAUL, I WILL NOT RETURN WITH THEE; FOR THOU HAST REJECTED THE WORD OF THE LORD, AND THE LORD HATH REJECTED THEE FROM BEING KING OVER ISRAEL."
—1 *Sam.* 15:26.

THE echo of that first glad shout of Israel, "God save the king!" has hardly died away in the distance before now we are summoned to behold his downfall in whose honor the people clamored. God is not going to save King Saul any longer; for he has committed one sin too much for the divine forbearance. But he is going to save the realm he has permitted to rise into being. The whole story upon which we enter to-day affords an extensive illustration of sin in almost all of its phases of manifestation as judged by the righteous law of God.

1. We discover the simple nature of sin: it is disobedience of a divine command. What Saul was bidden to do, he refused to do, and in the end did not do: that was sin. "Now go and smite Amalek, and utterly destroy all that they have, and spare them not; but slay both man and woman, infant and suckling, ox and sheep, camel and ass. But Saul and the people spared Agag, and the best of the sheep and of the oxen and of the fatlings and the lambs, and all that was good, and would not utterly destroy them." There is no need of bewildering ourselves with a subtle analysis: "Sin is any

want of conformity unto, or transgression of, the law of God."

There is one enactment recorded in the Pentateuch about nothing more or less than the eggs in a bird's nest (Deut. 22:6, 7): "If a bird's nest chance to be before thee in the way in any tree, or on the ground, whether they be young ones, or eggs, and the dam sitting upon the young, or upon the eggs, thou shalt not take the dam with the young; but thou shalt in any wise let the dam go, and take the young to thee; that it may be well with thee, and that thou mayest prolong thy days."

This the Jewish rabbis have always pronounced to be "the least commandment in the law." Yet they called a man a transgressor if he broke it. And this is the New Testament rule for all time; if a Christian offends at one point, he disobeys; and that is just the same as being guilty of all (Jas. 2:9-11): "For whosoever shall keep the whole law, and yet offend in one point, he is guilty of all. For he that said, Do not commit adultery, said also, Do not kill. Now, if thou commit no adultery, yet if thou kill, thou art become a transgressor of the law."

2. We learn, likewise, a lesson concerning the wide reach of sin. Saul felt quite independent in his disobedience; was he not the unquestioned general of an army of two hundred and ten thousand men? He did what pleased his own cupidity and satisfied his own pride, and took no account of other people. Now we see that this sin of his "grieved" Samuel so that it kept him crying in prayer all the

night. Moreover, it disinherited Jonathan, wrecked the new dynasty, mortified all the loyal subjects of the realm, and gave final offence unto God.

It is not possible for any man to keep his sin all to himself; when a human will meets the divine will in opposition, it is sure to cause a vast disturbance. This universe is balanced with great nicety. It cannot endure a sinner's perversity without suffering any more than an oarsman can tolerate a perverse boy in a boat; every time the self-willed creature steps across the thwart, he rocks the vessel, and makes it uncomfortable and perilous for each one who has anything to do with him.

3. Next to this, we discover an illustration of the bold effrontery of sin. Saul seems to forget that he agreed to send for Samuel whenever an exigency should arise, and wait for his arrival seven days in order to have his counsel in coming to a decision. He did not seek the prophet at all. Samuel came at the command of the Lord seeking him instead; and yet Saul hurriedly begins the conversation— begins it with a brag and a bluster and a blessing, all in one rush of breath: "And Samuel came to Saul: and Saul said unto him, Blessed be thou of the Lord: I have performed the commandment of the Lord."

Thus iniquity often tries to carry off shame with a show of daring, and attempts to restore its self-confidence with a complacency of self-congratulation. Its fair picture for all the ages is found in the sharp description of a wicked woman, which Solomon gives us in the book of Proverbs: "She eateth, and wipeth her mouth, and saith, I have done no wickedness."

4. Of course, now comes a lesson concerning the certain discovery of sin: "And Samuel said, What meaneth then this bleating of the sheep in mine ears, and the lowing of the oxen which I hear?" The very sheep gave their testimony with bleating, and the cattle lowed for a witness against this hypocritical king; he was betrayed by his triumphs.

Guilt always feels lonely; and yet, curiously enough, always imagines that everybody knows about the crime. Conscience keeps the culprit excited, for he understands that nature positively abhors transgression of law. The universe has a thousand voices with which to speak, when the time comes for wickedness to be known. "Be sure your sin will find you out."

5. Once more: the story gives us an illustration of the evasive meanness of sin: "And Saul said, They have brought them from the Amalekites; for the people spared the best of the sheep and of the oxen, to sacrifice unto the Lord thy God; and the rest we have utterly destroyed." Notice the language here carefully. Saul was evidently an adept in the use of pronouns. "The people spared the best of the sheep and the oxen;" but the rest of the spoils "we have utterly destroyed." When the guilt was proved "they" did it; so far as the slender obedience was admitted, "we" did it. One would think this king had been fairly outraged by the greed of his people, and at the same moment quite wonder-struck with their unusual devoutness.

Well, Adam set the example, when he charged his sin over to the woman who gave him the forbidden fruit, and over to God who gave him the woman; and the woman quickly followed the example, when she charged her sin over to the serpent. Meantime, Jehovah held all of these three accountable for their own personal share in the wickedness. It was most contemptible for a monarch like Saul to shirk his responsibility on the army, when he knew that if one of the soldiers had disobeyed him in a single act, he would have caused him to be hewed into pieces. But men who are caught in wrong are always doing the most unmanly things in order to get their punishment to be borne by others.

6. Then we have a lesson concerning the hypocritical excuses offered for sin: "And Saul said unto Samuel, Yea, I have obeyed the voice of the Lord, and have gone the way which the Lord sent me, and have brought Agag the king of Amalek, and have utterly destroyed the Amalekites. But the people took of the spoil, sheep and oxen, the chief of the things which should have been utterly destroyed, to sacrifice unto the Lord thy God in Gilgal."

Saul said that these excellent dumb creatures were brought home with him for the pious services of burnt offering. Ah, me! if those innocent animals could only have been heard once more, and could have made their language intelligible! This king even twice calls Jehovah "thy God" so as to compel Samuel to take the compliment of believing that he thought of him too, and expected he would be really pleased to know he had returned in such a good frame of mind.

Alas! this was not the first time, and it has not been the last, that human perversity has pleaded a religious motive for the vilest of sins. We have no reason to believe that Saul was overcome by an impulse of extraordinary devotion so as to forget the commands which had been laid upon him. Those flocks and herds were valuable; and Agag had been a formidable foe in the field. We presume that the young monarch wished to enjoy the wealth he had captured, and he wished the fame of dragging a conquered king at the back of his chariot: that was all.

7. Now just at this point we receive a lesson concerning the just condemnation of sin. Samuel appears decorous and kind in his dealings with the Lord's anointed. So he does not tell him that he sees through all his subterfuges, and knows him to be utterly false and fickle. He accepts his statement of fact so far as is necessary for his argument; and then he assures him that, even if he did come home to slay his sacrifices, the Lord preferred obedience to worship; so he was condemned: "And Samuel said, Hath the Lord as great delight in burnt offerings and sacrifices as in obeying the voice of the Lord? Behold, to obey is better than sacrifice, and to hearken than the fat of rams."

Here is the one open principle on which all men are to be judged. It runs through the whole Bible. The Psalmist sings it: "I will not reprove thee for thy sacrifices or thy burnt offerings, to have been continually before me. I will take no bullock out of thy house, nor he-goats out of thy folds: for every beast of the forest is mine, and the cattle upon a thousand hills. I know all the fowls of the mountains; and the wild beasts of the field are mine. If I were hungry, I would not tell thee: for the world is mine, and the fulness thereof. Will I eat the flesh of bulls, or drink the blood of goats? Offer unto God thanksgiving; and pay thy vows unto the Most High."

Isaiah repeats it: "To what purpose is the multitude of your sacrifices unto me? saith the Lord: I am full of the burnt offerings of rams and the fat of fed beasts; and I delight not in the blood of bullocks or of lambs or of he-goats. When ye come to appear before me, who hath required this at your hand, to tread my courts? Bring no more vain oblations; incense is an abomination unto me; the new moons and Sabbaths, the calling of assemblies, I cannot away with; it is iniquity, even the solemn meeting. Your new moons and your appointed feasts my soul hateth: they are a trouble unto me; I am weary to bear them. And when ye spread forth your hands, I will hide mine eyes from you: yea, when ye make many prayers, I will not hear: your hands are full of blood. Wash you, make you clean; put away the evil of your doings from before mine eyes; cease to do evil; learn to do well."

Jeremiah reiterates it: "Hear, O earth: behold, I will bring evil upon this people, even the fruit of their thoughts, because they have not hearkened unto my words, nor to my law, but rejected it. To what purpose cometh there to me incense from Sheba, and the sweet cane from a far country? your burnt offerings are not acceptable, nor your sacrifices sweet unto me."

Micah presses it also: "Wherewith shall I come before the Lord, and bow myself before the high God? shall I come before him with burnt offerings, with calves of a year old? Will the Lord be pleased with thousands of rams, or with ten thousands of rivers of oil? shall I give my first-born for my transgression, the fruit of my body for the sin of my soul? He hath showed thee, O man, what is good; and what doth the Lord require of thee but to do justly, and to love mercy, and to walk humbly with thy God?"

And our Lord quotes it in the New Testament: "Go ye and learn what that meaneth, I will have mercy, and not sacrifice; for I am not come to call the righteous, but sinners, to repentance." God will have obedience only: sin is an abomination to him.

8. There is likewise here an illustration of the aggregating force of sin: "For rebellion is as the sin of witchcraft, and stubbornness is as iniquity and idolatry. Because thou hast rejected the word of the Lord, he hath also rejected thee from being king." It is hardly worth while to attempt to enumerate the acts of wickedness which followed directly upon this first dereliction of Saul: treachery, lying, vanity, covetousness, hypocrisy,—these were among them. This king had been very zealous against rebellion, witchcraft, iniquity, and idolatry;

now the Lord tells him that his stubbornness and disobedience have been just as bad as anything else.

There are degrees of depravity, no doubt; but all sin is bad, and tends to what is worse. Sometimes we notice the workmen lift a great iron door in the pavement of the street; away down in the dark we discern a flight of stairs. The steps of sin are like those which run from the sidewalk to the sewer, down, always down; there is never so much as one of them that leads up to the plain level on which Christians ought to walk.

9. Still another lesson meets us here, and now it is concerning the inevitable result of sin: "And Saul said unto Samuel, I have sinned: for I have transgressed the commandment of the Lord and thy words: because I feared the people, and obeyed their voice. Now therefore, I pray thee, pardon my sin, and turn again with me, that I may worship the Lord. And Samuel said unto Saul, I will not return with thee: for thou hast rejected the word of the Lord, and the Lord hath rejected thee from being king over Israel."

Saul had reached the limit of divine forbearance. Indeed, he had already committed one sin too many. It was of no use for him to plead for pardon any more. There is something very strange in the subsequent career of this monarch; he seems bewildered and off his balance. Sometimes he prays, and then he consults the witch of Endor; sometimes he is superstitiously devout, and then he becomes blasphemous. He grows insane, then tries to murder David; at the last commits the final sin, from which there is no retreat. He disappears in the wild gleam of battle, dying by suicide.

All sin left to itself is hopeless. The kingdom was taken from this man so that he should not injure any one else any more. Even heathen people know that is just. When we were at school we used to declaim this sentence from Demosthenes' oration: "It is not possible, O Athenians! that a power should be permanent which is marked with injustice, perjury, and falsehood."

Every sin registers itself upon the line of association it belongs with. Iniquities are gregarious; they come in files silent and single, but they instantly affiliate themselves in dangerous herds. "And being let go, they went to their own company." The instinct that a wickedness has is almost like that of a living thing; it puts itself alongside of something like itself, and then grows swiftly organic and forceful for retribution. Nothing is ever lost, nothing forgotten.

Hence, finally, sin becomes massed and destructive. It is an Arab saying that we so often quote: "The last straw breaks the camel's back." No: it is the whole load that kills the camel, but it is the last straw which makes the load complete and intolerable. When the fall of the beast comes, all the burden tells. A time arrives at the last when just one more little act of rebellion against God discharges all the violence of divine wrath in an absolute reprobation. "He that being often reproved hardeneth his neck, shall suddenly be destroyed, and that without remedy."

X.

GOD'S ESTIMATE OF HUMAN AVAILABILITY.

"But the Lord said unto Samuel, Look not on his countenance, or on the height of his stature; because I have refused him.—1 *Sam.* 16:7.

This enunciation of one fixed principle in the divine government is of immense value as having a practical bearing upon all the mighty relations which each man sustains to his Maker. The narrative, in the midst of which the verse occurs, not only states it clearly, but shows it at work. We cannot fail to find profit, therefore, if we give such a passage our study in detail as an illustration of the Lord's dealing with a human soul in the precise moment when he was summoning it forth into activity and responsibility in the fulfilment of his purposes.

The tale of David's anointing by Samuel throws into luminous exhibition the way in which God searches and registers men; and it likewise informs us, once for all, what he accepts and what he rejects, in making up his estimates of their character and their availability.

In this procession of Jesse's sons Eliab came earliest: the head of their line, the pride of their household, the first-born of them in the tribal pedigree. Evidently Samuel was pleased and expectant, the moment he looked upon his vast proportions and his commanding mien; he exclaimed with enthusiasm, "Surely the Lord's anointed is before Him!"

"But the Lord said unto Samuel, Look not on his countenance, or on the height of his stature; because I have refused him: for the Lord seeth not as man seeth; for man looketh on the outward appearance, but the Lord looketh on the heart. Then Jesse called Abinadab, and made him pass before Samuel. And he said, Neither hath the Lord chosen this. Then Jesse made Shammah to pass by. And he said, Neither hath the Lord chosen this. And Jesse made seven of his sons to pass before Samuel. And Samuel said unto Jesse, The Lord hath not chosen these. And Samuel said unto Jesse, Are here all thy children? And he said, There remaineth yet the youngest, and, behold, he keepeth the sheep. And Samuel said unto Jesse, Send and fetch him: for we will not sit down till he come hither. And he sent, and brought him in. Now he was ruddy, and withal of a beautiful countenance, and goodly to look upon. And the Lord said, Arise, anoint him: for this is he. Then Samuel took the horn of oil and anointed him in the midst of his brethren: and the Spirit of the Lord came mightily upon David from that day forward."

I. Let us try to analyze the statement on the negative side, to begin with. The Lord does not look upon the outward appearance in fixing his judgment of any human soul. It so happens that this very narrative actually specifies many of those particulars which men are wont to regard as highest in value.

1. For example, the Lord does not look upon one's social rank. Samuel is sent to a village farm to choose a successor to King Saul. Bethlehem was a poor little insignificant town: a great prophet said of it, even many years after this, that it was "little among the thousands of Judah." The family of Jesse had no conspicuousness or remarkableness, as the world reckons.

Moreover, David was the one that made it royal, and when he was chosen he was by no means the head of it. It is worthy of our attention that the Bible makes such very short and sharp work with primogeniture as a condition of selection in exalted leadership. It would seem as if it had been settled that the first-born sons should be superseded. Isaac before Ishmael, Jacob before Esau, Joseph before Reuben, and here David before Eliab, so the inspired history runs on. It may be that this is designed to assert in Old Testament fact what is subsequently proclaimed in New Testament doctrine: "You see your calling, brethren, how that not many wise men after the flesh, not many mighty, not many noble, are called." Good Lady Huntingdon used to say she thanked God for the letter M, for he did not tell Paul to say "not any," but "not many."

Now it is certainly true that the best part of the world's highest worth has risen from what would by some be called its lowest sources. It is usual to sneer at the plebeian birth of Oliver Cromwell as well as that of Napoleon Bonaparte; but this had nothing to do with any vices they displayed or any virtues they possessed. These men were kings of other men by reason of a manhood which Charles the First never got from the contemptible Stuarts, nor Louis the Sixteenth from the more contemptible Bourbons. The pride of rank is prone to run into an extreme of superciliousness, of self-seeking, and of oppression. Cornelius Agrippa actually institutes an argument to prove that there was "never a nobility which had not a wicked beginning." Now it is not of any profit nor of any necessity that we should be harsh· it is enough for our present purpose to claim that God is not in any case a respecter of persons; "but, in every nation, he that feareth him and worketh righteousness is," as says the fisherman Peter, "accepted with him."

2. Furthermore, the Lord does not look upon one's family history. The lineage of Jesse, Obed, and Ruth was quite humble in its origin; the household stock had worth of piety in it, but there is no evidence that David owed his elevation to anything that had been done for him before he was born. His mother is not even mentioned by name in the Scriptures.

It is pitifully mean and conceited for any one to set himself up as meritorious because his family once had a hero among its members. When we were learning to write at school, one of the copies that ran along the top of two pages standing opposite was made up of this now worn and familiar couplet:

> "Honor and worth from no condition rise:
> Act well your part; there all the honor lies."

Four times in one chapter of ancient prophecy we are told by the Lord himself that when a land should be visited with pestilence, the most eminent merits of one's ancestors should not avail to save a wicked person from peril: "Though Noah, Daniel, and Job were in it, as I live, saith the Lord God, they shall deliver neither son nor daughter."

3. Again: the Lord does not look upon one's fortune. If any one supposes that the wealth of the "rich kinsman" Boaz had come down by inheritance into this family estate, we are surely without hint that the property had anything to do with the lot of the shepherd-boy David. He was not anointed king because of his father's possessions. It would not be fair to assert that God always chooses the poor before the rich, but he certainly does not choose the rich for their riches in any case.

In divine providence, so far as it can be read in history, there appears to be preserved a calm indifference to any recommendation that might be suggested, even if not pressed, by the fact that an individual belonged to what was called "the moneyed aristocracy" of his times. It is not necessary for any Christian to grow cynical. Old father Jerome left on record in his terse Latin this saying: "Every opulent man is either an iniquitous man or the heir of an iniquitous man who went before him." This saying was quoted, actually with enthusiasm, by the pulpit-orator Bourdaloue in his famous discourse on riches, wherein he improved the opportunity to assert, after replying to some objections and guarding against some possible perversions, that his mind also had come to the same conclusion. Such language seems ill-advised, and has to be pronounced extreme. For Abraham was rich, and Job was rich, and the Lord made him richer, and Nicodemus was rich, and Joseph of Arimathæa was rich; and if these men were therefore iniquitous, or sons descended from iniquitous fathers, it would be hard to find any just man even in the splendid biographies of Old and New Testament worthies.

As things turn out in modern times, we feel surer that religious hopefulness lies somewhere near the golden mean of moderation and competence. Wit does not always go with wealth either, as a matter of commonplace observation. That is a wise remark of Plutarch, as he contrasts two of his characters: "The poverty of Aristides was more noble than the wealth of Midas." In the presence of some of the hard and grasping men who wield the colossal fortunes of the present day, it is salutary sometimes to quote the words of inspiration as the rule: "Hearken, my beloved brethren, hath not God chosen the poor of this world rich in faith, and heirs of the kingdom which he hath promised to them that love him?"

4. Nor does the Lord look upon one's appearance. Hardly would it seem necessary to press this point, if it were not awkwardly true that vanity is sometimes discoverable even in aged men and women. In the story we are studying there is, in all

likelihood, an allusion to the ridiculous enthusiasm which the Israelites had previously manifested when Saul was elected king: they fairly shouted with admiration because he was so tall and comely. A man is not always great because he is big.

It is interesting to notice that in the margin of our English Bibles the words in the seventh verse of this chapter, "the outward appearance," are rendered more literally "the eyes;" and also the words in the twelfth verse, "a beautiful countenance," are rendered "fair of eyes." That is to say, David is not chosen for his good looks, nor is Eliab rejected because of his; they may both have had fine eyes, but the Lord does not regard such things in his selection of men for high service of himself. John Milton was blind, and Thomas Carlyle was not considered attractive in showy company. Plato tells us that Socrates resembled one of those misshapen pictures of apes and owls painted on the outside of an apothecary's gallipot; but he adds that although the figures were grotesque, the vessel was truly filled with sweet balsams. Paul was diminutive and half blind, in bodily presence weak and in speech contemptible; "but," says Chrysostom, "this man of three cubits' height became tall enough to touch the third heaven."

5. Once more: the Lord does not look upon one's age in making his choice of men. He sometimes selects children, and then trains them at his will. In the absence of any information on this point, some commentators have seemed to think, from calculation of dates, that David must at this

time have been about sixteen or seventeen years old. At any rate, he was the youngest of that large family, a mere boy out in the field tending the sheep of his father, and held in such small consideration as that Jesse had to be questioned about sending for him.

These repeated instances of passing by the elder and more mature members of a household for the sake of those in the very morning of youth must have in them a lesson as to the hopefulness of caring for the children in our own homes. Polycarp was converted at nine years of age, Matthew Henry at eleven, President Edwards at seven, Robert Hall at twelve, and Isaac Watts at nine. God chooses his best workers often in the beginning of their intelligent existence; they that seek him early are sure to find him. It does not require the wisdom of Lord Bacon to discover such a thing, but the aphorism gains authority from his having put it forth: "For the moral part, youth will have the preëminence, as age hath for the politic." It is less difficult for one to become a true and patient follower of Christ before the world's policies come in to warp the ingenuous soul.

II. But it is high time for us to turn to the positive side of the statement concerning the divine choice of men. The Lord does not look upon the outward appearance: what does he look upon? What is meant here by the word "heart"? "The Lord seeth not as man seeth; for man looketh on the outward appearance, but the Lord looketh on the heart."

It is not necessary that we try to be abstruse and philosophical in giving an interpretation to this familiar word "heart." The entire nature of the individual is brought into view. Our Maker does not intimate a mere curiosity in his search of character; he looks for actual availability. There was a work far on ahead for this young David's life; whether he was the one for this was the purpose of the inquiries in this instance. God does not look upon the surroundings a man shows when he wears a robe of wealth or station; he looks upon what the robe is thrown around. That is to say, he looks upon the soul itself; each choice of his divine wisdom turns upon the man's wishes and motives in the innermost recesses of his soul—his genuineness, his character.

We shall have to take up the remainder of the verse for study again; this is enough for our need just now. In a sober review of what has already been said, it seems as if there might be wisdom in picturing our own lives for a little while, in holding them out before careful and discriminating analysis. Then we can put some fair questions.

For example, this: *Do we hope for God's favor on the ground of a long line of personal recommendations?* It is hardly probable that our candor would be sufficient to meet such an inquiry plainly, if it were put in so bald and uncompromising a form. But some there are who conceive of their advantages as far higher than those of others, although many men with whom they compare themselves are on much superior elevations both in experience and in communion with God. There is a general superciliousness of soul out in the air nowadays, a kind of assumption of high-bred nearness to holiness and artistic piety, a knowledge of what is proper "form" in religion and fashionable decorum in ordinary worship, as well as what is saintly in demeanor and in contributions to charity. Really, are Christians trying to mock God genteelly?

Then again: this subject leads us to inquire whether our personal salvation is to be settled *by what the world around us thinks about our showy piety, or by what the Lord himself thinks.* There is an outward sanctimoniousness which looks very like sanctity: will it all end the same way? Krummacher, the German author, relates that he was once invited to a banquet given in honor of Goethe, at which all the mighty leaders of the continent had been gathered. The young writer was ambitious of making acquaintances in such a throng of celebrities. Watching his chance, he spoke to Thorwaldsen, the great Danish sculptor, at that moment standing on the height of his fame. He was met by the artist with a question, sharp and sudden, as if he had grown select in a fastidious choice of his companionships in such a company of foreigners: "Are you an artist?" The author of the "Life of Elijah the Tishbite," with due modesty, replied, "No; I am a preacher." The proud stonecutter straightened himself up as he cried out loud enough to be heard in the entire room, "Oh, how can it be possible that you should be only a theologian?" The youthful student was abashed; but he has recorded in his note-book of that date that he could not help even then reflecting on the fact that this self-satisfied sculptor had spent months on just fashioning the splendid statue of Christ which had made the world wonder, but evidently had a most inadequate notion of Christ himself. So he says quaintly, "From this moment I drew the conclusion that an enthusiastic admiration for Jesus, our Lord, is something very different from saving faith in him, reaching the heart and controlling the life."

Finally, in view of this subject, there would follow this question: *How much of what worldlings prize will vanish when the Lord makes known his register of actual worth?* Just lately you have noted in the missionary newspapers that the Maharajah of Travancore, in India, has at last prepared to revive the time-honored custom of his fathers, and is going to present the ceremony of "thooloparum." This is an old heathen performance, and consists in placing a living man upon one scale of a large balance, and then loading down the other scale with a splendid heap of pure gold: afterward the money is distributed among the attendant Brahmins according to each one's grade or station. Thus his Royal Highness is declared to be sanctified: and, best of all, thus those happy Brahmins are expected to shout aloud through the empire that for all time he is to be reckoned as worth his weight in gold to the Indian people. Now when we know, as we do, that the great God above, whom we worship as Christians, does not look on such things, but on the inner heart of the man who loves him and loves his fellow-man, what can any of us find really to admire in this ceremony of " thooloparum " ?

Calmly does that eye of God keep gazing down upon men: it registers us all justly; and that estimate will stand for ever undisturbed.

> " Life is the plaything of fortune, a medley of joy and sorrow :
> Lightly she tosses it up, lightly she tumbles it down :
> High in the heavens to-day, it is low in the dust to-morrow :
> Lightly she tosses it up, lightly she tumbles it down."

Calmly also does the Word of God utter its own counsel, whether the restless race of men will be content to listen or not:

"Love not the world, neither the things that are in the world. If any man love the world, the love of the Father is not in him. For all that is in the world, the lust of the flesh and the lust of the eyes and the pride of life, is not of the Father, but is of the world. And the world passeth away, and the lust thereof: but he that doeth the will of God abideth for ever."

XI.

GOD'S ESTIMATE OF HUMAN CHARACTER.

"THE LORD SEETH NOT AS MAN SEETH; FOR MAN LOOKETH ON THE OUTWARD APPEARANCE, BUT THE LORD LOOKETH ON THE HEART."—1 *Sam.* 16:7.

WE must consider this historic transaction as something more than the mere expression of a preference. The Almighty is selecting a successor to King Saul in the government of his people: one of the mightiest of all his decrees is rushing forward into exercise. So here can be found the revelation of a permanent and wide-reaching principle.

1. Observe, in the first place, that God's purpose claims a specific direction: the "Lord looketh on the heart." What does this mean?

David's own understanding of the examination through which he in company with his brothers passed in this instance comes to view afterward in the rehearsal of one of his historic Psalms for the temple use: "The Lord shall judge the people: judge me, O Lord, according to my righteousness, and according to mine integrity that is in me. Oh, let the wickedness of the wicked come to an end; but establish the just: for the righteous God trieth the hearts and reins. My defence is of God, which saveth the upright in heart."

The chief of all the words he here employs is "integrity:" this he accepts cordially for himself and repeats with equal candor for the aid of others. He remembers that the Lord judged him for his integrity in the beginning, and he prays that he may be worthy to be so judged even to the end. Now we know that the word "integrity" is derived from the Latin *integer;* and the meaning of *integer* is "whole;" and wholeness is our old strong Saxon for holiness. That is to say, what God means by stating that he looks upon, not the outside of a man, but his "heart," is, that he considers the wholeness of one's nature, and desires it to become holiness. He looks at each man through and through, and registers him by his soundness, his genuineness, his entire character.

2. Observe, also, that God's purpose erects a fixed standard. A man's "heart," as thus understood in the religious sense and as worthy of the divine regard, depends upon the thoroughness with which the man adjusts each exertion of his will to the divine will. That is to say, God's heart is the test of man's heart, God's wish, God's plan, God's purpose—in a single word, God's law—showing the perfect standard.

Here comes out, somewhat unexpectedly, but in a most interesting way, what is the true interpretation of that remarkable declaration about this man David which has given many people so much trouble. You recollect that in the earlier history God announced that he had already sought for himself "a man after his own heart;" and then, more than eleven hundred years subsequent to this, the apostle Paul declared, in one of his speeches, that this person was David. Now we are compelled to dwell carefully upon the explanation which the All-wise One offered instantly, in order that men might understand his exact meaning. Just because of Israel's wilfulness, he permitted the nation to choose Saul for their monarch; but he soon removed him for his sin, and "raised up unto them David to be their king: to whom also he gave testimony, and said, I have found David the son of Jesse, a man after mine own heart, which shall fulfil all my will." This final clause of the verse is what explains all the mystery: David was "a man after God's own heart," not because of any supreme holiness of his moral and religious attainments, but because of his fitness for fulfilling the Lord's will— his availability for the Lord's purpose.

If any one supposes that this shepherd-boy is in these words asserted to be, either in his youth, when Samuel pours the anointing oil upon his head, or in after years, while he is the crowned king in Jerusalem and the sweet singer of Israel, a perfect man— so excellent in manners or so supreme in piety that he had at last, through the disciplines of his turbulent career, reached all that even the heart of God could wish—he will surely be stumbled frightfully at some cruel recollections of David's mortifying weaknesses and terrible crimes, those awful and undisputed faults which led to the abasing penitences of the fifty-first Psalm. But if we understand that this son of Jesse was in these points human like the rest of us, and, in the sovereignty of divine wisdom, was chosen for what he was, simply to do the Lord's will, then we shall get a most valuable lesson for ourselves, and the difficulties of our exposition will disappear. It is the divine purpose in every case which fixes the final standard of judgment; and by this every human heart is to be tested as well as swayed. Whenever God is in his Word declared to look on a man's heart, the meaning is that he now is searching whether that heart is fully set to do his whole will.

3. Then observe, in the third place, that God's purpose starts a permanent revolution in a human character. The most interesting verse in this narrative, as well as the most valuable, is that which announces how "the Spirit of the Lord came upon David from that day forward."

It is wonderful to think of these changes now wrought upon this anointed stripling. He was the uncrowned king of Israel from the hour of Samuel's sudden visitation. It fairly arrests our imagination when we see the hitherto inconspicuous life of this shepherd-boy begin rapidly to advance into prominence; it is lifted into honor, exalted into strength, trained into majesty. He is instantly put into processes of discipline so as to be ready for his new destiny when his hour should arrive. Henceforth he is to be the shepherd of Israel; so he continues to manage his father's flocks a while longer, in order that he may learn the shepherd's duty. Henceforth he is to be the sweet singer of Israel; so he lingers out under Bethlehem sunsets and Syrian stars, in order that he may seek poetic images a while longer for some additional Psalms. Henceforth he is to be the monarch of Israel; so he is led a while longer among fierce outlaw experiences, consorting with the oppressed and the poor, in order that he may learn to understand his own subjects before he has hold of the sceptre by which he is to rule them wisely. And during this entire period this crownless king is hastening unconsciously forward in the lines of God's unfaltering purpose.

This is the interpretation of those passages which make allusion to his early career as a lad tending the sheepfold. The almighty Hand was guiding and moulding him; God's gentleness, as he gratefully takes pains to acknowledge, was making him great. And this is the secret of Asaph's eloquence, as he tells the story of the same educational years: "He chose David also his servant, and took him from the sheepfolds: from following the ewes great with young he brought him to feed Jacob his people and Israel his inheritance. So he fed them according to the integrity of his heart, and guided them by the skilfulness of his hands."

As we leave the detailed study of this incident, it might as well be urged earnestly that we should not exhaust the teachings of it upon the one man David as a mere historic hero: he is a representative king among kings, to be sure; but he is a representative man also among men of all ages. The principle which appears is of universal application. Hence the question that we must raise here at the close of the sermon is this: When the Lord leaves the outside show, which our pride pushes forward into notice, and looks down into the inner recesses of our own hearts, which we sometimes try to conceal, what does he actually see?

There is much that is full of suggestion in this conception of a fixed estimate of each one of us, just and conclusive, yet mysterious, and often quite out of our reach; how can we deal with it as a tremendous fact? In modern times, when village merchants come to the cities to purchase goods, asking for some easy credit on their bills, they usually are met with the calm reply that they will have to wait for the customary consultation of the firm just for a few moments or hours before they may expect a final decision. It has grown to be understood in our commercial communities that the great dealers are using such a delay, not altogether in talking to each other, but in searching pages and columns of what is called a Mercantile Agency for the exact standing of the would-be purchaser. The register of all possible customers is kept, filled with items of information, compiled quite independently, gathered from different tracts of the whole broad land, and covering the business career of each individual. By these particulars the man's genuineness and responsibility are tested, and thus the question is decided as to whether he is what the trading world calls "good" or not. The grade of his credit is fixed altogether distinct from his open professions or wishes, and uninfluenced by anything he himself may have to offer or may seek to urge. His name is on a list that has in the course of painstaking years been canvassed and settled before even his arrival in town. Hence, as the messenger returns and he receives his answer, he knows that it will not avail to wait any further or to plead any more. For his financial position is established, for better or worse, in the entire city. There remains this mysterious scrutiny, as well as this authoritative estimate, made up from a thorough investigation of his former history and his present circumstances. That is to say, he has been graded justly and absolutely for what he is worth.

So familiar has this method of registering men become now that a mere reference to it in illustration suffices to exhibit the whole admonition contained in the verse we have been studying. The Creator of this universe knows all the intricacies of its movement. He keeps the accurate account of each human character and standing as judged by his holy law. His estimate of every person in turn is made upon a private and exhaustive acquaintance with his intent, temper, spirit, and life. The Unseen One is the All-seeing One. He does not look on the outward appearance at all, save as one of his ways of knowing the man's heart.

This leads to another question: What is the use of wasting years of weary life in just trying to keep up appearances before men and women and before God? Oh, how full this old world is of those who spend their time and energy in fashioning parades of unreality and hypocrisy and emptiness, not one of which is looked on by God, not one of which is respected by men! And this, too, to the neglect of the heart, upon which are grounded the decisions of present favor and future destiny!

It makes us think of the child's story about the two boys in the street, who fought a battle blue and bloody over a shining ball which they chanced upon lying in the roadway, and which each claimed as his own. Yellow and beautiful the bauble seemed; silk covered its surface with gloss, the image of a crown was on either side of it. "Why," exclaimed one of them, and then the other, "it must be a casket containing the king's seal or some of the queen's jewels!" And so the foolish creatures fought like beasts over the possession of it. By-and-by a third lad, stronger than either of them, appeared on the scene, quietly picking up the trophy and making off with it for himself. So now a parley became necessary, and they reached an agreement to divide the treasure. With eager eyes they watched him when he unwound the silken threads which seemed actually without end: at last he came down in the middle to a poor little spool, a used-up spool of silk which after an anxious moment was soon to be not even that, but a bobbin, stubbed and uncomely, blackened by the oil of the loom. And the crown on the ends was but a patent-mark. The remnants of floss lay trampled in the dust; the small stick was worthless; nothing came out of it at all; the fight had been to no profit; the hands were weary; the heads were very sore.

What disappointments at the day of final reckoning there will be for men and women who have fought for a title, a star, or a ribbon, in the vain hope of being looked upon because of it! What disclosures of folly, what revelations of surprise! How ignoble their aims, how empty their achievements, how absurd their ambitions, how fierce their rivalries, how useless their victories, how unimportant even their worst defeats!

And finally, we ask, how is it with us in this grand age of the Lord's mastery of men? How is it with God's princes, anointed already for service of the living Christ—"kings and priests unto God and his Father"—but as yet unordained priests and kings still uncrowned? It is remarkable to note that, in all the subsequent history of David, he never alluded to this consecration of himself by the prophet. He never so much as once fell back upon his official selection for the royal place; whatever impression it made upon his life was quietly concealed in his own soul, and he went on trusting God. So we are not surprised to hear him singing in his Psalm: "The secret of the Lord is with them that fear him, and he will show them his covenant." When afterward he was brought into the presence of the delirious Saul, and was asked who he was, he answered only with the simplicity of a child, "I am the son of thy servant Jesse, the Bethlehemite." That was all he had to say.

The call of God does not confer on any one the privilege of pride or the indulgence of haughtiness; it calls a servant to service, and kingship comes further on. It only makes a true soul more knightly and more humble to know that he has been summoned in secret into the grand purposes of God.

And then during all the time of waiting and preparation what is a good and chivalrous man to do? Perhaps one of the best answers must be looked for in the fine words of Jesus, the son of Sirach, whom some suppose to have been inspired:

"Beware of a counsellor, and know before what need he hath; for he will counsel for himself; lest he cast the lot upon thee, and say unto thee, Thy way is good: and afterward he stand on the other side, to see what shall befall thee. Consult not with one that suspecteth thee: and hide thy counsel from such as envy thee. Neither consult with a woman touching her of whom she is jealous; neither with a coward in matters of war; nor with a merchant concerning exchange; nor with a buyer of selling; nor with an envious man of thankfulness; nor with an unmerciful man touching kindness; nor with the slothful for any work; nor with a hireling for a year of finishing work; nor with an idle servant of much business: hearken not unto these in any matter of counsel. But be continually with a godly man, whom thou knowest to keep the commandments of the Lord, whose mind is according to thy mind, and will sorrow with thee if thou shalt miscarry. And let the counsel of thine own heart stand: for there is no man more faithful unto thee than it. For a man's mind is sometime wont to tell him more than seven watchmen, that sit above in a high tower. And above all this pray to the Most High, that he will direct thy way in truth."

XII.

DAVID AND GOLIATH.

"AND ALL THIS ASSEMBLY SHALL KNOW THAT THE LORD SAVETH NOT WITH SWORD AND SPEAR: FOR THE BATTLE IS THE LORD'S, AND HE WILL GIVE YOU INTO OUR HANDS."—I *Sam.* 17:47.

THIS chapter upon the study of which we now enter ushers us at once into the midst of one of the most romantic tales of the Old Testament. Our childhood received it at the hands of pious mothers before our years were even mature enough to accept teachers outside of family circles. When we were boys, no story bore so many repetitions as this of the stripling and the giant; none ever sent the blood into our eyes and the spirit of war into our hearts as did this. It is on authentic record that one lad in a Sunday-school, when asked who it was he hoped to see as his first sight in heaven, chivalrously replied, "Goliath!"

John Bunyan recorded that in the Palace Beautiful were laid up among those "engines" enthusiastically shown to the pilgrims the sling and the stone with which David killed the giant of Gath. Hannah More, openly opposing the theatre with ordinary plays, constructed a spirited drama out of the grand battle scene there in the plain of Elah. It would be useless to rehearse the details of the picturesque narrative. Every child knows them; every child of mature years has told them over and over again to his growing household: for the whole world loves the tale of the boy who dared the chieftain in the name of the living God.

Of course the field is fairly covered with legends. But not an instance can be quoted in which the simple inspired rehearsal receives any help. The Mohammedans say that as David passed over the brook, or the "valley," as the margin of our Bibles renders it, three stones, one at a time, cried out to him, "Pick me up and take me with thee!" This he did; and it turned out that the first was the one wherewith Abraham had driven Satan away, when he had sought to keep him from offering up Isaac; and the second was that upon which the foot of the angel Gabriel rested when he opened the fountain in the desert for Hagar and Ishmael; and the third was that with which Jacob strove against the evil spirit whom his brother Esau had sent to destroy him in the old quarrel.

Then there is a new tradition, Mohammedan too, which declares as to the general result, that as David let go his sling the wind started to blow; this caught the helmet of Goliath, lifting it up into the air above his head, so that the stone struck him square upon the forehead, sinking in, and actually crushing his skull and strewing his brains over the horse he rode; thus the giant fell out of the saddle and died. Then David placed the second stone in his sling; and, casting it skilfully, it smote the right wing of the Philistine army; then he cast again, and the third stone smote the left wing and routed the host.

There is no good in such tales. In the apocryphal book Ecclesiasticus, which used to be bound up in our common Bibles as almost an integral part of it, there is an exquisite description of David, worth quoting for the poetry in it and for the bright picture it brings us:

As is the fat taken away from the peace offering, so was David chosen out of the children of Israel.

He played with lions as with kids, and with bears as with lambs.

Slew he not a giant, when he was yet but young? and did he not take away reproach from the people, when he lifted up his hand with the stone in the sling, and beat down the boasting of Goliath?

For he called upon the most high Lord; and he gave him strength in his right hand to slay that mighty warrior, and set up the horn of his people.

So the people honored him with ten thousands, and praised him in the blessings of the Lord, in that he gave him a crown of glory.

For he destroyed the enemies on every side, and brought to naught the Philistines his adversaries, and brake their horn in sunder unto this day.

In all his works he praised the Holy One most high with words of glory; with his whole heart he sung songs, and loved him that made him.

He set singers also before the altar, that by their voices they might make sweet melody, and daily sing praises in their songs.

He beautified their feasts, and set in order the solemn times until the end, that they might praise his holy name, and that the temple might sound from morning.

The Lord took away his sins, and exalted his horn for ever: he gave him a covenant of kings, and the throne of glory in Israel.

In almost every verse of the story which now comes under our study there may be found at least one homiletic lesson. It would be easy to group them together as usual into a plan with an orderly and logical connection. But perhaps in this instance they will fall with equal force if we follow closely the exact progress of the narrative. The moment the words are read the instruction will be seen.

1. Helps may sometimes be so multiplied as to become hindrances: "And Saul armed David with his armor, and he put a helmet of brass upon his head; also he armed him with a coat of mail." Never was a higher honor bestowed upon a shepherd-boy than this, when his king armed him with his armor, or, as the margin reads, clothed him with his own clothes. But no one needs now to exhaust his entire sympathy upon this overweighted champion. We might as well reserve a measure of our pity for the modern Davids in the pulpit who imitate popular preachers, and in the classes who seek to reproduce the rare excellences of famous teachers more tall and more brilliant, and so fail because they stalk around in unnatural panoply, and are borne down by a greatness they cannot fill out to its full swell.

2. There is always room in the divine purposes for proper originality in human methods: "And David girded his sword upon his armor, and he assayed to go; for he had not proved it. And David said unto Saul, I cannot go with these; for I have not proved them. And David put them off him." Paul the great apostle does indeed once say to the Corinthians, "Be ye followers of me," and then announce that he sends Timothy to tell them of his "ways;" but when he writes to Timothy what to do, he bids him not to neglect the gift that is in him, but stir it up. No counsel is more wise to give to any winner of souls than just this: Be yourself.

3. The best instrument for God's service is generally that which God has bestowed on the individual worker: "And he took his staff in his hand, and chose him five smooth stones out of the brook, and put them in a shepherd's bag which he had, even in a scrip; and his sling was in his hand: and he drew near to the Philistine." David's sling was "in his hand:" it was within reach; it was what the young man was used to handling. And indeed, if we may judge from Israelitish history, it was no mean weapon. The tribe of Benjamin was noted for its skill and courage in the use of it. At one time the army had twenty-six thousand of these slingers; and very odd and effective they must have been too, for we are told that "among all this people there were seven hundred chosen men left-handed: every one could sling stones at a hair breadth, and not miss." We are never to despise any instrument or tool or weapon or resource whatsoever until at least we learn to what extent one who knows just how to employ it can make it serviceable for good. It is simply silly for any spiritual martinet to bluster when he sees that Christians are doing well in winning souls, and insist that David shall put on armor like Saul's when he can accomplish far more in his own way as a slinger with his brook-stones. Let all wise men and women take what Providence has put within their reach.

Here comes again in a new history the old demand once made of Moses: "What is that in thy hand?" The crook he had used with the sheep in

Horeb became the "rod" which divided the Red Sea. Shamgar took his ox-goad, because he was accustomed to it. Samson seized the jaw-bone of an ass, because he found it "moist" and ready when he "put forth his hand." Dorcas did glorious good in Joppa with the needle her hand loved.

4. Giant-killing is yet the chief calling of the church: "And the Philistine came on and drew near unto David; and the man that bare the shield went before him."

This picture, so fine in its simplicity, is the one which childhood never forgets and age never disdains. The heathen "Philistine" is always coming on and drawing near to the believing "David." We may call the apparently mismatched combatants Good and Evil, Right and Wrong, Truth and Error; it is invariably the worst which seems colossal, and the better which appears insignificant. Error can generally find an obsequious armor-bearer; Truth sometimes has to stand alone with a sling. Often great leaders will contribute their cast-off clothing, but they do not offer to put their extra height into risk. Even brothers among the people will jibe the intrepid champion who finds "a cause." But the battle is watched from above; victory is eventually with the stripling shepherd; and Goliath of Gath falls upon his broken face, with his huge bulk stretched along the sand. And the lesson is full of counsel and cheer for chivalrous souls who are valiant for the truth, that they have patience, fight with courage, and trust God for ever:

"For the God of David still guides the pebble at his will:
There are giants yet to kill—wrongs unshriven;
But the battle to the strong is not given
While the Judge of right and wrong sits in heaven."

5. Here seems to be a register of the real worth of mere "muscular Christianity:" "And when the Philistine looked about and saw David, he disdained him: for he was but a youth, and ruddy, and of a fair countenance." Goliath answers very well to Matthew Henry's somewhat picturesque description, "a stalking mountain overlaid with brass and iron." David is a youthful champion, slightly dressed, fine-looking, red-haired, with beautiful eyes: that is all. The athletic advantage is plainly on the side of the giant. We hear even now some preachers declaiming about "more brain, brawn, and bones in our clergy." A few calm words from Canon Charles Kingsley might well be quoted here: "Better would it be for any one of you, young men, to be the stupidest and the ugliest of mortals, to be the most diseased and abject of cripples, the most silly, nervous, incapable personage who ever was a laughing-stock for the boys upon the streets, if only you lived, according to your powers, the life of the Spirit of God, than to be as perfectly gifted, as exquisitely organized in body and mind, as David himself, and not to live the life of the Spirit of God, the life of goodness, which is the only life fit for a human being wearing the human flesh and soul which Christ took upon him on earth, and wears for ever in heaven, a Man indeed in the midst of the throne of God."

6. It is the weakest sort of so-called honor which has to assert itself in bluster: "And the Philistine said unto David, Am I a dog, that thou comest to me with staves? And the Philistine cursed David by his gods. And the Philistine said to David, Come to me, and I will give thy flesh unto the fowls of the air and to the beasts of the field." "The first challenge of a duel that ever we find," says the shrewd Bishop Hall, "came out of the mouth of an uncircumcised Philistine; and whosoever imitateth him—nay, surpasseth him—in challenge to private duels, in the attempt partaketh of his uncircumcision; for of all such desperate prodigals we may say that their heads are cut off by their own sword, if not by their own hand."

7. The calmness of faith is always resolute and self-possessed: "Then said David to the Philistine, Thou comest to me with a sword and with a spear and with a shield: but I come to thee in the name of the Lord of hosts, the God of the armies of Israel, whom thou hast defied. This day will the Lord deliver thee into my hand; and I will smite thee, and take thy head from thee; and I will give the carcasses of the host of the Philistines this day unto the fowls of the air and to the wild beasts of the earth; that all the earth may know that there is a God in Israel. And all this assembly shall know that the Lord saveth not with sword and spear: for the battle is the Lord's, and he will give you into our hands."

"The battle is the Lord's;" there is a motto for all Christian life. John Bunyan has mentioned some of our modern giants: giant Despair, and giant Grim; giant Pope, and giant Pagan. Perhaps we could think of a few more who have come nearer yet to our own experience, and might have been named in the history of Christiana and the children. There is giant Pride, and giant Profanity; giant Untruth, giant Envy, giant Appetite; all of these confront us and with some of them we have had fights. But we can stand before them quite calmly if only we remember we come "in the name of the Lord of hosts."

8. The best defence against evil is found in a swift attack: "And it came to pass, when the Philistine arose and came and drew nigh to meet David, that David hasted and ran towards the army to meet the Philistine." We read with delight that David "hasted and ran to meet the Philistine." In this was found his safety. He rushed up swiftly towards the giant, and before the big blusterer could draw his sword, he received the stone crashing into his forehead.

Does any one want to know how this young shepherd learned a trick so fine? Saul raised the same question once. David told him that he "went out after" a lion and a bear, and smote him. There he gained his valuable experience; he modestly added that he knew that the Lord who had delivered him then would deliver him now, if he made the first onset. It is right to reason from every spiritual success over to new triumph. Growth in Christian courage is wrought out by a recollection of what God has done for us before.

9. There can be no providence in God's government that is not in some sense truly special: "And David put his hand in his bag, and took thence a stone, and slang it, and smote the Philistine in his forehead, that the stone sunk into his forehead; and he fell upon his face to the earth." The all-wise Creator has been pleased to people the universe with free-willed beings; an immediate interposition of a higher free-will is invariably necessary in times of unusual exigency. David never swung a sling with a more unhindered or more skilful sweep; but God guided that whirling stone with quiet sovereignty through the air till it lodged under Goliath's helmet. Only a small opening of the face was vulnerable, and the smooth pebble found it fairly in the middle and buried itself in the brain behind it. If that was not "special providence," what was it?

10. The weapons of the wicked are often at the last turned against themselves: "So David prevailed over the Philistine with a sling and with a stone, and smote the Philistine, and slew him; but there was no sword in the hand of David. Therefore David ran and stood upon the Philistine, and took his sword, and drew it out of the sheath thereof, and slew him, and cut off his head therewith. And when the Philistines saw their champion was dead, they fled." Goliath brought his shield-bearer with him; but he himself became the sword-bearer for David. His head was cut off with his own chief weapon.

When we search the teachings of conflict we

find this has almost invariably been the rule. Our Lord defeated Satan thrice in the use of retort. He turned back his antagonist's arguments and slew him with his own texts.

This principle should be kept in mind. Perhaps the highest illustration of the truth of it is found in the doctrine of the resurrection of our divine Redeemer. "Forasmuch then as the children are partakers of flesh and blood, he also himself likewise took part of the same; that through death he might destroy him that had the power of death, that is, the devil." Death was the chief weapon of the devil. Through this Jesus Christ destroyed him who had the power of death. That is why he is called in the hymn, "Death of death and hell's Destruction."

11. The victory of faith belongs only to Jehovah, and to him is the glory. This whole wonderful story closes without a word of praise for the nation's champion. It cannot be found that he anywhere ever alluded to this triumph as one of his exploits, nor does he ever sing about it in a Psalm. In the last verse of this chapter we see the picture of him as he stands before the haughty monarch Saul with the bloody head of the giant he came to offer to him. In wonder Saul asks him who he is. David does not answer, as he might, "I am the man already anointed, the uncrowned king of Israel in thy place!" He does not add one word beyond the sweet, modest reply, "I am the son of thy servant Jesse, the Bethlehemite."

XIII.

REAL FRIENDSHIP.

"And Jonathan said to David, Go in peace, forasmuch as we have sworn both of us in the name of the Lord, saying, The Lord be between me and thee, and between my seed and thy seed for ever. And he arose and departed; and Jonathan went into the city."—1 *Sam.* 20:42.

"All faithful friends went on a pilgrimage years ago, and none of them have ever come back:" so wrote one of the Puritan divines, whose heart was depressed at the time, most likely. It strikes us that it is possible to secure even now an affectionate regard from some whom we love which might be as bright and as true as that between David and Jonathan, if we understood it.

Perhaps the best definition of friendship is that given by Addison: it is "a strong and habitual inclination in two persons to promote the good and happiness of each other." Here it is intimated that to give, and not to seek, is its prime characteristic. Unselfishness is what lies at the base of it. Jonathan was the prince, and David could afford to receive just now, in the sweet bright hope that his turn to bestow would arrive by-and-by. Indeed, we do not believe that friendly feeling among genuine men could stand benefits all on one side. Some of us have read of the Scotch custom of burying their dead under heaps of stones. Those busy Highlanders deem it a vast compliment to have the cairn slowly rising, as one fragment of rock after another is flung upon it. To our minds this appears crushing. It brings a sense of suffocation under so much kindness and such indescribably heavy affection and so vast a weight of honor. Some people press us down in a way somewhat like this even while we are living. They put us under a cairn of favors, a stifling monument of obligation, never to be lifted, almost never to be borne either. Such a mistake is sure in the end to break friendship; for that is "a union which bespeaks reciprocated duties," and reciprocated privileges likewise.

This being our general understanding, therefore, we are ready to consider some peculiar conditions and characteristics of a manly affection like that between David and Jonathan.

1. True friendship requires some acknowledged basis of individual worth. The Septuagint closes the book of Psalms with another not included in our version, which it numbers as the hundred and fifty-first, and gives as the composition of David himself:

> I was small among my brethren,
> And the youngest in my father's house.
> I was feeding my father's sheep.
> My hand made a harp,
> And my fingers fitted a psaltery;
> And who shall tell it to my Lord?
> He is the Lord. He heareth.
> He sent his messenger and took me from my father's flocks
> And anointed me with oil of his anointing.
> My brethren were beautiful and tall,
> But the Lord was not well pleased with them.

> I went out to meet the Philistine,
> And he cursed me by his idols.
> But I drew his own sword and beheaded him,
> And took away reproach from the children of Israel.

We must go back a step in the story, and we shall find that the love which sprang up between these two young men was from the very beginning intelligent. Even while Saul was listening to the modest tale of victory over Goliath, Jonathan discerned the grand nature of the nation's champion; from that hour his soul was knit to David's: "And it came to pass, when he had made an end of speaking unto Saul, that the soul of Jonathan was knit with the soul of David, and Jonathan loved him as his own soul. And Saul took him that day, and would let him go no more home to his father's house. Then Jonathan and David made a covenant, because he loved him as his own soul."

To be popular is very different from being beloved. Frequently the multitude applaud a public officer, not because he is meritorious, but because some other multitudes have begun to applaud him before. It does not require the genius of La Bruyére to say that men "praise the man who is praised more than it is their habit to praise his praiseworthy qualities." But genuine friendship looks at worth, not at reputation.

It would be a mistake to assert that friends must resemble each other in forms of excellence. Often the liveliest interest arises between those of quite contrary dispositions. Only in a single thing do David and Jonathan seem to be positively alike:

they were both deeply religious. They were therefore true and honest, sincere and devout; and these are always great points. For wicked men cannot be real friends. Froissart says of Gaston de Foix, "In everything he was so perfect that he cannot be praised too much; he loved what ought to be beloved, and hated what ought to be condemned; and he never had miscreant with him."

2. True friendship demands courage and self-sacrifice in instant answer to the call. It seems that both Jonathan and David had at last become alarmed at the open violence of Saul. For the king was evidently set upon killing the young minstrel, of whom, since he had been so praised for slaying the giant, he had grown madly jealous. On one occasion David absented himself from the royal table. The monarch instantly missed him, inquired pettishly where he was, and threatened him with heavy explosions of wrath. At this point Jonathan interposed with a brave explanation which was perverted into an extenuation. So this drew down upon himself his father's insane anger. He was just able to dodge a dart which was flung at him; and then he was peremptorily bidden to go and fetch David back for a swift and deadly punishment.

When Jonathan rose up from the table there was more than one javelin in the air coming towards him; there was the mad king's wrath shooting lances of fire also. Which was the most required that day, moral courage or physical, it would not be easy to decide. On the one side was his father, on the other his friend; but in this instance Saul was wrong, and

David was abused. Jonathan chose instinctively for the one who was right, and so put his life in peril, before the whole court, for the one who was weakest.

They say that when a tiger has hold of a hunter, and is just going to break his bones, he will turn at once upon the intrepid man who dares to interpose for rescue; he will leave his prostrate victim with a kindling of tenfold wrath against the fresh foe; so that it is considered more dangerous, in such a case, to try to help a comrade than to be in the paws of the infuriated beast. Hence old campaigners in jungle fights are accustomed to say to their most faithful associates, "One could afford to go tiger-hunting with you." Are such friends to be met on every corner in our unheroic times?

3. True friendship becomes more disinterested as it becomes more loving: "And Jonathan answered Saul his father, and said unto him, Wherefore shall he be slain? what hath he done? And Saul cast a javelin at him to smite him: whereby Jonathan knew that it was determined of his father to slay David. So Jonathan arose from the table in fierce anger, and did eat no meat the second day of the month: for he was grieved for David because his father had done him shame."

It is one of the most delicate touches of nature that we meet in the story just here: what Jonathan cared most for was the shame done to David. For he does not mention the murderous flight of the steel dart across the room, hurled at him by his own father; he is "grieved for David."

We must remember that Saul's son had in a worldly sense almost nothing to gain from the son of Jesse. He perfectly understood that David was going to succeed his father in the kingdom; and that, to his own exclusion from the throne. But he willingly relinquished hereditary honors for the love he bore him. This was the taunt which his father was continually hurling at him: "Then Saul's anger was kindled against Jonathan, and he said unto him, Thou son of a perverse rebellious woman, do not I know that thou hast chosen the son of Jesse to thine own shame, and unto the shame of thy mother's nakedness? For as long as the son of Jesse liveth upon the ground, thou shalt not be stablished, nor thy kingdom. Wherefore now send and fetch him unto me, for he shall surely die."

But Jonathan would rather have his beloved friend on the throne than to reign there in person, for his soul was knit with the soul of the son of Jesse, and he loved him as his own soul.

Some few commonplace interpretations, offered us here by those who are familiar with the customs of speech prevalent in the East, will help our minds in understanding the feeling between these two men.

The expression in the first verse of this chapter is Oriental in two ways, but neither makes it much stronger than the Western ways of speaking. One is the use of "soul," where we would use "heart" or even "soul" itself; and the other is in the use of "knit," literally "bound up with" or "bound up in." Their hearts had a common tie, is the strong English expression. Yet we use stronger expressions for a less passion. We speak of being of one heart, or of one mind, of unanimity, and the like. The Latin *concors*, whence comes our "concord," is of the same class or figure. The German phrase "two hearts and one beat" is almost an equivalent expression; for it relates to passion, while the other expressions just mentioned relate to that which has become somewhat cooled by long standing. Perhaps, in Oriental parlance, the meaning of the phrase, "he loved him as his own soul," is to be understood as in other passages in the Bible, with "self" substituted in English for "soul." This is to say that Jonathan's love grew to be so unselfish that it seemed to make him happier to think that David would be king than that he would be himself. Once, not long after this, he made this perfectly clear, when his hunted friend became quite discouraged: "And Jonathan Saul's son arose, and went to David into the wood, and strengthened his hand in God. And he said unto him, Fear not: for the hand of Saul my father shall not find thee; and thou shalt be king over Israel, and I shall be next unto thee; and that also Saul my father knoweth. And they two made a covenant before the Lord: and David abode in the wood, and Jonathan went to his house."

Thus he offered to the ages the most exquisite illustration of the proverb written long subsequent to these troublous times by the son of David, who was in many things the wisest man in the world: "A man that hath friends must show himself friendly: and there is a friend that sticketh closer than a brother."

4. True friendship shows itself by delicate and sometimes mysterious signals of communication. Indeed, when two men become fast and sympathetic comrades, we sometimes fail to discover what they find in each other so companionable.

Take this little story which follows in the chapter—that about the shooting in the field, and the boy who waited upon them there. Jonathan kept his bow in most skilful and vigorous exercise: "But the lad knew not anything: only Jonathan and David knew the matter." We feel interested, not to say amused, as we contemplate this lad on his errands for Jonathan's arrows, with no sort of suspicion that he is holding converse for his prince with an outlaw of the realm. This small incident always arrests our imagination; for it offers a suggestion concerning that oneness of soul, that unbroken trust, that ingenuity of address, which together prove the existence of genuine affection between these two men. It seems inexplicable; we can appreciate it without understanding it any more than we can understand the strange vibrations of a harp's strings when a flute is played upon close beside it; we only know that one true heart answers to another as the one sensitive instrument in the corner replies to the other in the room by sympathetically reproducing the same melody over its wires.

One explanation is found in the fact that all real regard is observant of careful deferences and decencies of respect: "As soon as the lad was gone, David arose out of a place towards the south, and fell on his face to the ground, and bowed himself three times: and they kissed one another, and wept one with another, until David exceeded." Jonathan had come forth into the field to find his comrade; but he was the king's son. David bowed himself three times to show he knew his place. Piety is a sure basis for politeness, and a pledge that it will be rendered. Too much familiarity breeds contempt. The old adage says: "Thy friend hath a friend, and thy friend's friend hath a friend; so be discreet." All these apparently small considerations, the keeping of a comrade's secrets, the preservation of his honor, the acknowledgment of his position, the gentle watchfulness for his opinions and tastes; these are what show him that his friend truly and generously "cares for" him.

> "The man who hails you Tom or Jack,
> And proves by thumps upon your back
> How he esteems your merit,
> Is such a friend that one had need
> Be very much his friend indeed
> To pardon or to bear it."

5. So, finally, true friendship finds its highest model in the Lord of life and glory. We do not see how any one can be a genuine comrade for a Christian who is not himself a Christian. It was Merle d'Aubigné who wrote to Pasteur Anet at Brussels, four years before he died: "O my friend, may the true divinity of the Son, the power of his expiatory death, be ever the pillars of our faith and the foundation on which rests the indestructible affection that unites us!"

Our supreme delight in all this story we are

studying is the discovery that David is one of the Scriptural types of Christ. And so we seem sometimes to hear those familiar words of Jesus ringing through the air of Judæa: "Greater love hath no man than this, that a man lay down his life for his friends. Ye are my friends, if ye do whatsoever I command you. Henceforth I call you not servants; for the servant knoweth not what his lord doeth; but I have called you friends; for all things that I have heard of my Father I have made known unto you."

There is an Afghan proverb which says: "God will remain; friends will not." But if the Son of God be our friend, then surely there is one who remains, the same yesterday, to-day, and for ever. When President Edwards died, he summoned all his relatives to bid them his final farewell. Then he turned away positively and suddenly, saying, "Now where is Jesus of Nazareth, my true and never-failing Friend?" And so he fell asleep.

The close of our story is pathetically simple: "And Jonathan said to David, Go in peace, forasmuch as we have sworn both of us in the name of the Lord, saying, The Lord be between me and thee, and between my seed and thy seed for ever. And he arose and departed: and Jonathan went into the city."

We do not know that these two men ever met more than once thereafter. There came war, and they were on different sides. Jonathan fought loyally for his father, and was slain. Is it wrong to think that he was glad that his friend would profit by his disappearance? David, with his eyes full of tears, sang a song of mourning and brave hope, than which he never penned a sweeter. Then swift years glided by: "Therefore are they before the throne of God, and serve him day and night in his temple."

Fairer possession or finer has no man in this world than that of some dear old friend whom the flitting years only make truer and gentler and kinder. Absence need not be reckoned. Jonathan "in the city," David "in the wood," no matter where they are; each is sure the other "cares;" each is confident that in the hereafter of the blessed ones there will be kept the same regard, pure and changeless. For the kingly natures of the earth do bring their glory and honor into the New Jerusalem at the last.

XIV.

FORGIVENESS AS A FORCE.

"Then David arose, and cut off the skirt of Saul's robe privily."—1 *Sam.* 24:4.

The chapter we are to study to-day starts out abruptly in its pursuance of the history: "And it came to pass, when Saul was returned from following the Philistines, that it was told him, saying, Behold, David is in the wilderness of Engedi." *Engedi* means "the fountain of the kid," and the fountain so called lies among the hills on the western shore of the Dead Sea, and still bears its ancient name. "Then Saul took three thousand men out of all Israel, and went to seek David and his men upon the rocks of the wild goats. And he came to the sheepcotes by the way where was a cave; and Saul went in to cover his feet: and David and his men remained in the sides of the cave."

This cave grows picturesque as we look at it: the tired soldiers grouped in unsophisticated attitudes for rest, heavy shadows lying over them; the sudden entrance of their royal foe, whom the men in the dark could see, though remaining themselves unseen; the first flash of fear as they seemed entrapped by the misfortunes of the position, followed by the gleam of grim satisfaction when they perceived their enemy had put himself in their power; the whispered conversation between David and his rough comrades, which must have been conducted half in words and half in gestures; then at last the hushed breath of anticipation, as the giant king of Israel yawned and awaked, and swung his tall bulk out into the valley once more; all this is dramatic in the highest sense, and hardly needs the pencil of an artist to put it upon canvas so that our eyes may behold it.

The moral teaching of the incident will be easily reached if we notice the three steps of David's experience in turn; the temptation he endured, the magnanimity he displayed, and the victory he achieved.

I. What was the temptation which David was called upon to endure that night? Nothing less than this: here was King Saul, fatigued and wretched, entering the same rude shelter that covered David's homeless head, and offering himself a captive if he would take him. And several considerations really seemed to favor such a project and make it prudent.

1. This was David's most desperate antagonist. The king had openly declared that he would smite David even to the wall. He once told Jonathan his son, and all his servants, to kill him the moment they found him. The record says explicitly, "Saul became David's enemy continually." Hunted and driven, he now found himself in possession of his deadliest foe on earth.

2. Saul was completely in his power. How pathetic does it always seem to imagine a great strong man asleep! Why not terminate this destructive

campaign once and for ever, and bring the people to peace? Was it wise to continue possible bloodshed in further conflict? He knew that Saul was rejected of God; he had been told some years before that he himself was to be crowned in his place. Why not just put forth one stroke of the same sinewy arm which cut off Goliath's head, so smite the king and end the war? Was sentimental casuistry in order just now?

3. These men with David had their own case to be considered. Along the shadowy sides of the cavern lay fierce outlaws, whose hearts, outraged by ill-treatment, were burning with desire for revenge. Each one of them had a story of personal injustice to tell. David remembered that they had periled their lives in many a hillside battle, and were now ready to follow his command to the death. But here was the great destroyer in their own cave! why not destroy him? So they pleaded with their leader to put him to death as he lay there in the mouth of the cavern, the light falling on his most unwelcome face.

4. It appeared like a real providence proposing swift retribution. Even the undevout soldiers whispered to David that the covenanted day of the Lord had come for him: "And the men of David said unto him, Behold the day of which the Lord said unto thee, Behold, I will deliver thine enemy into thy hand, that thou mayest do to him as it shall seem good unto thee." They allowed their wish to be the father of their thought. God had never engaged that Saul should be murdered in se-

cret and by treachery. He had never sent the king into that cavern to render assassination lawful and wet David's hands in his blood.

II. We are now ready, in the second place, to consider the magnanimity which this generous leader displayed. We can well understand that a poetic, passionate man like David might have wrought himself up almost into a frenzy under such pressure: what did he do? "Then David arose, and cut off the skirt of Saul's robe privily." Only his robe, not his person! and he seems to have had some compunctions even over that: "And it came to pass afterward that David's heart smote him because he had cut off Saul's skirt."

1. Observe the sturdiness of his resistance to the evil thought: "And he said unto his men, The Lord forbid that I should do this thing unto my master, the Lord's anointed, to stretch forth my hand against him, seeing he is the anointed of the Lord. So David stayed his servants with these words, and suffered them not to rise against Saul." He utterly refused to harbor the suggestion of the excited men: he said, "The Lord forbid!" He put forth his hand to stay his servants. What silence and vigor there must have been in the rapid look and the forcible gesticulation with the authority of which he held back those exasperated creatures in the cave, so as not to awaken Saul by the peremptory command!

2. Notice also the reach of his generous meditation. The process of his mind is traced at length. His loyalty was touched: "But Saul rose up out

of the cave, and went on his way. David also arose afterward, and went out of the cave, and cried after Saul, saying, My lord, the king! And when Saul looked behind him, David stooped with his face to the earth and bowed himself." Bad as that enemy was, David knew he was Saul, the king of Israel. Perhaps he remembered likewise that Saul had given him Michal in marriage; what love there was between him and his cool-hearted wife would certainly not be improved by his ascending the throne through a murder. We feel certain that he recollected that Saul was Jonathan's father, and Jonathan he loved as his own soul. It seemed to occur to David there that this might be made an occasion of composing the strife which was racking the realm. There always appeared to him to be a vast mistake in the quarrel; he was not conscious of doing wrong to the king; he admitted Saul had his good points, his tender heart, his judicial mind, his gentle will, if only they could be found and touched. He made up his purpose to forgive his enemy and seek reconciliation; all the rest of the issues he would leave to God.

3. Consider the adroitness of his action. It would be a crime to kill the king, but it could not be wrong to conquer him. It was not therefore necessary that David should lose the supreme advantage of this singular opportunity offered. So he cut off a portion of the royal robe for a sign. He was dexterous at seizing the chance of making an impression. When one is going, as he says, to "leave events to providence," it is always prudent

to inquire whether providence has not left some easy expedients of effort to him as well.

4. Try to appreciate the tenderness of David's conscience. Never is a true Christian so considerate and careful as when his heart is anxious to do a magnanimous thing. This fugitive head of a rebellious band is so generous in spirit just now that he grows sorrowful, sad, and ashamed to think he has been guilty of disrespect even in touching the royal garments. Men may often measure their real sincerity in trying to do right by their solicitude against doing the slightest wrong.

5. See the moral courage of his decision. Out before all that astonished and exasperated crowd of lawless men this leader comes, and instantly gives away their case by surrendering his own. They look with consternation upon their trusted captain as they see him bowing himself before their common enemy. But what David thinks is right he carries at once into execution. He calls Saul "father." He pleads for a reconciliation. He enters into a passionate argument and appeal. For he hopes to close the war by kindness instead of crime: "And David said to Saul, Wherefore hearest thou men's words, saying, Behold, David seeketh thy hurt? Behold, this day thine eyes have seen how that the Lord had delivered thee to-day into my hand in the cave: and some bade me kill thee: but mine eye spared thee; and I said, I will not put forth my hand against my lord; for he is the Lord's anointed. Moreover, my father, see, yea, see the skirt of thy robe in my hand: for in that I cut off the skirt of

thy robe, and killed thee not, know thou and see that there is neither evil nor transgression in my hand, and I have not sinned against thee: yet thou huntest my soul to take it. The Lord judge between me and thee, and the Lord avenge me of thee: but my hand shall not be upon thee."

III. This leads us straight on, as might have been expected, to the victory which David achieved: "And it came to pass, when David had made an end of speaking these words unto Saul, that Saul said, Is this thy voice, my son David? And Saul lifted up his voice and wept." There could be only one result to an endeavor like this; "Hearts are not steel, and steel is bent."

1. We learn here how humble is a forgiving mind. There cannot be anything of exaggerated self-depreciation in David's comparison of himself to a dead dog or a flea. He doubtless expected to mollify Saul's jealousy in some degree by these strong expressions of meekness. He made appeal to his kingly dignity as being too high to suffer him to follow up one so ordinary and insignificant as himself. When a Christian sets himself about forgiving an enemy, he is willing to do it thoroughly. He will surrender all pride, and become modest to the extreme of civility, lest his pardon shall seem like patronage and do harm.

2. We learn also how trustful is a forgiving heart. The issues between Saul and David were real, pertinent, living, just as ever. What was to become of them? These men behind David, too, had the same grievances as before. Facts were not

changed because feelings were altered. But this brave son of Jesse exacted no pledges for Saul's good behavior; he felt he was safe in the Lord's hands. He could afford to leave judgment and vengeance to heaven: "As saith the proverb of the ancients, Wickedness proceedeth from the wicked; but my hand shall not be upon thee. After whom is the king of Israel come out? after whom dost thou pursue? after a dead dog, after a flea. The Lord therefore be judge, and judge between me and thee, and see, and plead my cause, and deliver me out of thy hand." He believed, as every really good man believes, that if he continued to do right, the Lord would deliver him always.

3. We learn, finally, how forceful is a forgiving spirit. Saul is conquered: "Is this thy voice, my son David?" A sword might have killed this hard man, but only magnanimity could make him weep. There is a strength in moral courage that does not reside in physical power. David overcomes evil, not with arms, but with good. He spares his enemy, and cuts off a little part of his enmity instead. He actually leads the stubborn monarch to confession and apology. Before those two armies on the hill there is a strange spectacle: David is triumphant, and Saul is defeated; but David is on his knees, and Saul is weeping brokenly as he exclaims, "Thou art more righteous than I; for thou hast rewarded me good, whereas I have rewarded thee evil."

XV.

THE DEAD MARCH OF SAUL.

"SO SAUL DIED, AND HIS THREE SONS, AND HIS ARMOR-BEARER, AND ALL HIS MEN, THAT SAME DAY TOGETHER."—1 *Sam.* 31:6.

"TO-MORROW shalt thou and thy sons be with me:" so said the solemn voice of the spectre which the witch of Endor in some mysterious manner had summoned from the grave. And now that morrow of fate and doom has arrived, and Gilboa is to become a monument of the truth of Samuel's prediction of speedy death and ruin to this king of many glad hopes and keen disappointments to the nation.

From this crisis the story advances with the august pomp and funereal stateliness of a procession. Each verse resembles a strain of melancholy music in a dead march; and at times there breaks in a new catastrophe that reminds one of the strokes of a muffled drum.

Our lessons of practical instruction are only reiterations; perhaps they can be best stated in words which have been inspired.

I. We begin with this: "Sin, when it finished, bringeth forth death." The career of the first monarch Israel ever had is now actually completed: his life is a failure; the wrong beginning has reached the fatal end. The narrative is unsympathetic and cheerless: "Now the Philistines fought against

Israel: and the men of Israel fled from before the Philistines, and fell down slain in Mt. Gilboa. And the Philistines followed hard upon Saul and upon his sons: and the Philistines slew Jonathan and Abinadab and Melchishua, Saul's sons. And the battle went sore against Saul, and the archers hit him; and he was sore wounded of the archers. Then said Saul unto his armor-bearer, Draw thy sword, and thrust me through therewith; lest these uncircumcised come and thrust me through and abuse me. But his armor-bearer would not; for he was sore afraid. Therefore Saul took a sword and fell upon it."

The parallel has more than once been drawn between the rejected Saul and the Roman Brutus at Philippi. They seem to have had a warning in very similar terms the night before they died. And the terrible destruction of their respective forces, the entire rout and ruin of their cause, worked the same maddening result. Each fell on his own sword, and so sealed his guilt with suicide.

One thinks of the story which naturalists tell concerning the scorpion, which, girded by a circle of fire, coils up on itself into narrower and narrower folds, till, when it can endure the heat no longer, it turns its deadly venom against itself and buries the sting of destruction in its own brain. Saul knew he must die before nightfall that day; it was not necessary he should let himself be tortured.

II. So there is a second text of God's Word illustrated here in the incident: "None of us liveth to himself, and no man dieth to himself." The lines and links of connection which bind us to our fellow-men are often very subtle, and sometimes unexpected; but they are certainly always very strong. We do not know that Saul cared much about others' interests, but his guilt was visited on many innocent souls: "And when his armor-bearer saw that Saul was dead, he fell likewise upon his sword and died with him. So Saul died, and his three sons, and his armor-bearer, and all his men, that same day together."

By a tradition of the Rabbins we are told that the armor-bearer mentioned here was named Doeg, and the tale adds that both of these men were slain by the same weapon, that was indeed the one with which the Lord's servants had been massacred at Nob. Just how it came about that this attendant soldier should deem it necessary to die at such a moment and in such a way, we are not informed. It might be surmised, however, that his loyalty, perhaps his personal affection, possibly even his fear, led him into following the royal example with an impulse worthy of a far better deed. But he died, and is now forgotten.

Still more yet do we pity the family of this wretched king. In the Chronicles the record says that "all his house died together." It followed rather as a matter of course that they should be swept mercilessly down with the fate of the head of their line. Perhaps they in their respective parts of the field fought bravely for his crown and for his honor. It may be they did not know, as he himself knew, that this sacrifice would do no good. Their prowess had been hopeless away back at the beginning of the battle; it was pitiable at the end. For in the death of Saul the dynasty died, and their prospects perished.

III. Notice, therefore, closely in this connection that another of the Bible texts phrases for us a new lesson: "One sinner destroyeth much good." There was more in this tremendous catastrophe at Gilboa than an individual wreck. Great public interests were shaken almost as if the nation had been rocked by the force of an earthquake: "And when the men of Israel that were on the other side of the valley, and they that were on the other side Jordan, saw that the men of Israel fled, and that Saul and his sons were dead, they forsook the cities and fled; and the Philistines came and dwelt in them. And it came to pass on the morrow, when the Philistines came to strip the slain, that they found Saul and his three sons fallen in Mt. Gilboa. And they cut off his head and stripped off his armor, and sent into the land of the Philistines round about, to publish it in the house of their idols and among the people. And they put his armor in the house of Ashtaroth: and they fastened his body to the wall of Bethshan."

Clear over on the other side of the Jordan the panic of the rout extended. The villagers rose in a frightened mass and deserted their homes. They surrendered costly territory without an instant's stand for defence, and suffered the victorious Philistines to occupy their houses and reap their fields. Humiliation lay like a pall over all the land. And when the ghouls of war came on the succeeding day greedily stripping the dead, they found not so much as a squad of soldiers in the plain to receive them or resist their horrible errand. So they tore from the royal person of Saul the raiment; they cut from the tall shoulders the head; they nailed the mutilated limbs of that once beautiful monarch against the dull wall of Bethshan among the hills.

It has been revealed, as a principle of the divine government, that those who have sown the wind, they shall also reap the whirlwind. But men do not always seem to remember that inspiration has likewise said, "One soweth and another reapeth." The mighty misfortune which attends evil-doing is sometimes intensified by the fact that those who have done the sowing are not by any means the only ones who have to do the reaping afterwards. Saul reaped the wind before he died, and when he died too; but it was his people that, with sickles of humiliation and loss and shame unutterable, reaped the whirlwind in his stead.

IV. Happily there is another side even to this. We choose again from the utterances of inspiration, and we read, "The triumphing of the wicked is short, and the joy of the hypocrite but for a moment." It has been noticeable in human history that the Almighty deals somewhat surprisingly with remnants; even in great devastations there is often left a seed that tries to serve him and retrieve the disasters: "And when the inhabitants of Jabesh-gilead heard of that which the Philistines had done to Saul, all the valiant men arose, and went all night, and took the body of Saul and the bodies of his sons from the wall of Bethshan, and came to Jabesh, and burnt them there. And they took their bones, and buried them under a tree at Jabesh, and fasted seven days."

It does our hearts good just now to learn that Jabesh-gilead was aroused: somebody after all was alive in the land. A good turn often comes back again. Years before this Saul had saved the inhabitants of that town from losing their eyes at the hands of some brutal enemies; now they sent a faithful band to take reverently down from the spikes the bodies of the royal victims and give them decent burial at last.

And this was the type incident of hope for Israel's future. For a while it did appear as if the Lord had forsaken his people. All the gains of honest industry and of hard conquest for many an anxious season were swept away. Strangers were in possession of the large walled towns. Fields were devastated. Hearts were sad and half broken. Irreligion was flourishing. Obscene and idolatrous worship was offered in high places and on conspicuous hills. But Jehovah had not left his chosen nation yet. Saul's head was deposited in the temple of Dagon; but the son of Jesse was coming to the throne. The temper of the warriors among the tribes was rising. We read in the Chronicles that "at that time day by day there came to David to help him, until it was a great host like the host of God." It became evident that before long affairs would alter for the better and the kingdom would recover its advantage.

It is wiser always to side with the Lord of hosts, no matter how discouraging the present prospect may be. He will help the faithful ones to retrieve fallen fortunes. The wicked will soon cease to spread himself like a green bay tree; soon he will be "not." And in the new return of favor there will be peace, if only there shall first be purity. When Crates the Egyptian saw the men rebuilding Thebes, he passionately exclaimed, "For my part, from this time forth I want a city which no future Alexander can overthrow."

V. Once more, we find an illustration also here of the text that has grown so familiar in our times: "In the place where the tree falleth, there it shall be." For we cannot leave the story of Saul without making up an estimate of his career, and trying to settle what the causes were which led to his downfall. It appears to us, from our sober point of view, that here, as in the old case of Esau, there is the sad picture of what the world is apt to call a great lost chance.

Everybody recollects now how the enthusiastic people lifted up their shouts when this magnificent chieftain came to the throne. The very children in the Sunday-school could recapitulate this instant the circumstances which promised so well for him in the beginning of his reign. But when we study the mournful story of his end, we find not a single suggestion of any one's mourning genuinely for him except generous David whom he tried ever so many times to murder. He had certainly outlived his welcome; he had died without being desired. No patriot sighed for any more of him. What was the real reason for all this?

He lost his chance through his sinning against God. Imagination grows busy with thinking of his final experiences. We wonder whether, in that last wild moment while he was pleading with his awe-struck armor-bearer to kill him, he wished for the old times and the former opportunities to come back. It is not worth while to inquire further as to his remorseful regrets; it is too late now; it was too late then; a mere sentence spoken by the wisest man in the world is enough to show us what would be his fitting epitaph; so he passes out of our sight: "There is no man that hath power over the spirit to retain the spirit; neither hath he power in the day of death: and there is no discharge in that war; neither shall wickedness deliver those that are given to it. All this have I seen, and applied my heart unto every work that is done under the sun: there is a time wherein one man ruleth over another to his own hurt. And so I saw the wicked buried, who had come and gone from the place of the holy, and they were forgotten in the city where they had so done. This is also vanity."

He lost his chance: but ours remains to us yet; and this is of vast importance and demands our notice as living men. "The memory of the just is blessed; but the name of the wicked shall rot." While the hours linger salvation is possible to any one who will come with penitence seeking it, and even a great bad record may be blotted from the book of God's remembrance by the blood of Christ.

XVI.

GREATNESS BY GENTLENESS.

"And David went on, and grew great, and the Lord God of hosts was with him."—2 *Sam.* 5: 10.

"Thy gentleness hath made me great." So wrote David when he rehearsed the history that had culminated in his advancement to the throne of all Israel. He admits, therefore, that he was a "made" man, but not a "self-made" man. Here in the narrative of his prosperity he confesses that it had been the Lord who established him king, who also exalted his kingdom; and then in a Psalm of devotion he ascribes all his glory to divine grace.

We can reach the instruction now offered us better, if we spend a little time in considering the greatness David had just reached and the gentleness he instantly acknowledges.

I. At last this monarch had attained the height of power and was established in a throne loftier than that which Saul had forfeited. Six successive steps, at the least, had the eternal God taken in his behalf on the way to his advancement.

1. He caused that a full and loyal call should come from the realm over which he was now to rule as the second king: "Then came all the tribes of Israel to David unto Hebron, and spake, saying, Behold, we are thy bone and thy flesh."

We must study this verse: it is evident from it

that some gracious influence of God's Spirit had been working among these people, preparing them for such a king as he was. The blending of the two forms and phases of feeling which they here display is remarkable; they do not in the least reject the notion of an overruling authority from Jehovah himself, but they couple with it a hopeful and happy recognition of David's relationship, as a man whom they felt to be one of themselves. Here was an early instance of a divinely-ordered government which was designed to be "from the people, by the people, and for the people."

2. The Lord trained David for the position he was to occupy by a long and intricate process of providential discipline: "Also in time past when Saul was king over us, thou wast he that leddest out and broughtest in Israel: and the Lord said to thee, Thou shalt feed my people Israel, and thou shalt be a captain over Israel."

This official deputation of the tribes admitted that God had been dealing with him for many years before to render him a shepherd who should "feed" and a "captain" who should lead Israel. Frederick the Great used to say, "A king is but the first of subjects." He must have meant by this that only he who had been taught how to be obedient to law and order could be fitted to rule over masses of men. David had gone through great versatilities of experience; he had known what it was to abound and what it was to be abased. Once he had sat at the feet of Saul, the monarch, and once he had been out on the hills homeless and pursued; once he had heard the maidens singing about the victories he had gained and the thousands he had slain, and once his wife had let him down through a window that he might escape for his life. On the slopes of Bethlehem hills he had tended flock after flock as his father grew in wealth; and there under those Syrian skies he had learned the song of the night from the chiming of the stars that gave to him the figures of the eighth and the nineteenth Psalms. And then, years afterwards, he had been a fugitive and an outlaw, hiding among the same caverns and fleeing along the same paths. Out of all this had come growth, and out of all of it had come experience for his present charge.

3. Moreover, God had chosen David intelligently, years before, and announced him as the man who should come after Saul: "So all the elders of Israel came to the king to Hebron; and King David made a league with them in Hebron before the Lord: and they anointed David king over Israel."

It is true the people anointed him now, but God had caused him to be anointed a long time previous to this; a promise that was given then had made him the uncrowned king of Israel for an unreckoned period of fifteen years. This monarch's history furnishes one of the brightest and most affecting illustrations of the fact that every true man's life is a plan of God. No words can be found in the Old Testament annals more profoundly pathetic than those with which Asaph closed the seventy-eighth Psalm: "He chose David also his servant, and took him from the sheepfolds: from following the ewes great with young he brought him to feed Jacob his people, and Israel his inheritance. So he fed them according to the integrity of his heart, and guided them by the skilfulness of his hands."

4. Then, too, God helped on David's greatness by providing for the stability of his government a capital and a royal abode: "Nevertheless, David took the stronghold of Zion; the same is the city of David. And David said on that day, Whosoever getteth up to the gutter, and smiteth the Jebusites, and the lame and the blind, that are hated of David's soul, he shall be chief and captain. Wherefore they said, The blind and the lame shall not come into the house. So David dwelt in the fort, and called it The city of David. And David built round about from Millo and inward."

And now with this acquisition of new territory begins the strange long story of a wonderful old town; here first it finds itself enrolled as a true city of God's providence and love, as well as the centre of Christian interest and inquiry for nearly three thousand years: an ancient stronghold of the Jebusites in wild and warlike days, suddenly converted into an Israelite citadel, by-and-by becoming "Ariel, where David dwelt," then as Jerusalem, "habitation of peace," becoming a type of heaven—the "Jerusalem above, which is free, which is the mother of us all." When this enthroned king took his earliest outlook from the palace he could see Bethlehem in the distance, and send his recollection over all the past path along which God's providence had led him. Good and pious resolutions appear to have swelled his heart: the one hundred and first Psalm is believed to have been composed at this time, and certainly seems to have foreshadowed all the best policies of this king's long reign. We might read it over, for with these purposes he committed his future to God:

"I will sing of mercy and judgment: unto thee, O Lord, will I sing.

"I will behave myself wisely in a perfect way. Oh, when wilt thou come unto me? I will walk within my house with a perfect heart.

"I will set no wicked thing before mine eyes: I hate the work of them that turn aside; it shall not cleave to me.

"A froward heart shall depart from me: I will not know a wicked person.

"Whoso privily slandereth his neighbor, him will I cut off: him that hath a high look and a proud heart will not I suffer.

"Mine eyes shall be upon the faithful of the land, that they may dwell with me: he that walketh in a perfect way, he shall serve me.

"He that worketh deceit shall not dwell within my house: he that telleth lies shall not tarry in my sight.

"I will early destroy all the wicked of the land; that I may cut off all wicked doers from the city of the Lord."

5. Once more: God's gentleness made David great in that a perpetual presence was vouchsafed to him for his entire life: "And David went on, and grew great, and the Lord God of hosts was with him."

At the height of his fame Agamemnon is recorded to have said that his nobility imposed upon him the dignity and the duty of being foremost in enduring labors for others. It is not everybody that sees this clearly when he rises into a position of honor and force. This newly-crowned son of Jesse had gained a vast experience already. His outlaw years had taught him the responsibility of leadership. He knew what he was now going to undertake. "He sure must conquer who himself can tame." But a peculiar element in his instruction had shown him that he could succeed only when God was with him. It is to edification to us all that we find here in the very first battle he fights against his old enemies the Philistines, that he rests entirely upon an answer to his prayers; he waits for a mysterious messenger from on high; he will not bestir himself till there is the "sound of a going in the tops of the mulberry-trees;" by that he is to be certain that the "Lord shall go out before" his armies. It has deepest meaning to a believing heart that God cares and helps.

6. Then, also, God had made this monarch great by opening his intelligence so that he should understand the meaning of divine providence, past and future, and admit its special reach: "And David perceived that the Lord had established him king over Israel, and that he had exalted his kingdom for his people Israel's sake."

When we read over this verse we must be sure to attach unusual importance to that word "perceived." Not every king is alert enough to find out, nor humble enough to acknowledge, that he owes his fortune not to adroitness or address, but to the positive arrangements of history written beforehand in God's books. Nebuchadnezzar walked along the roof of his palace once, and in the vast distances below and around him saw his mighty capital: "The king spake, and said, Is not this great Babylon, that I have built for the house of the kingdom by the might of my power, and for the honor of my majesty?" But David knew that Jehovah had ordered and adjusted his entire career for him. His devotion was now at its highest point. He seemed to be keeping, about these days, his harp in his hand almost all the time. One of the old commentators once called the Psalms of David "a spiritual library." He was by no means unduly enthusiastic, for they have lived in the hearts of God's people for thousands of years. The experience crowded into those lyrics of the shepherd-king is so extensive only because he accepted his whole life as a plan of God. He "perceived that the Lord had established him," and then he thoughtfully admitted it before the ages to come: "Thy gentleness hath made me great."

II. It is time for us now to move onward to the consideration of the second point that was mentioned at the beginning of this sermon: the gentleness in the divine dealing with him from his first recognition as a shepherd-boy to this final establishment of him in the throne of Israel: it is that in particular among the attributes of God which he acknowledges just now.

The poet Goethe has left behind him, in his autobiography, this somewhat curious sentence as a revelation of personal fact: "I was especially troubled by a giddiness which came over me every time that I looked down from a height." Many people, since his day and before it, have had the same characteristic disturbance; but it has more often been a height of ambition than merely a height of tower or precipice. It would have been no astonishing surprise to us, if we had been, here in the story we are studying, confronted with a sort of superciliousness in the manners and speech of this Bethlehem lad so suddenly raised to the very summit of power, and now summoned to look across the years and trace the steps of the steep declivity up which his history had been climbing. But there is no symptom of giddiness in the quiet ascription of his gratitude: "Thy gentleness hath made me great." We have seen how the providence of God had lifted this man up to such an eminence, and have discovered the particulars; it remains for us now to inquire how it comes about that David speaks more concerning the gentleness with which he was led on.

1. For one thing, God's gentleness had borne with David's want of memory. There is something very singular in the foreboding, which was noticeable more than once in David's experience. Recall for a moment one incident in which Jonathan helped him: "And David saw that Saul was come out to seek his life: and David was in the wilderness of Ziph in a wood. And Jonathan Saul's son arose, and went to David into the wood, and strengthened his hand in God. And he said unto him, Fear not: for the hand of Saul my father shall not find thee; and thou shalt be king over Israel and I shall be next unto thee; and that also Saul my father knoweth." Why was it left to this friend of his to assure him that he had been an-

ointed to be king in Saul's place? Had David really forgotten it? Yet here was the prince of the kingdom announcing a succession that would dispossess him of all hereditary position in his own right—a fact which he and his father knew, but David seems to have allowed to slip out of his mind altogether in his estimate of his peril. It was surely a culpable disrespect of the divine promise; and still God bore with it gently and patiently, and took the hand so frankly laid over into his again.

It is not wise to find fault with this son of Jesse, lest we condemn ourselves. Many a Christian professes to be abiding in the Lord and living on a promise; he is bold and brave till some real onset of the adversary summons him to his defences at an instant's warning; then he forgets his covenant. Few in our time know what it is to rely upon God with a sense of absolute communion with him. Not every one can say, as did one of those rough cavaliers of whom we read in the old "Morte d'Arthur," "It is more than a year and a half since I have lain down ten times in a dwelling where men rest; but in the wildest forests and in the mountains God has ever been my surest comfort and my stay."

2. Then, also, there was David's want of faith, with which the Almighty bore in a like spirit of gentleness. Here again a fraternal interposition of Jonathan alone saved him from making shipwreck of his future; for Jonathan's confidence was unbroken: "And David fled from Naioth in Ramah, and came and said before Jonathan, What have I done? what is mine iniquity? and what is my sin

before thy father, that he seeketh my life? And he said unto him, God forbid; thou shalt not die: behold, my father will do nothing either great or small but that he will show it me: and why should my father hide this thing from me? it is not so. And David sware moreover, and said, Thy father certainly knoweth that I have found grace in thine eyes; and he saith, Let not Jonathan know this, least he be grieved: but truly, as the Lord liveth, and as thy soul liveth, there is but a step between me and death." Think of the steps of service and honor, and duty and obedience, which, during the forty years of reigning in Jerusalem, were between David's coronation and death!

We can only admire the long-suffering and patience of God which was shown in the gentleness that forbore with such wretched unbelief. If the Lord had fallen heavily on him with the retribution due to it, David might have had no salutary penitence with which to meet the blow; for he was of a passionate temperament, and might have ruined himself by a hot answer. It is not easy to walk by faith when sight is so much more flattering to our human pride. "It is one thing to believe," said Des Cartes, "but another thing for a man only to imagine that he believes." "Delight thyself also in the Lord, and he shall give thee the desires of thy heart. Commit thy way unto the Lord; trust also in him; and he shall bring it to pass."

3. To this we may add that God's gentleness is disclosed in his patiently bearing with David's want of courage: "And David said in his heart, I shall

now perish one day by the hand of Saul: there is nothing better for me than that I should speedily escape into the land of the Philistines; and Saul shall despair of me, to seek me any more in any coast of Israel: so shall I escape out of his hand." It is plain that he had lost all hope and given over all trust, and so surrendered himself a prey to simple cowardice in the immediate presence of danger. He decided to give himself up into the hands of his enemies. He was going to become traitorous in his desire to escape from his personal peril. It is pitiful to be obliged to read a record like this, for we must admit one inevitable inference, that David was foolishly afraid.

We must arrest the discussion now: indeed there is nothing in the story which is more fitting to fix its impression on our minds than this we have just observed. We may all find it much to our edification to take a stand where we may review our past history and examine our future prospects in the light of this abiding principle: it is God's gentleness which makes any believer great. It is an affecting thought for each of us to bear in mind, that divine love has been very patient with us. Even far inferior successes have the same explanation as David's, and we may well keep singing his song, praising the gentleness of God.

> "A sacred burden is the life ye bear;
> Look on it, lift it, bear it solemnly:
> Stand up and walk beneath it steadfastly;
> Fail not for sorrow, falter not for sin,
> But onward, upward, ever, till the goal ye win."

XVII.

SEEKING THE ARK OF THE COVENANT.

"And David arose, and went with all the people that were with him from Baale of Judah, to bring up from thence the ark of God."—2 *Sam.* 6 : 2.

For sixty-five or seventy years this Ark of the Covenant had been permitted to remain in almost total neglect and forgetfulness. Those Israelites had fallen into the habit of bearing it at the head of their attacking columns in battle; the Philistines were afraid of it; but, on one occasion, they captured it nevertheless. They recognized it as the symbol of Jehovah, and they complimented it with a place by the side of their deity Dagon in their temple. But Dagon got the worst of it in the impious association, and was broken to pieces down to the stump. In their consternation they then gave it to Ekron; and there was a deadly destruction through all the city, and the frightened inhabitants sent it forward to Bethshemesh. There the Lord smote fifty thousand men for looking into its sacred recesses. These poor people moved it along till at last it was restored into Israel's hands; after that it rested in the little border town of Kirjath-jearim, beneath the roof of Abinadab, and under the official care of Eleazar, who was constituted its priest.

There it had remained during all the stormy period of the monarchy so far. At length the time had come for David to interpose and, in the exercise of his royal authority, bring it back into prominence and reverence in the worship of the people.

I. Our study to-day will require us to answer a few questions concerning the Ark itself, before we enter upon the story of its removal with so much pomp and ceremony to Jerusalem.

1. What was the so-called "Ark of the Covenant"? It was a mere chest or box of wood, covered with golden plates, with its elegantly-wrought lid, above which hovered the figures of the two cherubim. Between these the sacred light of the Shechinah presence of Jehovah was wont in the Holy of Holies in the Tabernacle to shine; and just there was the Mercy-seat of prayer. The contents of this strange receptacle were peculiarly interesting: a pot of manna such as that which fell in the wilderness, the two tables of the law given to Moses, and Aaron's rod that budded.

2. Of what was it the symbol? Of the presence of Jehovah as the "covenant-keeping God" of his people Israel. In the New Testament there is found very little of appeal to men's imagination. That which gave to this former dispensation its richness and splendor was suffered to pass out of sight and use in order that the spiritual teaching of the gospel might not be obscured by mere sensuousness of external forms. The present worship of God is very plain, but to the eye of faith or the heart of love there is that in it which is far more valuable than simple show and glitter of ritual. "If that which is done away was glorious, much more that which remaineth is glorious."

3. Of what is the Ark a sign now? This question needs an answer in order to open the line of instruction between the Old Testament and the New. We shall make a better use of this narrative now, if we recollect that what the Ark of the Covenant was in those days to David, sometimes an *institution* is to us. For example, the Sabbath, as a period set apart for the Lord; while we have it and observe it, it is as if the divine presence were abiding in the midst of us. Just so the Ark is often represented in an *organization* like the church. Christ loved the church, and gave himself for the church, which is his body. Where this company of believers is compact in strength and fidelity, there is prosperity and peace in the presence of the Redeemer. Then, too, the Ark becomes the sign sometimes of an *ordinance*, like the Lord's Supper. There have been days in which the true Sacrament needed to be brought back from among the Philistines as evidently as the symbol of a divine presence needed to be brought in David's reign. Now and then in a *duty* likewise does the Ark become our sign in these days of open Bibles and secret sin. The family altar of prayer is in every one's mind the moment we think of the blessings of that sacred symbol in the prospered house of Obed-edom. Often in even a *doctrine* likewise does the Ark find its representative in modern times: truth is betrayed when righteousness is low in men's hearts. An old creed may be lost in polemic battle, and then a procession of singing people may have to be sent for it, or the church cannot hope to be prospered. However we

may look at the narrative before us, it will not be for want of suggestion that it may seem foreign to our need, for of that it is full.

4. What does the absence of the Ark involve? The lonely heaviness of work done without a helper or a promise of success. And let us understand that, when the Ark of God's presence is away from one's kingdom or one's house or one's heart, he must go after it; it will not start on its path unless it is sought. In our Christian days we have some advantages and encouraging motives for zeal. That ancient Ark was only a symbol; Christ's presence is to us a wonderful fact. That was but a sign that divine companionship was near; now we may be sure that Jesus, the Master, is really under our roofs and in our hearts. That stay in the house of Obed-edom was but for a while; the residence of Jesus Christ with us may be permanent: he has promised that he and his Father will come to a believer, and will make an "abode" with him for ever. Then, moreover, this presence is extensive enough for every man: we do not read that any one received the Ark cordially during all that period of its wandering, and the record does not tell of anything but disaster from its nearness, until it is lodged in the house of this Gittite; then all shows prosperity and peace. Our promised presence of Christ is offered to each seeking believer as much as it ever was to Obed-edom.

II. Thus we are ready to take up the narrative of David's removal of this ancient symbol of the theocratic government; it was of no use to him to have a great town for his capital or a fortified stronghold for his citadel; he knew then what he sang afterwards in his Psalm, that "Except the Lord build the house, they labor in vain that build it; except the Lord keep the city, the watchman waketh but in vain."

It will be necessary that you bear constantly in mind the representative character of this transaction, as it has already been before us, or you will gain no spiritual help from it. It will furnish us with some suggestions concerning different methods of treating the presence of God when vouchsafed to us.

1. To begin with, we can see here how the Ark of God must be treated with a becoming honor. There are times when good or modest people should be quiet and retiring; and there come also times when they need to be spectacular and even showy. True humility can be shown in forwardness; for there are occasions in which it costs more to go forth into necessary conspicuousness, and brave the criticisms of public opinion, than it would to remain in concealment, withdrawn into a quiet of deepest reserve.

"Again, David gathered together all the chosen men of Israel, thirty thousand. And David arose, and went with all the people that were with him from Baale of Judah, to bring up from thence the ark of God, whose name is called by the name of the Lord of hosts that dwelleth between the cherubim." That must have been a splendid pageant, when the king led out in person the very flower of his army, thirty thousand veterans in number. They must have nearly lined the road along the stretch of nine miles, and filled the ways with glitter of arms. Nothing is too much for a soul that loves God, in that glad and affectionate moment when it finds it can pay him his due honors.

2. We see, also, how the Ark of God can be treated with a culpable carelessness: "And they set the ark of God upon a new cart, and brought it out of the house of Abinadab that was in Gibeah; and Uzzah and Ahio, the sons of Abinadab, drave the new cart." It had been decreed in the beginning of its history that this singular chest should be carried on men's shoulders; for this purpose of handling it had been constructed with rings through which poles might be passed so that it could be borne by the priests. Here we observe that Abinadab mounted it in a cart; and in this he patterned not after Moses, but after the Philistines, who once did the same disrespectful thing.

It is of no use to say this was of no consequence. It is always of much consequence that one obeys God, and pays respect to every one of his commandments exactly as he gives them. The sequel of this story will tell us whether such thoughtless disobedience passed without notice from God's sovereignty. When finally David really brought the Ark into the city, he took eager pains to have men detailed to carry it on the staves prescribed. Men must serve Jehovah, but it is part of the obedience he asks that they shall be content to serve him in the way he commands.

3. We see how the Ark of God can be treated with the highest exuberance of joy: "And David and all the house of Israel played before the Lord on all manner of instruments made of fir wood, even on harps, and on psalteries, and on timbrels, and on cornets, and on cymbals." It is impossible for an ordinary reader to go over this history without finding his imagination all on fire with exhilaration. The music in this case constituted one of the grand features of the occasion. The account in the chapter from which the text is taken must be supplemented by that which is added in the book of Chronicles: there we learn that a great school of training in music was set up at Jerusalem in patient preparation for this ceremony. There is nothing too good in poetry, in instruments, in singing, for God who is over all.

In this procession David himself took part. He wrote the words of the hymns which were sung. They had in their band all sorts of curious instruments: "harps" that were stringed across metal, and "psalteries" that were stringed over wood; with "timbrels," which were what we call tambourines, and "cornets," which were loud-ringing blast-givers made out of the horns of chamois goats or rams, with "cymbals," which were brazen disks like our own in these modern times, and full of tremendous vibration in that clear atmosphere; and the account in Chronicles says they had "trumpets" also; and with all these, a chorus of men's voices—a mighty body of nine hundred and sixty-two priests and Levites, of whom it is declared, they "played before

God with all their might, and with singing." Ah, that must have been congregational music worth hearing, when King David lifted the Psalms, a choir of a thousand male voices joined the strain, and thirty thousand soldiers had a chance to do what they could to help on!

4. We see, again, how the Ark of God can be treated with a fatal presumption: "And when they came to Nachon's threshingfloor, Uzzah put forth his hand to the ark of God, and took hold of it; for the oxen shook it." The grand procession moved on along its way, making the air quiver with the usual songs which were sung when this sacred symbol was advancing: "Arise, O Lord, into thy rest; thou and the Ark of thy strength!" They reached one of those open spaces common in that region, where the rock had been swept clear for a threshing-floor; the oxen, perhaps, slipped on such a treacherous spot; the cart was shaken. Uzzah, one of the two sons of Abinadab, seeing the catastrophe or fearing one, suddenly seized hold of the golden chest. There is no proof that his hand more than touched it; but presumption proved to be profanity: "And the anger of the Lord was kindled against Uzzah, and God smote him there for his error; and there he died by the ark of God." He was not a priest, he had no rights, he was not responsible for any duty. God's holiness would not bear it; Uzzah fell dead beside the cart. Now was seen the folly of putting the sacred symbol in a wagon to be drawn by beasts; now was disclosed the wickedness of an unauthorized anxiety about God's affairs.

Is it likely that any one could now commit such a sin, or rush into any danger of such a punishment? We have become somewhat familiar with the warning. It is possible that even a modern Christian should imagine himself a champion for the defence of the church, and all the time be only fighting for a denomination; or that one should suppose he must stand for the truth of the living God, when what he suffers for is only a creed or tradition. And it is possible that one should strive to defend an institution of the gospel, or a doctrine of the faith, with ill-chosen zeal or uncalled-for temerity or fanatic determination, or even with unlawful measures or tricky deceit. If the Almighty God does not strike him down in an instant for his profanity and presumption, it is because he is long-suffering and patient, and is willing to wait his retributions until the rash shall become prudent and the wrong shall discover the right.

5. We see, once more, how the Ark of God might be treated with a half-hearted timidity: "And David was displeased, because the Lord had made a breach upon Uzzah: and he called the name of the place Perez-uzzah to this day." This great pageant came abruptly to an end: the king's purpose was but half of nine miles long.

He was "displeased:" the word means vexation akin to petulance; he was disappointed in all his plans. There was a sense of humiliation under the discovery of an unexpected exercise of divine sovereignty. His complacence in his own action was altogether disturbed. Jehovah had not asked this king's permission to inflict retribution on a subject; he was the King of kings: "And David was afraid of the Lord that day, and said, How shall the Ark of the Lord come to me?"

He was "afraid." There was likewise a sense of penitence under the revelation of infinite holiness. He must have discovered that they all had gone about their work in a hurried and a self-seeking way. He could admit now that he had rather prided himself on undertaking so creditable a thing as this journey after the Ark. Fear fell on his heart under such a reminder of a jealousy and a power so sensitive and supreme. What if his own sins should be visited on him with a punishment as swift?

He was inconsiderate: "So David would not remove the Ark of the Lord unto him into the city of David: but David carried it aside into the house of Obed-edom the Gittite." He seems not to have had the least compunction or care concerning the danger he might bring to the house of this stranger, Obed-edom. He dared not take the Ark any farther, but deposited it beside the way as quickly as his alarmed attendants could remove it from the wheels.

The admonition here would be addressed to such persons as start out in a religious career, and leave their surrender to a life of consecration only half accomplished. They go after the Ark of God with enthusiasm in the beginning; but, finding it an unexpectedly serious thing to continue in the line of duty, the purpose becomes irksome, and the surrender is surrendered.

6. We see, finally, how the Ark of God may be

treated with an appropriate and affectionate devotion: "And the Ark of the Lord continued in the house of Obed-edom the Gittite three months: and the Lord blessed Obed-edom and all his household." The fearless courage of this unhistoric stranger contrasts finely with the selfish alarm of his sovereign. He was a Korathite by birth; this was a help to him; he belonged to the family which had originally carried the sacred symbol through the wilderness travel. He now opened the doors of his home; and no one can doubt that he offered cheerfully the best of his rooms for the Ark to rest in, and the best of his care in the reverent protection of it afterward.

Of course he received his reward; for God is good to the men whom he finds to be faithful to any trust. Josephus is quoted as saying that, whereas before Obed-edom was poor, on a sudden, in these three months, his estate increased, even to the envy of his neighbors. Matthew Henry says, with his usual brightness, that the Ark "paid well for its entertainment; it is good living in a family that entertains the Ark, for all about it will fare the better for it."

Household piety is always profitable; we suppose that the whole career of this devout man felt the temporal and spiritual uplifting which religion brings with it. We can have God's actual presence with ourselves and our children, if we accept his Word for our guide and his love for our shelter evermore.

XVIII.

PROSPECT AND RETROSPECT.

"WHO AM I, O LORD GOD? AND WHAT IS MY HOUSE, THAT THOU HAST BROUGHT ME HITHERTO? AND THIS WAS YET A SMALL THING IN THY SIGHT, O LORD GOD; BUT THOU HAST SPOKEN ALSO OF THY SERVANT'S HOUSE FOR A GREAT WHILE TO COME."—2 *Sam.* 7:18, 19.

WHEN King David ascertained precisely what the Lord's will was concerning the erection of the temple, he hastened to make known his grateful acquiescence. He was to be granted the privilege of raising the money for the vast undertaking; but it was Solomon his son who was to build the edifice. The devout monarch seems fairly borne down with the weight of the promises vouchsafed to him. He goes immediately into the tabernacle, where the ark was resting under curtains, and there presents his thanksgivings and his prayers: "Then went King David in, and sat before the Lord, and he said, Who am I, O Lord God? and what is my house, that thou hast brought me hitherto? And this was yet a small thing in thy sight, O Lord God; but thou hast spoken also of thy servant's house for a great while to come."

At this precise moment our text brings the picture of him before our imagination: he is on his knees in the presence of God's majesty.

Only for a single use do I bring to your minds to-day an incident so familiar and yet so foreign to our general conception of such an occasion as that which assembles believers together at the Lord's Supper. We are then sitting before the Lord's majesty and kneeling fervently at his mercy-seat under circumstances not so very dissimilar as might at first sight seem. The ark was not Jehovah to David any more than the communion-table is Jesus Christ to us. But as the ark was to him a symbol of the divine presence, so the elements used in this church ordinance are symbols to us of the Saviour's body and blood. And the words of the king's meditation as he bowed himself there are singularly appropriate for any devout and grateful believer to repeat while partaking of the feast.

There appears to us always, as these seasons of celebration occur with a stated regularity, to be a kind of crisis in our religious lives. We pause as on an isthmus of time; the past and the future are alike open to view. There are no utterances which more fitly express our emotions, as we glance back over the years, than these used here: "Who am I, O Lord God? and what is my house, that thou hast brought me hitherto?" And there are no words better for us to speak, as we are looking forward into the eternity we are rapidly nearing, where the fruition of our best hopes is erelong to be, than these which the king employed in his gratitude then: "And this was yet a small thing in thy sight, O Lord God; but thou hast spoken also of thy servant's house for a great while to come."

I. Let us try the retrospect first; this will open the way for us to note the prospect afterwards.

1. In the history the review of the past was laid upon David himself. Thus came to him the message sent by the prophet Nathan: "Now therefore thus shalt thou say unto my servant David, Thus saith the Lord of hosts, I took thee from the sheep-cote, from following the sheep, that thou shouldest be prince over my people, over Israel: and I have been with thee whithersoever thou wentest, and have cut off all thine enemies from before thee; and I will make thee a great name, like unto the name of the great ones that are in the earth."

What a series of reflections must have thronged upon that king's mind as he sat there in silence alone with the ark of God! His memory would run back through the years that passed while he, a fair and ruddy-cheeked boy, had tended his father's flocks in Bethlehem; he would recall the scene when, flushed with his hurried summons from the field, he had come suddenly into the presence of Samuel, and been startled by the announcement that he was one time to be the king of his nation, and must consent to be solemnly anointed now. This was the first occurrence, flung like a stone into a lake, to ripple the calm serenity of his pastoral life, and disturbing it ever afterward with restless harassments and forebodings. How swiftly he had grown up from that low estate, to be at last the ruler of Israel upon a glorious throne!

He had not journeyed along over the hills and valleys of years by ways of pleasantness and by paths of peace. He would well consider his dangers and his deliverances too. He could not have forgotten the hour in which, as a stripling lad, he had slain the Philistine giant with the pebble from the brook, only by trusting in the Lord God of Abraham, Isaac, and Jacob. Then that would make him think of the terrible manner of Saul's attacks upon his life while he as a simple-hearted minstrel was trying to soothe him with his harp. He would seem to see at this moment of review, perhaps as he had never seen before, that his defences must have been actually divine. Who could have turned in their course those javelins that went quivering through the air out of the mad monarch's hand? Then would come up the reminiscences of those months of wild outlaw life, from the time when the malcontents rallied around him at the cave of Adullam until at last, worn and weary, and almost without enthusiasm because he was so tired of battle, he journeyed up to Hebron out of the wilderness country to be crowned. This was a career that might well be reviewed with the words, "Who am I, O Lord God? and what is my house, that thou hast brought me hitherto?"

Now it is to a like historical rehearsal of past incidents and experiences that we, my Christian friends, are always called by such a festival as this ordinance creates; but the history in our case is almost entirely spiritual. There is the choice of us first, like that of David in one respect at the least, in that it was unexpected and undeserved; but unlike it in another respect, in that it was made by Infinite Wisdom in the counsels of eternity. Our souls were anointed to the celestial kingship before we were born; after that came our effectual calling, when God's Spirit of grace constrained us to close in with the offers of salvation. Then, for us to think of, there come very closely along these merciful and providential experiences which have followed in train since our early espousal to Christ. Who can ever forget them?

The call, therefore, is very plain to us: "Look unto the rock whence ye are hewn, and to the hole of the pit whence ye are digged." David might sometimes wonder why, among all that band of brethren of his, so stalwart and strong, he, the weakest and the youngest, had been selected for this wonderful place of honor as the king of Israel. But we may marvel the more that we were made to be the recipients of this grander honor still as kings and priests unto God. Among the private papers of John Howard was found after his death one bearing only these pathetic words: "Lord God, why *me?*" Such a reflection must have been suggested in the very spirit of David's exclamation there before the ark: "Who am I, O Lord God, and what is my house, that thou hast brought me hitherto!"

2. The result of this retrospection upon the prayer of the king is the special thing to be observed, because there comes to view the true temper which on every such occasion as this ought to be found in the heart of the Christian. One might suppose that an exaltation like that, in the case of a shepherd-boy lifted at a stroke to be a sovereign, a token of divine favor so evidently supreme would be likely to puff up his pride and inflame his vanity. But there ap-

pears nothing of superciliousness nor of self-conceit, nor even of satisfied complacency, in David at this moment. On the contrary, no words can be found which in more vigorous terms could express his humility and utter self-abnegation than these he employs for himself: "Who am I, O Lord God!"

Matthew Henry commenting in his own inimitable way, exclaims in a kind of expostulation at his self-abasement: "Why, he was upon all accounts a very considerable and valuable man! His endowments were extraordinary. His gifts and graces were eminent. He was a man of honor, success, and usefulness; the darling of his country and the dread of its enemies." But David here evidently counts himself nothing before his Maker, and attributes everything to God's sovereign grace to him.

Nor is this all: he disclaims also any credit for his relationship and family connection: "And what is my house, that thou hast brought me hitherto!" David was evidently an essentially modest man. He made very much the same remark as this to his royal predecessor on the occasion when he was offered the hand of his daughter in marriage: "And David said unto Saul, Who am I? and what is my life, or my father's family in Israel, that I should be son-in-law to the king?" Then, and in such circumstances, he had much less ground for his self-depreciation than now, as it afterwards proved in his domestic history. His family was not a mean one; he was descended from the regal tribe. But he renounced his princely descent before the people and before God as any real reason for his pride.

The same motive was in his mind now. His reflections had made him diffident in temper. He felt that he had not been advanced by his own worthiness, but it was the "gentleness" of God alone which had made him "great." So he says: "For thy word's sake, and according to thine own heart, hast thou done all these great things, to make thy servant know them. Wherefore thou art great, O Lord God; for there is none like thee, neither is there any God beside thee, according to all that we have heard with our ears."

A calm and candid review of his past religious life always humbles a genuine Christian, rather than exalts him into self-importance. There are so many falls for which he is responsible; there are so many neglects for which he is to blame; there are so many weaknesses in his character and so many errors in his walk, that he feels he has little reason to grow self-complacent. It is better to keep saying with this king before the mercy-seat: "Who am I, O Lord God? and what is my house, that thou hast brought me hitherto?"

II. This leads us directly to the second clause in David's question: "And this was yet a small thing in thy sight, O Lord God; but thou hast spoken also of thy servant's house for a great while to come." Having now considered the believer's retrospect, we turn to consider his prospect, as he sits at the table of the Lord.

You cannot fail to observe how, in the utterance of the text we have chosen, the comparative value of these two was reckoned. Glorious indeed were the remembrances which thronged upon David— the deliverances, the honors, the communings; he dismisses them them at once when he begins to think of the anticipations he is permitted to cherish. He calls them "a small thing." Not that he deemed these past experiences insignificant; he had shown by his acknowledgments how he prized them. But the transcendent worth of what now remained eclipsed them wholly.

What was this outlook, the peculiar splendor of which caused him to value the retrospect less than the prospect? Some of the promises had reference to Israel as a kingdom under his reign: "And what one nation in the earth is like thy people, even like Israel, whom God went to redeem for a people to himself, and to make him a name, and to do for you great things and terrible, for thy land, before thy people, which thou redeemedst to thee from Egypt, from the nations and their gods? For thou hast confirmed to thyself thy people Israel to be a people unto thee for ever: and thou, Lord, art become their God." Some of them had reference even to the Messiah's kingdom; for the Old Testament words are quoted by the apostle in the New Testament as if concerning Jesus: "Thy throne, O God, is for ever and ever."

Christian friends, here we stand; I have likened the communion season to an isthmus; but it resembles an isthmus which links a peninsula to a continent. We look back, and we behold a beautiful land, it is true; how many a bright valley it has, how many a high hill; how many green pastures, how many still waters! This past life of ours since first we learned to know the Saviour is very dear to us; it ought to be. How many a glad hour we have spent in it after all; how many a joyous companionship we have known! But we do not regret to turn our eyes forward away from it. For we step at once upon the mainland of the grand continent of the future. On every side it is stretching its vast area. Fair fields and beautiful valleys are before our vision; mountains as majestic, Pisgah-tops as sightly, as ever we have known.

The one peerless characteristic of the believer's outlook is its permanency; it concerns "a great while to come." This feast points to the marriage supper of the Lamb, the Father's house, the inexhaustible provision, the residence of the blessed, from which they shall go out no more for ever. Then the children of God shall all come home, shall partake of the true bread and drink the new wine in the kingdom.

Observe, finally, that David's acknowledgment passes on almost imperceptibly into a prayer. *He asks for the same favors that he has just thanked God for promising.* This is all according to rule. Even to Ezekiel, rehearsing the terms of the Better Covenant, the Lord said, "I will yet for this be inquired of by the house of Israel to do it for them." Pray, then; pray, and the Lord will keep his covenant.

"And now, O Lord God, the word that thou hast spoken concerning thy servant, and concerning his house, establish it for ever, and do as thou hast said."

XIX.

DAVID'S SIN AND NATHAN'S PARABLE.

"AND NATHAN SAID UNTO DAVID, THOU ART THE MAN."—
2 *Sam.* 12:7.

RAPID reversals of feeling are to be expected when one gives attentive study to the progress of history in the Old Testament. For it seems to be the plan of the Almighty, in issuing the biographies of so many human beings at once, to show the fitful changes more vividly, as they pass across our field of vision, by contrasts of striking color.

We left King David on his knees before the ark of God, humbly obedient, praying for greater grace and pledging constant piety. Here now we find him upon his knees again, but it is because his wickedness has cast him down to the uttermost depths of shame and remorse.

I. It is necessary that we indicate, in the outset, the occasion upon which the monarch disgraced himself and the touching little story of the slaughter of a poor man's ewe-lamb was told as a parable.

The king of Israel had committed a fearful and degrading sin, so public and so scandalous that there was need of direct rebuke. He had beguiled the wife of Uriah, one of the generals in his army, away from her duty and her home. He had then by a deceitful plot compassed the death of her brave husband in order to conceal his shame. To the crime of adultery he had added murder. Time passed on:

a wicked year wore slowly away. The calm, dispassionate record of the Scripture at this point is all the more impressive because the inspired writers are not wont to express opinions as to the moral character of the transactions they place on the historic pages. Here, however, we are tranquilly told, as if to guard against any false inference from the divine forbearance with this guilty monarch, that "the thing which David had done displeased the Lord." Sharp rebuke was near at hand.

II. This was the occasion, therefore, for the utterance of the parable. Nathan, the commissioned prophet, suddenly appeared in the palace for its recital. This man was the old and tried servant of the king. He meets us often in the midst of the turbulent history of those days. David had learned to trust him as a counsellor and lean upon him as a friend. For years this servant of the high God had been the messenger between the king and Jehovah, as well as the medium of information between the king and his people. Many a case of injustice, or act of unneighborly dealing, had he brought to the ears of the monarch, that the wrong might be righted and the weak succored against the strong. To all appearances this was the errand he came upon, when, unsummoned by any order, he came into the king's presence:

"And the Lord sent Nathan unto David. And he came unto him, and said unto him, There were two men in one city; the one rich, and the other poor." Alas, how familiar are these words even to our ears! How many a perplexed tale opens thus!

how many a demand for redress starts with an announcement precisely similar! Men seem to know how to manage every relationship but one—the rich man and the poor in the same city. Now it is fair to say that David was usually very keen-sighted in such cases as these. His long training of outlaw life under Saul had fitted him to understand them better than most rulers. Singular illustration does this parable present of human blindness to personal guilt: he who was a prophet as much as Nathan now needs a prophet himself; he who could detect the sin of any one else instinctively is most unsuspicious of any purpose to expose his own.

> "Oh, wad some power the giftie gie us
> To see oursel's as ithers see us!"

But Nathan went on to state his case more particularly: "The rich man had exceeding many flocks and herds: but the poor man had nothing save one little ewe-lamb, which he had bought and nourished up: and it grew up together with him and with his children; it did eat of his own meat, and drank of his own cup, and lay in his bosom, and was unto him as a daughter. And there came a traveller unto the rich man, and he spared to take of his own flock and of his own herd, to dress for the wayfaring man that was come unto him; but took the poor man's lamb, and dressed it for the man that was come to him."

The touching beauty of this little apologue cannot be passed carelessly by. Its appeal forces its way to the most sensitive centres of our feeling. But the general shrewdness of its conception is heightened by the fact that it entered at once into the historic experience of this king. He knew what it was to be poor; he knew what it was to have and to love one little ewe-lamb. In those early memories of his Bethlehem home he held most affectionate reminiscences of shepherd life, and he understood well the depth of attachment which a lonely man would have for a pet from the flock which he had taught to feed from his own hand and lie in his bosom. To think that any rich man should plunder a poor man, and in the name of sacred hospitality should do an act of such ineffable baseness as to select meat from another's fold when his own was full—this was enough to rouse the fiery indignation of a man much less impulsive than David.

But the story of the one little pet ewe-lamb had already touched his feelings: and when Nathan told him that the rich, mean neighbor had stolen and killed the creature which the poor man cherished in his bosom as a daughter, his anger was at its height. The old soldier-king seemed to leap up from his throne and fairly dilate with terrible wrath. His violence exploded into a sentence of unparalleled severity: "And David's anger was greatly kindled against the man; and he said to Nathan, As the Lord liveth, the man that hath done this thing shall surely die. And he shall restore the lamb fourfold, because he did this thing, and because he had no pity."

III. This was precisely what Nathan wanted. The explication of his skilful parable was instantaneous: "And Nathan said to David, Thou art the man. Thus saith the Lord God of Israel, I anointed thee king over Israel, and I delivered thee out of the hand of Saul; and I gave thee thy master's house, and thy master's wives into thy bosom, and gave thee the house of Israel and of Judah; and if that had been too little, I would moreover have given unto thee such and such things. Wherefore hast thou despised the commandment of the Lord, to do evil in his sight? Thou hast killed Uriah the Hittite with the sword, and hast taken his wife to be thy wife, and hast slain him with the sword of the children of Ammon."

It is easy to draw a picture of that most impressive scene before the imagination, however difficult it may be to describe it in words. The king must have been startled beyond all power of self-control. How rapid was the transition of feeling through which he passed! One minute he was on his feet in all the flush of indignation at another's sin, fairly exulting in the proud sense of unutterable contempt at injustice so apparent and so unmitigated in its foul stroke. In that happy moment how did his heart swell under the lofty consciousness that he had full power to right so heinous a wrong! How satisfied he was to believe that the poor man's thanks would be given him, while the rich man's superciliousness should be humbled to the very dust; and he, David, the just, the noble, the friend of the injured, would be theme of many a maiden's song.

The next minute he perceived the countenance of Nathan changing towards him. Around came that long scornful finger, which had been pointing at an imaginary offender; and now in reply to the implied inquiry for that offender's name, its index slowly reached his own face, and then the sober words were spoken—"Thou art the man."

Could his discomfiture have been more complete? Could Nathan's triumph of rebuke have been more successful? No invective had been used: not a word of upbraiding had been spoken. But in the instant when David's judgment had been pronounced against indescribable meanness and unmitigated wrong he now discovered that his lips had pronounced sentence on himself. And of the two cases his sin was the more abominable. If it was wrong to pilfer a lamb dear as a daughter, what was it to steal a daughter? What was it to cheat a man of his life and his wife? So, in broken tones, and with covered face, he owned it: "And David said unto Nathan, I have sinned against the Lord!"

IV. In attempting to draw our lessons of present instruction from this parable it is easy to see that it does not come legitimately within our reach to consider the sin of David, to attempt to apologize for it, or to examine his penitence. These can be touched only incidentally. The main teaching of the narrative is centred upon the one doctrine concerning fraternal Christian rebuke.

I say fraternal, for here you find one inspired man rebuking another: a prophet rebuking a prophet: a subject rebuking a king. Sin levels the loftiest man to the lowest rank. Zeal for God lifts the lowliest man into a vantage unquestioned. Any man has a right to be heard when he challenges a wrong, wherever he finds it. And every Christian man has a charge from high heaven sturdily to confront sin in all times and places.

Still, there is a right way and a wrong in which to do this. So confused are our notions of real indignation at wickedness, and the consequent recoil from it; so apt are we, in a kind of sanctimonious self-congratulation, to mistake a satisfied arrogance for a true zeal of righteousness; so likely are we to confound spite with spirituality, that it may as well be confessed here as anywhere how feebly this duty of Christian rebuke is performed by most of the people of God, and how utterly injudicious are most of its commonest forms.

If a man is proud, it seems to poor human nature rather a fine thing to be instrumental in taking him down; if he is rich, it gratifies our ill-concealed envy to detect a meanness in him and expose it; if he is conspicuous, it pleases our vanity to have bystanders observe how fearless is the faithful attack we make upon him.

Hence it is well for us to study this famous rebuke with much penetration.

1. Observe then, first, that in all cases conscience is the arbiter in the wrong, and must be the centre of aim in the reproof.

It would have helped Nathan's cause in no respect whatever to force David to fear public opinion. Any threat of violence from the great nation he had outraged would only have misled the king. Just so any endeavor to compel David to appease Uriah's relatives with gifts of fortune or position would have entirely missed the point. David must be led to see that he had done his wrong in the full sight of God. And unless Nathan's rebuke was levelled with this direct purpose, and unless it actually reached its aim, there would have been a most serious harm from it. It succeeded, as we have seen; but how inimitably it was pressed, and how thorough was the triumph, no one is aware until he enters into the depth of repentance disclosed in the fifty-first Psalm, where the royal poet's contrition appears. There David seems to have actually forgotten almost everything but the vileness of his crime before God, for he says, "Against thee, thee only, have I sinned and done this evil in thy sight!" We are to lead transgressors to this confession, or our most ingenious reproofs will utterly fail.

2. Observe, secondly, that absolute rectitude is the only standard to be admitted in all processes of rebuke.

Nathan might have paused long before he had reached this humbling crisis. But once in the chariot of divine retribution, he drove that terrified king up to the very verge of ruin. He made him see that his entire soul had been defiled; that it was not the single act of debauchery which was offending the Infinite Purity, but the whole inner defilement it left behind it. David must perceive not less that he had *done* wrong, only the more that he *was* wrong. So we find in that Psalm of which I have spoken the words: "Behold, thou desirest truth in the in-ward parts, and in the hidden part thou shalt make me to know wisdom. Create in me a clean heart, O God, and renew a right spirit within me." It will do little good merely to reprove one outbreak of sin, and leave the internal source of all the evil, the wicked heart, untouched.

3. In the third place, observe that tenderness is the dominant spirit in all truly Scriptural, or even successful, rebuke.

There is not one word of violence in all this address of Nathan. The story of the poor man's ewe-lamb cannot even be repeated in a loud, coarse voice. Its tranquil incidents are conceived in a temper of elevated simplicity. Nathan is not angry. It is true that David becomes so: this feeling is what is speedily turned upon himself. He is indignant at last in tearful wrath over his own miserable defection, and mourns out, feeling that all reparation comes too late: "The sacrifices of God are a broken spirit: a broken and a contrite heart, O God, thou wilt not despise." He pours forth a confession full of contemptuous scorn; but in no words of Nathan is there found even a passionate intonation towards him.

And there can be no doubt that in this particular there is furnished our most admirable lesson. Remember that even under the Old Testament, when it was said, "Thou shalt in any wise rebuke thy neighbor, and not suffer sin upon him," it was added, "Thou shalt not hate thy brother in thy heart." Paul told Timothy to "reprove, rebuke, exhort;" but he bade him do his delicate duty "with all long-suffering and doctrine." We have no example, no precept, no intimation, that will give us an apology or excuse for proud upbraiding, even of the worst malefactors. The servant of the Lord must not strive, but be patient with all men. Even Michael, the archangel, when contending with the devil, did not dare to bring against him a railing accusation, but said, The Lord rebuke thee! It was well that David's agitation should in a salutary outburst be addressed towards his own discovered sin; but Nathan would have defeated his own parable if he had allowed the king to pervert the counsel and become indignant with him for having uttered it.

4. Observe, in the fourth place, that courageous fidelity is the measure of all Christian duty in administering rebuke.

There is a limit here; one may be betrayed, and suffer himself to go too far. Hence the wise man says: "He that reproveth a scorner getteth to himself shame; and he that rebuketh a wicked man getteth himself a blot. Reprove not a scorner, lest he hate thee; rebuke a wise man, and he will love thee." Just whereabouts this line is to be drawn cannot be stated in any rule, however elastic it may be. But our danger does not generally lie in going too far. We are much more apt to be backward in challenging high sins. We are afraid of giving offence. We are more afraid we shall be attacked in our turn by that terrible rejoinder, "Physician, heal thyself!" Now men demand honesty from Christians above everything else. The ancient declaration holds true still: "He that rebuketh a man, afterwards shall find more favor than he that flattereth with the tongue." It has been made our duty to help each other in just this way. "Open rebuke is better than secret love." The precept is imperative: "Them that sin, rebuke before all, that others also may fear." It will be a mean evasion of this when any one of us beats about, and winds around, or in any way stops short of courageously saying, "Thou art the man."

Suffer me now, in closing, to ask how a theme like this bears upon our own habits and history. Are we up to this standard in helping each other? Has not the day of honest fraternal rebuke pretty much passed by? And are we not ourselves to blame for many of those defections to the common cause which make such sudden scandal? It may oftentimes check grievous sin, oftentimes lay hold of waning penitence, for us merely to speak one true word of warning to a perplexed and wavering brother in the faith.

Another question, quite akin to this, is likewise suggested by this theme: What ought to be expected of every faithful ministry in a time like that we live in? What does *close preaching* mean? Is there any sin so peculiarly delicate that the messenger of God is debarred from saying, "Thou art the man"?

And one more question still: What lesson is there here for unrepentant sinners to learn? We make parables: we tell you of a child and a father— a rebel and a government—a steward and a householder. We carry your decision at once with us;

what is to hinder your own self-condemnation when the definite application is made? David repented when Nathan told him, "Thou art the man." Yet how long many of you linger, even under pressure of the truth! How many men stand self-convicted every time the clear gospel is preached! You are quick to perceive others' wickedness: your mind responds with instinctive decision. Now it is yourself! "He that being often reproved hardeneth his neck, shall suddenly be destroyed, and that without remedy."

"Almighty God, the fountain of all holiness, who by thy Word and Spirit dost conduct all thy servants in the way of peace and righteousness, inviting them by thy promises, winning them by thy long-suffering, and endearing them by thy loving-kindness; grant unto us so truly to repent of our sins, so carefully to reform our errors, so diligently to watch over all our actions, so industriously to perform all our duty, that we may never willingly transgress thy holy laws: but that it may be the work of our lives to obey thee, the joy of our souls to please thee, the satisfaction of all our hopes and the perfection of all our desires to live with thee, in the holiness of thy kingdom of grace and glory; through Jesus Christ our Lord."

XX.

DAVID'S PENITENTIAL PSALM.

"Wash me, and I shall be whiter than snow."—*Psalm* 51:7.

For many years the Moravian missionaries labored among the inhabitants of Greenland with no apparent success. One preacher came, and tried to prove to his simple-minded hearers that there must be a Supreme Being called God. They laughed at him for attempting to teach them what they knew as well as he. Then came another, urging morality, insisting that they should leave off drunkenness and cease to thieve and lie. They sent him away in quickened impatience, bidding him go to his own people, who needed such counsel far more than Greenlanders did. Thus one messenger after another arrived and departed. Yet no good seemed settled in the hearts of men.

At last one meek and holy man determined to ask what most they wanted; and they answered that they wished for something that would cleanse them from the guilt and defilement of sin. He proceeded to preach the pure simple gospel of redemption, the forgiveness of sin through the atonement made by the Lord Jesus Christ; he taught them the prayer: "Wash me, and I shall be whiter than snow," and showed how they could be made clean. With one heart and voice the people cried out around the pulpit, "Oh, that is what we have been longing to know this many a day!" Then began the glorious work of divine grace, which soon filled the cold regions of the north with the warmth and lovelight of the gospel and brought glory to God's name.

I. Here is a prayer which is *universal*, and yet *personal*. "Wash me, and I shall be whiter than snow." If the whole world of sinful men raised their voices together, they would still be compelled to say "me," as if only one soul had been pleading. It is not possible for God to pardon and cleanse communities in a vast penitent bulk; he pardons each soul among the multitude by itself, when the cry reaches his ear and he sees the penitence.

Such a petition takes fresh meaning from the fact that in its set terms it was first offered by a very good man. But David had fallen into grievous and direful wickedness. He was at this moment driven to the lowest depths of humiliation and self-loathing; his conscience was lashing him unsparingly with whips which had a sting in each thong that struck him. He poured his penitence forth in an agony of intense supplication for pardon: "Have mercy upon me, O God, according to thy loving-kindness; according unto the multitude of thy tender mercies blot out my transgressions. Wash me thoroughly from mine iniquity, and cleanse me from my sin. For I acknowledge my transgressions; and my sin is ever before me."

"My transgressions—I acknowledge my transgressions:" ah, there is something unutterably pathetic and solemn in the sense of admitted ownership in wrong! When any human being settles back on these fixed conclusions, and in his deepest reserves confesses that a great guilt claims him as its master; when, with no exculpation of self and no inculpation of others, a man simply says, "This is mine, unshared, solitary, direct violation of God's law," he feels he must go farther than the mere act; he must admit greater trouble still; he must say not only, "I have sinned," but also, "I am a sinner;" then he will cry out like David again: "Behold, I was shapen in iniquity; and in sin did my mother conceive me. Behold, thou desirest truth in the inward parts: and in the hidden part thou shalt make me to know wisdom. Purge me with hyssop, and I shall be clean: wash me, and I shall be whiter than snow."

But now the moment any one of us is tempted to insist in any instance that the cry is that of the Psalmist alone, and is to be used only in a spirit of accommodation by the rest of the world, we are met by the discovery that Paul says quite the same thing in the seventh of Romans. Thus we find it everywhere—a personal and a universal cry of the human soul through the races and the ages. Like some great battle-plain at nightfall, where the wild hosts have contended, leaving the shade to cover the dying and the dead, the whole world is vocal with wailings and desperation and pain and hopeless agony. Pierced and bleeding, souls suffer and cry, and each one says "me" and "my" with a dreadful sense of ownership. Such prayers are personal and universal.

II. Then, further, it is to be confessed that this prayer is intensely *special*, and yet thoroughly *inclusive*. As we fasten our attention upon David's words, possibly they seem strained: "Against thee, thee only, have I sinned, and done this evil in thy sight: that thou mightest be justified when thou speakest, and be clear when thou judgest."

We admit that every petition ought to be clear and have a specific aim, towards which all the energies of our faith are to be directed. And no doubt this royal sinner had offended a God of infinite purity. But then think how he was placed, and remember what he had done. He was very unhappy; why did he not plead for comfort? He had just laid his little child in the silence of a sepulchre. He was humiliated: a prophet of the high God had just given him a public and withering rebuke. He was aware of all the aggravations of his wickedness. He had sinned against Uriah, whom he had despoiled and murdered; he had heavily sinned against his whole people, whose trust he had betrayed; he had sinned against Bathsheba, whose imagination he had royally corrupted; he had sinned against his own manhood, by blindly covering his eyes from consequences of his weakness. But now a great passionate cry bursts forth from his soul, "Against thee, against thee only, have I sinned!" What can such words mean?

One of the best of our modern scholars has told us that a single term has been employed in the fifty-first Psalm to designate the generic idea of sin: this originally means to be noisy, to be tempestuous;

thence, with a transition to the notion of a moral disorder, it is used with the meaning of breaking in pieces with a crash; and so it comes to signify an evil action. Beyond this, however, there are three other words in the same old formula of confession. Each one of these describes a different aspect of the idea of sin. For example, the first implies that, God's will being the aim which a man rightly pursues, sin is a missing of his true goal in life; sinning is a stumbling on the way to the soul's proper end; it is a moral action with a total failure in it. Then another of the words regards sin as a twisting or perversion of the will from the right way; for it means *to be bent* or distorted; and so *evil* is the departure from man's appointed path. And the last word brands all wrong-doing as a rebellious transgression of divine law, the law which every human being is bound to obey; for it signifies in itself a faithless rejection of God's covenant with his creatures for their good and his own glory. Hence, out of the use of all these terms surely comes a definition of wrong-doing which centres the whole force of it against the Supreme Ruler of the universe; and we can understand now what David means when he says, "Against thee, thee only."

The fact is, he had learned that all specific sin is hopelessly embraced in the generic sin. Breaking the divine law is what constitutes one a sinner. Sinning against one's neighbors is sinning against God. So if one can only get his pardon from God, he can arrange for his pardon from all others. If only he can be washed from guilt in God's sight, he may be sure that infinite grace can make him "whiter than snow."

III. Observe, again, that this is a prayer which is characterized by *utter desperation* coupled with a supremely *confident hope*. When the guilt-burdened penitent prays, "Wash me," he is certain that he has reached a point at which he cannot wash himself.

He feels precisely as David did when in this Psalm he exclaimed, "Thou desirest not sacrifice, else would I give it." A settled conviction rests upon his soul: "Thou delightest not in burnt offering." He is driven at last to God himself. He lets go of all dependences he had previously tried to lean upon, precisely as Naaman did when he gave up his pleading for the rivers of Damascus, and started for the Jordan commanded, in order that he might bathe there and be clean. He keeps repeating the inquiry of an old prophet: "Wherewith shall I come before the Lord, and bow myself before the high God?" This question he cannot answer; for an instinctive sense of the fitness of things shows him that he has nothing to offer for an atonement that the Judge needs; the Lord will not "be pleased with thousands of rams, nor ten thousands of rivers of oil." He cannot give his "first-born for his transgressions, the fruit of his body for the sin of his soul."

Singular indeed is that profound consciousness, which every guilty person has, that he is all the time in pursuit of what he plainly knows will elude him. Did you never dream, and feel at the same moment that you were dreaming? You were aware that you were toiling with all your might to attain something, which after all you understood would amount to nothing. For you were going to awake soon, and then these struggles would not count.

It is not an act of sin that we deplore, nor even are its consequences what we dread; it is the deep, loathsome pollution of our nature behind and beneath it. One of the old martyrs, said to have been betrayed into a moment's recreancy, signed a recantation of his faith; but renouncing his renunciation afterwards, and being a second time led to the stake, he thrust his shrivelling right hand into the flame where it burned the hottest; then he exclaimed, "This hand did the wrong, it shall suffer the earliest!" Now we have no sympathy with such an act of reparation, save mere admiration of its fortitude; we feel the brave man only made a mistake. The hand was not specially to blame; it was the heart behind it which was vile and full of condemnation.

Just there comes in the hope on the background of despair. We are sure David was right when he said that God desired truth "in the inward parts," and when he believed that "in the hidden part" He would make him to know wisdom. Most of us would cheerfully accept his prayer on the instant as our securest hope of relief: "Hide thy face from my sins, and blot out all mine iniquities. Create in me a clean heart, O God, and renew a right spirit within me. Cast me not away from thy presence; and take not thy Holy Spirit from me. Restore unto me the joy of thy salvation; and uphold me with thy free Spirit."

For up to the moment in which God himself interposes with an entire revolution of our being, equivalent to a new life out of death, a desperate fear holds us in its grasp; we are perfectly certain that it is hopeless for us to contend with our fate. We may keep pursuing and pursuing, until our souls are convulsed with repeated failures; we are no nearer deliverance until we are absolutely helpless—fallen on the earth, with our faces in the dust. Never, till driven out of even the expectation of relief, and shut up to God, are we on the way to pardon for our sins. It is in the brokenness that there is the beginning for a fresh strength; out of weakness are we to be made strong. See for a moment how the Psalmist here reiterates that somewhat striking word in his acknowledgment. When one feels that his courage is broken, confidence is broken, his whole self is broken—broken—then he suddenly discovers he is safe, for he lies in the hollow of his Father's hand: "Make me to hear joy and gladness; that the bones which thou hast broken may rejoice. The sacrifices of God are a broken spirit: a broken and a contrite heart, O God, thou wilt not despise." In his swift surrender of all his refuges of lies he finds rest, perfect and fearless, trusting in the unalterable truth and mercy of God.

"A guilty, weak, and helpless worm, on thy kind arms I fall:
Be thou my Strength and Righteousness, my Saviour and my All!"

IV. Once more: this prayer is unusually *extrava-*

gant in utterance, and yet entirely *legitimate in its meaning:* "Wash me, and I shall be whiter than snow." It is important that you see how close is the connection here between the means and ends.

Observe the very form of expression: "I shall be whiter." David makes us know that he has the strongest kind of expectation. He was praying for the washing for the sake of the whiteness. He felt far away from God, but he propelled his petition with the dauntlessness of a determinate faith. "Prayer," wrote an old nonconformist once, "is the rope in the belfry; we pull it, and it is sure to ring the bell up in heaven. We may not hear the strokes, but they sound aloft in the tower."

This petition is legitimate, because God wants the answer as much as man does. Sin is an abomination in his sight; it is the one thing he hates supremely. He has made provision for an entire abolition of it. We may ask for wealth; but whether any one will get it or not depends on circumstances; we may ask for long life, and God may deem it wiser for us to go up into Mt. Nebo and die *now*, as Moses did, with bodily strength unabated and eye not yet grown dim. But if a man penitently asks for pardon, he will certainly get it; for God knows that sin is never of advantage to anybody, and holiness is always a thing of grace and of glory. This is what the gospel was proclaimed to secure for sinners. In the early twilight of history stand three figures, which we recognize as the three sons of God, Lucifer, Adam, and Christ. The first of these asked the omnipotent Father for his throne; he would rival him in the might of his power; but for a daring so wild he was thrust into the outer darkness. Then the second of these sons asked the omniscient Father for his wisdom, for he planned to rival him in the limitless reach of his knowledge; but for this presumption he was driven forth from his happy home in paradise. But the third of these sons of God only opened his lips to say, "Lo, I come; in the volume of the book it is written of me, I delight to do thy will, O my God!" And when the voice was heard coming forth out of the excellent glory, it said, "This is my beloved Son, in whom I am well pleased." God exalted that chosen one of his three sons above both the others, for he made him the Judge of the fallen angels and the Redeemer of fallen men. That Son is our intercessor; and God loveth him specially, and "hath given all things into his hand." So these prayers for pardon will surely and always be answered.

But we are constrained to admit that even a provision for answer does not relieve this petition from extravagance in form. "Whiter than snow:" what can be whiter than snow? It does seem strange to use a comparison so extreme. But then we might well remember that the reason why snow is so white is because it has been lit with that which is whiter. Snow is soft and loose and crystal, and the light from the sun rests in among its flakes over all its glittering surfaces; but the sunshine itself is whiter than any snow-rift it falls on. And while a pardoned man's sins are cleansed and purified and brightened by the sweet shining of Christ, the Sun of Righteousness, upon his heart, yet it is certainly true that Christ himself is purer than the man can be in a world like ours where the dust and soot keep falling on his life. To pray to be "whiter than snow" is only to ask that one may be as pure as the Lord Jesus Christ is pure; indeed, an inspired expression has been given to this very thought: "Every man that hath this hope in Him purifieth himself even as He is pure." We are not satisfied with becoming as white as other heroes and sages and leaders and worthies, of whom the world grew proud while they lived, and to whom fair monuments were erected when they died. We long to be whiter than such snow as that of an unsullied reputation or an uncontaminated character; we pray that we may be likened to Immanuel himself, the Prince of Light.

Herein is found the explanation of David's neglect of everything else in his supplication except his sin. His guilt lay out before his mind; of this he desired to be free, first, most of all. He could bear his affliction. He could defend himself from the enemies he had made. He could make it right with Israel whom he had scandalized. But this great, foul stain on his soul he could not endure. No one can fail to notice the extreme purity which this royal sinner desires, nor the extreme earnestness with which he desires purity. He wants to be "whiter than snow," because he wants to be white as the sunshine of God.

XXI.

DAVID'S PSALM OF PARDON.

"Blessed is he whose transgression is forgiven, whose sin is covered."—*Psalm* 32:1.

By its date it is understood that this Psalm of David was written certainly after the commission of his great sin in the murder of Uriah and the theft of his wife. It is entitled "Maschil," and was used in the synagogue at the conclusion of the service on the Day of Atonement. The commentators tell us that ten of the temple songs bear the same designation. One of the chief scholars renders the title "an instruction of David;" Gesenius, speaking somewhat more simply, names it "a poem of David." It is likely that the margin of our English Bibles contains the best suggestion of all: "A Psalm of David giving instruction." The meaning of the word *Maschil* is thus perfectly preserved.

The quaint Izaak Walton chose the second verse of this composition as the motto of his spiritual life. In closing the biography of Bishop Sanderson he says: "It is now too late to wish that my life may be like his, for I am in the eighty-fifth year of my age; but I humbly beseech Almighty God that my death may be, and I as earnestly beg of every reader to say Amen. 'Blessed is the man unto whom the Lord imputeth not iniquity, and in whose spirit there is no guile.'"

It is not necessary to our present exposition that

we attempt an analysis of this sacred song. The poetic paragraphs of it fall apart very easily, and may be profitably taken up, each in its order.

I. To begin with, the Psalmist pictures the present happiness of a pardoned soul: "Blessed is he whose transgression is forgiven, whose sin is covered. Blessed is the man unto whom the Lord imputeth not iniquity, and in whose spirit there is no guile." The reason why the words here have such a familiar sound is found in the fact that we have become used to them in the New Testament. A thousand years before the Epistle to the Romans was written David was singing the same gospel in one of his penitential Psalms. For the apostle quotes: "Now to him that worketh is the reward not reckoned of grace, but of debt. But to him that worketh not, but believeth on him that justifieth the ungodly, his faith is counted for righteousness. Even as David also describeth the blessedness of the man unto whom God imputeth righteousness without works, saying, Blessed are they whose iniquities are forgiven, and whose sins are covered. Blessed is the man to whom the Lord will not impute sin."

When Martin Luther was once asked which were the best songs for a Christian, he answered, "The Pauline Psalms;" and these he defined as Psalms which Paul adduced as his proofs in discussing the plan of salvation by grace; among them he reckoned this that we now are studying. Its whole significance may be stated in one verse of Paul's argument: "Therefore being justified by faith, we have peace with God through our Lord Jesus Christ." This is not a Messianic Psalm, and so has not much to say about Christ; but it has more to say about the gospel of Christ.

The word "blessed" here is the same and in the same form as that which appears at the beginning of the first Psalm; it is used explosively and is in the plural number: "Oh, the blessednesses of the man whose transgression is forgiven!" Good Robert Leighton observes the grammatical peculiarity and cries out: "This is to denote the most supreme and perfect blessedness; as the elephant, to denote its vast bulk, is spoken of as *behemoth* in the plural number!"

The Psalmist thus draws upon his own experience. He had sinned and had been forgiven; he now appreciates the wonderful joy of peace and safety, and proclaims his discovery and possession of it as if with a full and grateful heart. It is forbidden for any one to cover his own sins with secrecy; it is commanded that he should have them covered for him by the atonement of the Lord Jesus Christ: "He that covereth his sins shall not prosper: but whoso confesseth and forsaketh them shall have mercy."

II. Having thus stated the theme of his song, David passes on in his thought to review the past. The Psalm, therefore, in the second place, rehearses the sad experiences of his impenitent life before he reached the sense of pardon through grace: "When I kept silence, my bones waxed old through my roaring all the day long. For day and night thy hand was heavy upon me: my moisture is turned into the drought of summer."

The figures he employs are very forcible, and seem to have been taken from his early history when he was a shepherd-boy out on the exposed hillsides night and day tending his father's flocks. We draw at once the inference that David, even after he had received the rebuke from Nathan, did not seek to make his peace with God by acknowledgment of his wickedness. His crimes had been simply atrocious; and yet this proud sinner would not, at least did not, confess them and implore the pardon which alone could bring him relief. His conscience meanwhile kept him in a state of torturing remorse and chronic alarm. His very physical nature succumbed. He shut himself up in the silence of his sullen reserve till his bones ached with the sighs he repressed: then he went around venting his anguish with roars like those of an infuriated beast caught in a trap. The language is almost violent. He must have raged like a brute under the pain he felt in his innermost soul.

But such suffering counts for nothing when it comes not from the pangs of a broken heart and a contrite spirit, but from the strain of a stubborn will which tires itself out with resistance. Indeed a sinner's sufferings are never valuable any way. Christ's sufferings have merit, but ours do not. The imagination is fairly arrested with such a picture as this of David, storming around like a wild animal in unappeased and unappeasable pain; but what good did it all do?

It really looks as if, during this wretched year that succeeded Nathan's visit, this royal transgressor had been working himself into illness with his compunctions of conscience and his hardness of will. Perhaps he brought on a state of feverish heat and dryness of his body, and suffered with disease under the pressure of his frightened remorse. More likely the expression means that all refreshment and spiritual enlivening of soul went away from him, so that he languished like a tree burned and exhausted, with the heat of fierce sunshine wilting all moisture out of it. He must have pined in uselessness and joylessness of spirit through those miserable months. The whole springs of his being were dried up; life lost its cheer; there remained only a fearful looking for of judgment which might fall upon him at any moment.

III. Just here the whole tone of the Psalm turns. In the third place, David traces the steps of the process by which he secured forgiveness and so obtained relief from his pain: "I acknowledged my sin unto thee, and mine iniquity have I not hid. I said, I will confess my transgressions unto the Lord; and thou forgavest the iniquity of my sin."

He began with confessing his guilt. It does not seem as if any illustration could be needed to make this whole transformation clear to every experience. When friends are estranged because of wrong that has fallen between them, when we have done a neighbor an injury, when we have been betrayed by passion into speaking the wild word which has given another pain, our instant relief and our only relief is sure to come with the frank admission, "I did wrong; forgive me!" It is like rolling off a stone from our limbs when it is crushing the bones and the sinews with intolerable excruciation; everything rights up at once, and we find we were not injured half as much as it seemed while we imagined we were all going to pieces. Forgiveness arrives in answer to confession, and all the old suffering is gone. The correspondence is immediate, like that of a telephone. Human frankness speaks: "I admit my sin." Divine clemency replies: "I forgive the iniquity."

The force of the whole Psalm is centred here. We are to confess our sins, and God will, for Christ's sake, forgive us our sins. This is the doctrine of the New Testament found here in the Old. The basis of pardon is the atonement made by the Son of God when he died upon the cross at Calvary. We are not forgiven because we repent and confess, but because Jesus Christ died: we are forgiven when we repent and confess, because that is the condition which God has made.

And we need no intervention of any priest or penance between us and God. Christ is the only priest recognized in the Bible. There is only one mediator, and that is the man Christ Jesus. He now sits at the right hand of the Father, and says, "No man cometh unto the Father save by me." All this talk about confession and absolution and priestly mediation is simple folly, hindrance, and shame. The story is told in Martin Luther's "Table Talk" of a German penitent in his day who offered himself to an Italian ecclesiastic for penance and acknowledged his crime. He was absolved, promising to keep a secret of what was bestowed upon him until he had reached home; whereupon he received a leg of the ass on which Jesus rode into Jerusalem, neatly bound up in silk. Of this the man boasted so loudly when he reached the Rhine that four of his old comrades suddenly came out from their promised secrecy too; they showed how they had been to Rome also, and each had gained a leg of the same animal with the same promise of reserve. With great wonder therefore they were laughed at by their neighbors, for thus their journey far away for pardon had proved that one beast had five legs! Oh, why will wise men suffer themselves to be so cheated and mocked, when the Word of God continually speaks with such clearness of warning: "The blood of Jesus Christ his Son cleanseth us from all sin. If we say that we have no sin, we deceive ourselves, and the truth is not in us. If we confess our sins, he is faithful and just to forgive us our sins, and to cleanse us from all unrighteousness."

IV. In the fourth place, the Psalmist offers the grand results of his restoration to all who would come and take them on the same easy conditions: "For this shall every one that is godly pray unto thee in a time when thou mayest be found: surely in the floods of great waters they shall not come nigh unto him. Thou art my hiding-place; thou shalt preserve me from trouble; thou shalt compass me about with songs of deliverance."

Protection and prosperity were the chief spiritual advantages he claims to have received; and he says that any one can have them by the asking; each sinner must pray, and must not be dilatory about it. David intimates that there may come a moment when the Spirit of grace is going to withdraw; and then the guilty man might learn that it was too late for God to be found. But to any one who would now confess and ask for pardon, grace would prove accessible and sufficient. The everlasting God would be a hiding-place to him, and put into his mouth a new song full of gladness, the song of a soul thoroughly redeemed from sin.

There is nothing in all this vain world that can satisfy a soul except the mercy and companionship of a pardoning God. All else leads only to despair. I have just read of a distinguished lady who came to the height of what people call wealth and fortune. She built a magnificent palace for her residence, and called it "Satis House:" that is, Satisfaction House: for she said she expected to be perfectly happy in it all the rest of her days. But she found that money could not buy rest; she grew tired and lonely; and in the end the neighbors came to find her, and she had hanged herself in the beautiful "Satis House."

But God has never failed to satisfy completely every one who has come to him with penitent confession, accepted the free pardon, and so rested upon him with unbroken trust. Indeed, the new life is more far than a mere restoration. Making up after estrangement always increases the affection of friends. No joy is like that which a saved sinner feels when he knows what God has done for him and now is going to be to him in all the inexhaustible future of love. A converted Indian was once asked, "What has your Maker done for you?" He took a worm on the path and placed some straw all around it in a circle; then he set fire to the heap. The creature began to suffer from the heat, and endeavored to escape, but without avail, for the flame was on every side, whichever way it turned. But in the midst of the fright and agony the worm showed, suddenly the Indian opened a part of the blazing ring and it crept out into peace and safety. "That," said this simple son of the forest, "is what Christ, God's Son, has done for me; the flames of hell were gathering around me when Jesus came and set me free!"

V. Finally, in this Psalm which records the peace that David attained through God's pardoning grace, he repeats for others the counsels he received for his future life and conduct from his reconciled God. The rest of the Psalm is highly dramatic. He represents Jehovah as speaking to him in person, almost as if he heard a mysterious voice calling to him out in the air overhead with the words of confident love.

This remarkable address begins with a promise: "I will instruct thee and teach thee in the way which thou shalt go: I will guide thee with mine eye." The Almighty engages to furnish guidance to the pardoned believer with the mere glance of his eye, such as dear parents are wont to bestow in answer to the upward look of their delicate and loving children.

Then with this promise comes a precept likewise: "Be ye not as the horse, or as the mule, which have no understanding; whose mouth must be held in with bit and bridle lest they come near unto thee." Of all creatures the mule is said to be the most obstinate and rigid. The horse is dull enough, the mule is hopeless; both have to be taught and held by harness of bridle and bit lest they turn upon the hand that feeds them. The Lord pleads with his children that they will not grow stupid and brutal in their service so as to need curbing and spurring.

To enforce this he adds another warning: "Many sorrows shall be to the wicked: but he that trusteth in the Lord, mercy shall compass him about." He gives fair and open caution as to the melancholy results of any return to courses of sin when one has once been pardoned and restored.

And the voice of God closes its sweet communication with an exhortation that the believer should come home to his comfort and enjoy his privileges: "Be glad in the Lord, and rejoice, ye righteous: and shout for joy, all ye that are upright in heart." It may interest you to listen to just a little story told of Alexander Peden, as we end the study of this Psalm. He was the old Covenanter who wandered before his enemies for years in the south of Scotland. His prayer was often that God would "cast the skirt of his cloak over him;" and more than once, when pressed by the troopers out on the moors where he could find no hiding-place, he would have the mists strangely grouped around him, and so even the fogs saved his life. These fogs and mists he used to call "snow and vapors fulfilling God's word." Once on a time, when he and his trusty comrades were brought to a breathless stand, they crept into a sheep-house and a few went to sleep. Alexander Peden rose early, and went up by the burnside and stayed long. When he came in he sat quiet, and only broke the silence after a while singing this thirty-second Psalm, from the seventh verse through to the end. As he finished, he repeated the seventh verse over again, and then he said: "These are sweet lines which I got at the burnside this morning, and I will get more to morrow, and so we shall get daily provisions:

"Thou art my hiding-place; thou shalt from trouble keep me free;
Thou with songs of deliverance about shalt compass me:
Ye righteous, in the Lord be glad, in him do ye rejoice;
All ye that upright are in heart, for joy lift up your voice."

XXII.

THE REBELLION OF ABSALOM.

"And there came a messenger to David, saying, The hearts of the men of Israel are after Absalom."—2 *Sam.* 15:13.

It would not be exactly generous, perhaps, for us in easier times to rejoice over another's adversity, but it is certainly a happy thing for the church in all ages that the periods of sore disaster for David were most prolific of Psalms which have brought peace to many sufferers since. The heading of that one which is numbered as the third in our Psalter is a motto which might be placed at the head of many others also; for each was "a Psalm of David, when he fled from Absalom his son." Evidently this was a period of deep solicitude as well as of high poetic inspiration. Things fell down from their plane of happiness and success, and had to be adjusted in painful recollection of what was better and brighter. As we often say: "Sorrow's crown of sorrow is remembering happier things."

But the most remarkable among these Psalms are the sixty-ninth and the hundred and ninth; for in the first of these have been spoken the words which we think our Lord repeated while on the cross, and sought to fulfil as a prophecy of his thirsting. He certainly said, "I thirst," and the evangelist has added the singular explanation of so personal a complaint; we are told in the narrative that he did this "that the Scripture might be fulfilled;" and the Scripture was written by David in this time of his sorrow and shame when Absalom was seeking to dethrone him. Think how strange such words sound when referred to Jesus Christ, yet spoken over a thousand years before he was crucified: "They gave me also gall for my meat; and in my thirst they gave me vinegar to drink."

And then in the other Psalm occur the words which were applied by the apostles when they tried to fill the place made vacant by the traitorous defection of Judas; it is likely that reference was made in this instance also to the treason of Ahithophel; but there is significance in the use which was given it in that crisis of the New Testament church: "Let his days be few; and let another take his office."

I. Let us take up the story of this wretched rebellion just as a close reading of the sacred narrative gives it to us. We shall find a vivid illustration of certain characteristics of this son of David.

1. Notice, in the beginning, that Absalom's conduct began in the exercise of the basest ingratitude. Somewhere along in those dreadful months between David's sin and his repentance Absalom's eldest brother committed an outrage of the vilest sort against his sister Tamar. David visited upon him all that was possible in the private explosion of his wrath; but he could not punish him publicly, for the simplest reason in the world: his son had done nothing more than his father had, in full view of the nation, just done before him. But in this juncture it was that Absalom constituted himself the champion of his sister's honor. This long-haired youth

felt the shame of the family, and possibly thought he could wash out the stain with the crimson blood of a murder. He assassinated Amnon at a banquet, and then fled to his grandfather's city Geshur for a refuge. There he remained for some years; the popular soldier Joab caused the woman of Tekoa to go to David with a parable and an entreaty; and the king reluctantly permitted his son to return to Jerusalem, but he would not meet him in the palace. That gave Absalom a chance again. And now we have two lessons to learn at once.

One is this: *what a man sows he must also reap*. David's boys divided up David's crimes between them, and repeated his guilt there under his own roof. The king had betrayed Uriah's wife, and then slain Uriah: Amnon reproduced the betraying, and Absalom reproduced the murder. That was an instance of sowing the wind and reaping the whirlwind. It is wise to remember that harvests are greater than seed. It is just as well to look along the life of David, when we see so potent a monarch in such floods of tears. This king had nobody to thank for his troubles but himself. He sowed the wind while he was seeking Absalom's mother to wife, against the law which forbade him to marry a Canaanite; he had betrayed Bathsheba and reared Absalom in misgovernment; he was reaping vast whirlwinds of anguish now in the death he deplored, the rebellion he felt, the shame which humiliated him, and the losses which he endured.

The second lesson is, *there is no gain in discipline unless it leaves behind it a better heart*. "Even after a shipwreck," the old philosopher Seneca remarks, "there are hosts who still will seek the sea." Here was Absalom, just returned from a flight into the outside world for refuge, punished with continued banishment for his miserable crime in his father's house, forbidden a sight of the king's face for two whole years, now restored by a generosity as kind as it was religious, and yet using the first opportunity he had of starting a rebellion anew. It is not for any man to say that affliction sanctifies; of itself it sours a heart which is not sanctified beforehand. And he has lost much who has lost a discipline at God's hand; he has had all the weary pain of it without any of the good; he has had the roughness of the ploughing without any of the fruit from the furrows.

2. But now, in the second place, we perceive that this rebellion disclosed itself in the mere show of personal vanity. That is the only significance of such gorgeousness of equipage, and a half a hundred men to run before this conceited creature Absalom's chariot. There is not a sign of patriotism in his course. He had no *case* in starting an uprising in his father's realm; he was a self-seeker of the lowest degree. His ostentation, and the crowds who were attracted by it when he appeared on the street, must have arrested David's attention in a measure. For expressions occur in some Psalms which show his mind was becoming disturbed. We think we detect in his singing a subtle sense of some new force levelling itself against him; the music is plaintive, as if he were worried. But he keeps up courage; he is

not going to yield to violence. His fears and his faith find vent sometimes all at once: "Lord, how are they increased that trouble me! many are they that rise up against me. I will not be afraid of ten thousands of people that have set themselves against me round about."

So here we have another lesson to learn. In this instance it is the epistle which gives it to the Psalm: *all true leadership is taught by the discipline of endurance under fierce distress.* It was with David as with Jesus Christ; he that is to be a Captain of salvation unto God's people must consent, as our divine Saviour consented, to be made "perfect through suffering." We sing David's songs of courage without any conception of the pain of him who was preparing them for us. They receive new significance when we recall the fact that real trouble was driving him away from his palace, and his boy, Absalom, the beloved and trusted one, was the chief in insurrection. The fifty-fifth Psalm seems like a fresh inspiration when we know this: "And I said, Oh, that I had wings like a dove! for then would I fly away and be at rest. For it was not an enemy that reproached me; then I could have borne it: neither was it he that hated me that did magnify himself against me; then I would have hid myself from him: but it was thou, a man mine equal, my guide, and mine acquaintance. We took sweet counsel together, and walked unto the house of God in company." Many a broken-hearted Christian has cried out for "wings like a dove" who has not happened to consider that this king gained his experiences in the midnight while he was climbing up the slopes of the Mount of Olives, pursued by the army of his ungrateful son. That is what gives a sacred song like this its power; the suffering brought the leadership.

3. Once more: we see that this outbreak of Absalom was conducted with the hypocrisies of malicious deceit. How plausibly the man talked; how venomous were his insinuations; how false were his kisses; yet thus it was that he won the people's hearts and undermined his father's throne. David understood it at the last, and described it in the song he sang as he wandered forth an exile in his own city: "The words of his mouth were smoother than butter, but war was in his heart: his words were softer than oil, yet were they drawn swords."

The lesson that comes to us just here is rather commonplace, but it may have its help to offer to some who are relying upon conspicuous graces: *there can be no dependence on mere personal advantages unless they are put to a serviceable use.* The record which is familiar to us all reminds us of the old commendations of Saul in the day when he came out before the people a head and shoulders above any one of those who cried, "God save the king!" We have a kindling picture of Absalom's attractions of person and form: "But in all Israel there was none to be so much praised as Absalom for his beauty: from the sole of his foot even to the crown of his head there was no blemish in him. And when he polled his head (for it was at every year's end that he polled it; because the hair was heavy on him, therefore he polled it), he weighed the hair of his head at two hundred shekels after the king's weight." Such elements of popularity as kingly looks and a fine presence are not to be derided or despised. But if one swells his heart with vanity and puffs his soul with wild conceits because his hair is heavy and his step light, there is no manhood in the possession. The old honest historian of the Greeks says with a creditable frankness that Themistocles was able to make his insipid son, Cleophantes, a good horseman, but he failed in every particular when he endeavored to make him a good man. And that same failure has been reached a great many times since.

4. In the fourth place, we notice that this insurrection was relentlessly continued through a long period of time. Not "forty years" surely, as one of the verses seems to say; such a chapter can be found neither in David's nor in Absalom's biography. It is impossible to put the reckoning anywhere. Here occurs the mention of a numeral which it is difficult to manage; not even the wisdom of the new Revision avails to give relief, for the word is not displaced there, and the margin is content to tell us what we knew before. Josephus states the time, with the authority of the Syriac and the Arabic version behind him, as being four years instead of forty. And that is long enough certainly for an ungrateful son to continue mischievously to plot against his father in so villanous a way. That son of David's admiration and love lived under the palace roof; he was tolerated because he was of the

royal family. He traded upon the fact that he was his father's darling, and no living man would dare to harm him. Such a space of prolonged trickery and treachery is sufficient to show the contemptible soul of Absalom.

There can be no value in a noble lineage unless the position is employed nobly. Absalom had nothing to do with the item of his birth; it would be a credit to him or a shame according to what he should do with it. Honor and wealth from no condition rise. The Bible makes short work with primogeniture; in almost every instance the chieftainship goes away from the sons earliest born. Later history is suggestive. Cleanthes lived by watering gardens; Pythagoras was the child of a silversmith; Euripides was brought up to help his brothers till the fields; Demosthenes was the son of a cutler; Virgil's father was a potter. There is no pretension more impertinent than that which is forcing itself forward on the merits of mere parentage and position.

5. Once more: we observe that this wild rebellion is consummated at last with a lie in the name of religion. This was at once the meanest and the shrewdest of all Absalom's subterfuges. He knew how sorely his father had been wont to bewail his want of piety; he understood how pleased he would be with such signs of improvement in his son. In order to cover his absence from suspicion, and put David off his guard in Jerusalem, he trumped up this pretext of an old vow. Then he withdrew to his own birthplace, Hebron, and from there de-

spatched a series of trumpeters, a sort of relay of heralds, along the roads, each ordered to proclaim that he was reigning instead of David— actually established in power in the town which used to be the national capital.

From Hebron he also sent back for Ahithophel, the best counsellor David had in his government, and a man of utmost wisdom and adroit resources. Bathsheba, whom David had maltreated, was his granddaughter: he was chill in his loyalty, but really the strongest partisan in the nation. The defection of this adviser seems to have wounded David intensely. He cries out with pain; the forty-second Psalm, written at this period, is full of a sense of bereavement and betrayal, cheered only by his trust: "O my God, my soul is cast down within me; therefore will I remember thee from the land of Jordan and of the Hermonites, from the hill Mizar. Deep calleth unto deep at the noise of thy waterspouts; all thy waves and thy billows are gone over me."

Our lesson as before is very simple: *God sometimes leaves wicked people to the retribution of apparent success.* Absalom comes to Jerusalem, is actually crowned as king, has a few military victories; then his downfall is swift and heavy; the triumph of traitors is short. In a part of one year is dissipated all the fortune of the four years the treacherous son had plotted against his father. Ahithophel closes his career with a suicide, and erelong the rebellion is ended; David sits in his throne and sings brighter songs even while he mourns in his heart.

II. But let us now move forward a step; we can mention, in the second place, a few reflections concerning the death which this rebel prince died. The lessons continue to grow deeper.

1. *There is a limit beyond which patience, both human and divine, cannot be expected to go.* When the heart of this royal ingrate became fixed in his wickedness, the Lord simply withdrew from all interposition; so he was left to his fate; he died the rebel he had lived. Remember, this man Joab had been for years the frankest, the truest, the steadiest friend Absalom ever had. He pleaded with his father for his restoration while he was banished: he personally went after him to bring him to the palace. But when this creature turned against everything honest, Joab openly pulled away from his fortunes. For a while he was forbearing, as if the old soldier longed for him to come into a better mind; and perhaps he remembered how well the king loved him. A day came, however, in which there could be no more toleration of war: "And Absalom rode upon his mule, and the mule went under the thick boughs of a great oak, and his head caught hold of the oak, and he was taken up between the heaven and the earth; and the mule that was under him went on. And a certain man saw it, and told Joab, and said, Behold, I saw Absalom hanging in an oak. And Joab said unto the man that told him, And, behold, thou sawest it, and why didst thou not smite him there to the ground? and I would have given thee ten pieces of silver and a girdle. And the man said unto Joab,

Though I should receive a thousand pieces of silver in my hand, yet would I not put forth my hand against the king's son. Then said Joab, I may not tarry thus with thee. And he took three darts in his hand, and thrust them through the heart of Absalom, while he was yet alive in the midst of the oak."

So this picturesque ending of Absalom's career is as quaint and as sad as it is terrible. Caught by his beautiful hair in the tangled branches of an oak-tree, under which his frightened mule hurried him as he ran away from the defeat of his troops, there he stuck, between heaven and earth. Friends swept by, but no favorite cared for him in his despair; the mule ran right on, precisely as if it still kept a rider: and no scene in the Bible awakes more stern comment than this, when God holds up a king's son in the air, while Joab, the king's commander, thrusts three javelins straight through his heart, "while he was yet alive." Here is an inspired warning: "Some men's sins are open beforehand, going before to judgment; and some men they follow after."

2. *When a false leader falls, he drags down his favorites in the failure.* The most interesting feature of this story has always been the immediateness with which the rebellion subsided when those darts went through Absalom's heart. What ultimately became of those who had perilled all their fortunes upon his success, we are not informed. Their hopes failed; they had attributed many excellences to that young and beautiful prince; possibly they had not studied the future carefully,

into the abysses of which they had now plunged. Hereafter they were outlaws and wanderers. There is nothing men are so careless about, and yet nothing men are so often ruined by, as the wrong choice of leaders, in the Church and the State alike. Nothing in all this delusive age of ours can be trusted but truth and uprightness and justice. "The world passeth away and the lust thereof, but he that doeth the will of God abideth for ever."

3. *There can be no advantage in having "a fair chance" in life unless one hastens to improve it for the good of others.* The fact is, we instinctively hold this man Absalom responsible all the more sternly because he had opportunities so fair and abused them so basely. His sin was the more heinous on account of his conspicuous position. His father was a doting and affectionate parent even to weakness; to outrage such love was quite beyond the limit of forgiveness, for there was nothing to start the slightest provocation to it. The great critic Ruskin draws a suggestive line of discrimination: "It would be well if moralists less frequently confused the greatness of sin with its unpardonableness; the two characteristics are altogether distinct. The greatness of a fault depends, partly upon the nature of the person against whom it is committed, partly upon the extent of its consequences; its pardonableness depends, humanly speaking, upon the degree of temptation which has led to it." On this basis of decision Absalom stands convicted of guilt for which no apology could be received; he simply perverted the chances that God's providence gave

him into hindrance and wrongs to others. Absalom also had come to the gathering of his bad harvests. For he had begun with murder, and now by a murder he was likewise dying; he had deceived his friends and betrayed his adherents in a reckless selfishness, and now they betrayed him in turn, when it was death to desert his cause; he had hated his followers in their fidelity; now he died detested, without a sigh among them: "And they took Absalom, and cast him into a great pit in the wood, and laid a very great heap of stones upon him: and all Israel fled every one to his tent."

4. *The hour of retribution is likely to be an hour of melancholy review.* Confidence in the successful issue of evil purposes only deepens the humiliation of defeat. There is even to this day pointed out in the valley close by Jerusalem a lofty structure of stone called "Absalom's Tomb." The Scripture has given us a hint concerning its true origin, but not of its date: "Now Absalom in his lifetime had taken and reared up for himself a pillar, which is in the king's dale: for he said, I have no son to keep my name in remembrance: and he called the pillar after his own name: and it is called unto this day, Absalom's place." That particular structure is perhaps replaced by this: tradition says it is not a sepulchre, but a monument; and Josephus goes so far as to insist that it was called "Absalom's Hand," and bore at its summit a hand as the symbol of power and victory. The egregiously vain rebel, in full and fond anticipation of triumph over his father in the battle, had reared this ostentatious

pillar to commemorate his victory before he won it. We wonder how the swift thoughts surged through his aching head as he hung in the tree and remembered the folly of his hope. The most dreadful pain of a man's career comes when he is still on the field of his existence, but his life is all finished. He must look over the whole line of his history, and find nothing for comfort. Ambition which is simply for self, and not for God or truth or hope or heaven, is a fateful crime. By-and-by it makes a hateful master. Sometimes it would be well for even the best of us to read over the lamentation of Rodrigo, in old chivalric days:

"Last night I was the king of Spain; to-day no king am I:
 Last night fair castles held my train; to-night where shall I lie?
 Last night a hundred pages bold did serve me on their knee;
 To-night not one I call mine own, not one pertains to me!"

5. *A wicked man is reckoned according to his deserts when history makes up its final verdict.* The world knows its heroes: "the memory of the just is blessed, but the name of the wicked shall rot." In a brief time that monument in the king's vale by the side of the Kidron had become a derision and a mockery. We now find the men and boys always casting stones against the battered structure, to show their utter contempt for a rebellious child; the memorial has become the symbol of perpetual shame.

XXIII.

MOURNING FOR ABSALOM.

"AND THE KING WAS MUCH MOVED, AND WENT UP TO THE CHAMBER OVER THE GATE, AND WEPT; AND AS HE WENT, THUS HE SAID: O MY SON ABSALOM! MY SON, MY SON ABSALOM! WOULD GOD I HAD DIED FOR THEE, O ABSALOM, MY SON, MY SON!"— 2 *Sam.* 18:33.

AFTER the death of Absalom and the defeat of his forces in the field—which of course was the end of the rebellion—there remained nothing more than the communication of the news of the victory to King David. Ordinarily this would have been a post of honor that any joyous soldier would have hastened to fill at once. But now the whole affair was complicated by the fact of Joab's vengeance on the prince whose safety David had specially ordered to be regarded. Absalom was dead; and how to break the tidings becomingly was what was disturbing the minds of them all. Just at this moment one of the eager men came with a proposal: "Then said Ahimaaz the son of Zadok, Let me now run, and bear the king tidings, how that the Lord hath avenged him of his enemies. And Joab said unto him, Thou shalt not bear tidings this day, but thou shalt bear tidings another day; but this day thou shalt bear no tidings, because the king's son is dead. Then said Joab to Cushi, Go, tell the king what thou hast seen. And Cushi bowed himself unto Joab, and ran."

Many conjectures have been hazarded by commentators as to Joab's reason in holding back this first soldier and substituting another man in his stead: it is likely that the plainest explanation is the best. The tidings were most perilous to carry. Kings are never well constrained in moments of exciting trouble. David had shown how dangerous it was to bring news to him which would be unwelcome, when he heard of the death of Saul and Jonathan. Now Ahimaaz was the son of Zadok, the high priest of God, and so himself of sacerdotal lineage and rank; but this unknown man Cushi was only an Ethiopian, and perhaps a slave. If David slew him with his scimetar, it would count less perhaps than if a priest should feel the royal stroke in an instant of wrath.

Still, Ahimaaz persisted in having his share in the errand. Soon after the blackamoor had gone he pleaded for his chances: "Then said Ahimaaz the son of Zadok yet again to Joab, But howsoever, let me, I pray thee, also run after Cushi. And Joab said, Wherefore wilt thou run, my son, seeing that thou hast no tidings ready? But howsoever, said he, let me run. And he said unto him, Run. Then Ahimaaz ran by the way of the plain, and overran Cushi."

Now the scene suddenly shifts, and the narrative shows us the king waiting with eyes and ears to gain knowledge of Absalom. It is pathetic to notice his reasoning; he sees a single runner; that means tidings: then he sees another; that means good news. Cushi is doing his duty bravely, but

Ahimaaz now has permission to follow, and he proves the swifter footman: so Ahimaaz begins the parley. Startled, however, by that first question of David, which was about—not the victory at all—but about the safety of his beloved son, this priest evades the answer, and then his abrupt dismissal makes way for honest black Cushi to come up in his turn. Without waiting for a question, he breathlessly tells the king of the victory. But David has only one thought still: "And David sat between the two gates; and the watchman went up to the roof over the gate unto the wall, and lifted up his eyes, and looked, and behold a man running alone. And the king said unto Cushi, Is the young man Absalom safe? And Cushi answered, The enemies of my lord the king, and all that rise against thee to do thee hurt, be as that young man is."

So now the whole truth was told: the son of much love was no longer a traitor, but was no longer alive. This was all that the fond and doting king could open his mind to receive on such a subject. His boy was no more. He burst into a cry of agony, a great unreasoning, uncomforted, inconsiderate cry of human pain: "And the king was much moved, and went up to the chamber over the gate, and wept; and as he went, thus he said: O my son Absalom! my son, my son Absalom! would God I had died for thee, O Absalom, my son, my son!"

It is this manifestation of feeling which becomes instructive to all God's children. Sooner or later we all fall into a stress of sorrow. How shall we meet our heavy experiences? It may teach us to moderate our sensibilities much just to study a demonstration so conspicuous as this of the man who wrote large portions of the most comforting Psalms, but who appears strangely unhelped. We reach the series of reflections, with which we may fitly close the study of the story, concerning the mourning made for this rebel prince by his father. Indeed, we do not discover that he was very seriously mourned by anybody else.

1. *For even a fond parent, it is very weak to grieve more for a loss than for the crime which brought it on.* This wild outcry of David is essentially mistaken in its sentiment. That he was patient was evident enough; but that he saw God's hand avenging wrongs done against God, and launching the retributions of the divine law upon an offender who had defied God, nowhere appears. The utterance of grief he makes assumes only soreness and pain. Absalom was his favorite; this downfall had come suddenly; the catastrophe was remediless. His boy had died in the act of rebellion against his father and his king. But not even a word of sorrow or shame or humiliation passes his lips. Sometimes mourning reaches so supreme a height of personal grief as that it is mere egotism and tends towards sheer selfishness.

Now let us be careful to be always just, and let us be intelligent as to what is the exact lesson here. Heed might well be paid to a thoughtful caution of Chateaubriand when he says: "One can never be the judge of another's grief; that which is a sorrow to one, to another may be joy. Let us not dispute with any one concerning the reality of his sufferings; it is with sorrow as with countries—each man has his own." This is true: a sincere pity swells every heart that tries to comprehend so burdensome a trial as this of the king. But what we feel needs an explanation is the fact that this man once wrote a verse which told us what he should do first when he should be overwhelmed: "Hear my cry, O God; attend unto my prayer. From the end of the earth will I cry unto thee, when my heart is overwhelmed; lead me to the rock that is higher than I." But instead of this, he cries unto his dead child. He does not say, "O God, my Father!" he says, "O Absalom, my son, my son!"

And the issue which is raised is this: a true Christian opens his heart to receive comfort, not when he blindly and passionately explodes into outcries of pain, but when he draws nigh to God and pleads for help. It does not follow that every trouble has sprung directly out of sin, as this bereavement of David certainly did, but that each child of God ought to inquire diligently whether the Lord is sending an inquisition for wrong.

2. *It is better to live honestly for one's children than just to wish to die for them when their retribution comes.* The fact is, we miss the proper feelings of the occasion here in David's form of expression. His language is extravagant; it was very rough to tell those soldiers, who had imperilled their lives again and again that day to sustain his kingdom, that he wished a gracious providence had taken his life instead of that of the chief rebel they had fought.

Think how almost brutal it was to say that he would have died happy if only Absalom were alive again! With that creature for a king, what would have become of the kingdom? A mere sense of personal bereavement moved him. He became unmanly, unknightly, and inconsiderate.

But our main trouble must be found with the absence of every sort and measure of self-examination in David; he sends not one glance of his eye backwards over those vast mistakes of the past which he had committed in rearing that child. He makes no allusion to an offended God, except to point his reckless asseveration with the mention of his name. One would think that the king must have had, even in these successes, some misgiving now and then; something like those thoughtful acknowledgments which history records in the dying utterance of William the Conqueror: "Although human ambition rejoices in such triumphs, I am nevertheless seized with an unquiet terror when I think that, in all these actions of mine, cruelty marched with boldness." We wish David had lived always for Absalom's instruction and mourned a little less for his defeat. We wish he had thought of those actions of his own life in which wickedness had marched with hardness of cruelty to Solomon's mother and Bathsheba's husband, as his son was growing up and becoming sadly like him in his crime. For David had other children around him increasing in years; it would have given him help in bringing them on better if he had been more penitent for the dreadful failure made with Absalom.

> "Life is strong; and still
> Bears with its currents onward us who fain
> Would linger where our treasures have gone down,
> Though but to mark the ripple on the wave,
> The small disturbing eddies that betray
> The place of shipwreck: life is strong, and still
> Bears onward to new tasks and sorrows new,
> Whether we will or no."

3. *Public duties should check the indulgence of noisy personal griefs.* We all admit that the human feeling of the king in an instance so severe is pathetic and poetic. But at that time an awful field of blood was wild with cries of desperate pain from the dying and around the dead. Twenty thousand of Israel's loyal soldiers lay on the plain of battle; and all that David seemed to care about it was that his boy Absalom was killed likewise: "The people of Israel were slain before the servants of David, and there was there a great slaughter that day of twenty thousand men. For the battle was there scattered over the face of all the country: and the wood devoured more people that day than the sword devoured."

It does one good to read those brave words of the devoted warrior Joab in a rebuke: they sound like the rush of a cool breeze: "And it was told Joab, Behold, the king weepeth and mourneth for Absalom. And the victory that day was turned into mourning unto all the people: for the people heard say that day how the king was grieved for his son. And the people gat them by stealth that day into the city, as people being ashamed steal away when they flee in battle. But the king covered his face, and the king cried with a loud voice, O my son Absalom! O Absalom, my son, my son! And Joab came into the house to the king, and said, Thou hast shamed this day the faces of all thy servants, which this day have saved thy life, and the lives of thy sons and of thy daughters, and the lives of thy wives, and the lives of thy concubines; in that thou lovest thine enemies and hatest thy friends: for thou hast declared this day that thou regardest neither princes nor servants: for this day I perceive that if Absalom had lived, and all we had died this day, then it had pleased thee well. Now therefore arise, go forth, and speak comfortably unto thy servants: for I swear by the Lord, if thou go not forth, there will not tarry one with thee this night: and that will be worse unto thee than all the evil that befell thee from thy youth until now. Then the king arose, and sat in the gate. And they told unto all the people, saying, Behold, the king doth sit in the gate. And all the people came before the king: for Israel had fled every man to his tent."

Once we saw in the palace at Amsterdam a bas-relief representing the sternness of the ancient Brutus. Everybody recalls the classic story of the Roman ruler whose two sons, Titus and Tiberius, were among the conspirators that planned the overturning of the government. He sat in judgment upon the enemies that had threatened the realm; nor did he hesitate to do the justice they deserved upon all alike. He caused those two sons "to be scourged with rods, in accordance with the law, and then beheaded by the lictors in the forum, and he neither turned aside his eyes nor shed any tears over them, for they had been false unto their country and had offended against the law." And then the well-known dictum of his was pronounced, which these patriotic Dutchmen have perpetuated in their king's judgment-hall: "A man may have many more children, but never can have but one country, even that which gave him birth." David certainly had very little of that firm justice which made Lucius Junius Brutus historic.

4. *The death of an infant child may quite possibly become a greater comfort to its parents than the rebellious life of another child who grows up to be a pain and a shame for ever.* The counsel was long ago given to bereaved Christians by one who understood what it was to be in mourning: "Do not ask that the enveloping cloud be ever entirely taken up from your home; it never will be; but it may become so luminously transparent that you can see bright stars through it." When David's little child in earlier times was stricken with death, he fell down heavily sorrowing over the affliction before the Lord; but he said in wise and strong confidence of a submissive faith, "I shall go to him, but he will not return to me." But now he could only pour out hopeless wails of grief; for Absalom appeared to have no future in which he could expect or in which he wished to share.

The loss of children is a sore trial, but it may bring to some bereaved hearts a sort of satisfaction to remember that infants who are taken away in infancy are saved from the evil to come in the chances of this worried life of ours, and are kept safely where by-and-by they may be found and loved again. Many of us have seen over in Westminster Abbey a beautiful alabaster cradle, with an infant's face just showing itself from beneath a coverlet wrought in delicate stone apparently spread over the figure. It is the tomb, as the inscription relates, of Sophia, daughter of James I., who died when only three days old, in 1607, and to that brief record is added this verse for an epitaph:

" When the archangel's trump shall blow, and souls to bodies join,
Millions will wish their lives below had been as short as thine."

5. *There is a sad meaning in the words "too late."* Most of us wish we could live parts of our lives over again, to make some corrections. Especially we think of the example we set or the words we speak or the deeds we do in the presence of our intimates, perhaps even of our children. David does not help the case much with any behavior of his in this story. But we begin to feel, I am sure, that his wrong-doing had something to do in the formation of Absalom's character and in the fixing of Absalom's doom. For we carry in mind the truth of the old couplet:

"Who saws thro' a trunk, tho' he leaves the tree up in the forest,
When the wind casts it down, is not his the hand that smote it?"

But there comes a moment in which one feels that all regrets arrive too late for any good to come forth from them: no hope now!

Yet out of this ought to grow some benefits to ourselves or to others, or life is a failure. It would be to edification if we could know how much the wisdom of one of David's sons was drawn from the behavior of another. Solomon was reared in this tempestuous period, and must have been a thoughtful observer of what was going on. Did he gather from these storms of feeling wildly sweeping over his father's experience any of the sober maxims he has given us in the book of Proverbs? As the fateful years rushed by him, and this studious brother of Absalom moved forward towards the kingdom he was soon to wield, did he reach the conclusion that there was "a time" for everything? "a time to get and a time to lose, a time to keep and a time to cast away." There is a limit set; there is an hour that is too late.

Could Solomon have been thinking of Absalom's death, and of his father's failure, when he penned those sad and gentle sentences: "Hear, ye children, the instruction of a father, and attend to know understanding. For I give you good doctrine; forsake ye not my law. For I was my father's son, tender and only beloved in the sight of my mother. He taught me also, and said unto me, Let thy heart retain my words: keep my commandments, and live."

XXIV.

THE VOICE OF A ROCK.

"The Rock of Israel spake to me."—*2 Sam.* 23:3.

It is comforting and edifying to find King David at his very best when he bids us farewell. He sings a great song which he gives afterwards to the Psalter, and thus sends out into the public service of the Lord's house. Then he sings a shorter one full of tenderness and trust, which he leaves to be the crown of his history among the annals of Israel: "Now these be the last words of David. David the son of Jesse said, and the man who was raised up on high, the anointed of the God of Jacob, and the sweet Psalmist of Israel, said, The Spirit of the Lord spake by me, and his word was in my tongue."

Now it will be better for us in our present exposition to bring before our minds the peculiarities of David's experience first, so that we can fully appreciate what will help us most in our own.

I. The whole story of this dying king might be illustrated by a brief analysis of still another sacred song which he had written during the same period of his later disciplines, and then we can give our direct study to the terms of that in which the text appears.

No one can read the twenty-seventh Psalm

without becoming certain that it was written by a man who was at the moment far down in the depths of spiritual conflict, and yet was holding a steady front against his troubles after all. He prays so passionately, that we should deem him weak even to cowardice if it were not for the fact that he praises so jubilantly, and lifts his head with a most unsubdued ring in his voice. The Psalm is like a summer cloud just before a storm, in that it reserves an overcharge of power to be driven on by a sort of induction into the very verge of the final verse, from which it explodes with a glorious flash of lightning, which clears the air instantly.

This closing counsel, coupled with the apprehension of a failure, mentioned before, has been rendered into exquisite poetry:

> "Oh, if I had not believed verily
> To see the goodness of Jehovah
> In the land of the living!—
> Wait on Jehovah, be strong, and let
> Thine heart take courage,
> Yea, wait on Jehovah!"

"Here," says the German commentator Hengstenberg, "is the strong part of the soul just speaking to the weak: the Psalmist is not exhorting others, but exhorting himself: it is a kind of monologue."

It is because each believer has these two "parts" in him always—the strong and the weak—that such a sacred song serves him with such a mysterious welcome. He studies it until he can read it fluently; he reads it till he knows the words by heart; he begins to sing it softly to himself, when all of a sudden he finds his voice rising in exultation, his heart growing into a dauntless courage, his eyes filling with tears as he sings on.

Put with this now the beautiful song which forms the theme of the present discourse. The subject-matter is the same. David avows his implicit trust in Jehovah. He calls him by an old name and also by a new: "The God of Israel said, the Rock of Israel spake to me." Of these two the first is the historic designation of the true and living One who had chosen, guided, loved, and protected the nation from the beginning. The second seems to be a fresh appellation coming from the innermost heart of the grateful monarch as he now reviews the past and anticipates the future. The phraseology is peculiarly dramatic and picturesque. The Rock has a voice; the Rock of Israel had been speaking to him ever since he had been in the kingly seat of power. David's wild and outlaw life had made him know what was the value of a stronghold, a shelter, a refuge. Rocks had been in his experience his best friends for many a year. Rocks were unchanging in their affection for him; they were immovable in their stability; they were impregnable for defence; often he had found rest under the "shadow of a great rock in a weary land." What had this Rock of Israel said to him during this wonderful career?

For one thing, it had told him, as a counsel of superior wisdom, that he ought to reign righteously all his life: "He that ruleth over men must be just, ruling in the fear of God."

For another thing, the Rock had spoken the terms and the conditions of a fine promise. A just ruler would be prospered in proportion to the purity and piety of his administration: "And he shall be as the light of the morning when the sun riseth, even a morning without clouds; as the tender grass springing out of the earth by clear shining after rain."

And for the best thing of all, the Rock had assured him graciously of a permanent continuance of the divine favor: "Although my house be not so with God, yet he hath made with me an everlasting covenant, ordered in all things, and sure: for this is all my salvation, and all my desire, although he make it not to grow." The wicked should fall before him; he must keep on his guard against them, for they would soon be destroyed from the kingdom: "But the sons of Belial shall be all of them as thorns thrust away, because they cannot be taken with hands; but the man that shall touch them must be fenced with iron and the staff of a spear; and they shall be utterly burned with fire in the same place."

Thus the song ends; and it leaves the king peaceful and tranquil in the repose of his faith. Living or dying, he would now be the Lord's own servant. The grace of his heavenly Benefactor had passed by the imperfections of some of his family and the soiled fame of his "house." There had been made with him "an everlasting covenant, ordered in all things, and sure:" upon this he would now be content to abide for ever.

II. Hence, we are prepared to take the whole thought with us, as we come, in the second place, to consider modern religious experience. The doctrine we have traced through the history and the Psalms, and in these final words of David especially, is this: God has given to those who are willing to receive it an everlasting covenant, ordered in all things and sure, and he invites believers to come and rest in it.

What are the conditions of implicit trust in the Lord of our salvation, such trust as will insure peace and comfort? It is likely that most of God's children, sooner or later, are permitted to journey on wearily over what seemed a highway, only to find, at the last, the sign inscribed, "No thoroughfare here." A grim kind of consolation enters one's heart as he murmurs, "Some one has been here before to put up the guideboard, at any rate!"

1. The main condition of resting in the Lord is found in looking outside of one's self. There is a habit of morbid self-examination which needs to be shunned. The more conscientious any believer is, the more apt he is to press unnecessary scrutiny of introspection. Some experiences there are which are too delicate to bear this rude analysis. A woman's love for her husband, a child's confidence in his father, could be disturbed fatally and for ever, if only half as much violence were brought to bear upon it as some Christians are accustomed to exert upon their religious feelings. One can tear himself all to pieces, to no sort of profit, and to every sort of harm. Whoever will read over the

first six verses of this Psalm must be constrained to see that the Lord is the one to look at, not ourselves.

2. The next condition of spiritual repose is found in the avoiding of unwise counsellors. Once a Christian friend wrote a letter to me, saying that she had just, after a long struggle, come to something like peace in believing, when along came a "so-called evangelist to torment her before her time," telling her that "all we have to do is to accept salvation as we would accept a book from Christ's hand." She could not do this so easily, and hence she was informed again that her faith had no foundation upon which to be "secure." It would break up two-thirds of the business firms in the United States if an evangelist were to keep going round among the counting-rooms, telling people that they were in jeopardy every hour unless they could come to absolute confidence in their senior partners; and then they must be sure, still, that they have the right kind of confidence in them; and then they must be modest, and become surest of all that they are not becoming over-sure of anything this side of heaven. Human beings cannot get on with this; they cannot live so with God or with man. We must cultivate some measure of unquestioning trust. We must learn to trust our trust, and not keep rooting it up. No plant grows which is continually being rooted up.

3. Another condition of rest in God is found in drawing a clear distinction between historic faith and saving faith. What secures to us a perfect sal-

vation is spiritual trust in the Saviour, and this is the gift of the Holy Ghost. And whoever says that we receive divine grace as we would receive a book from a man's hand, is simply mistaken in ignorance, or is misunderstood in his statement. Mechanical acts are frightfully poor illustrations of deep religious exercises. Some sort of fervor, some degree of emotion, is needed in order to appreciate divine grace and receive it fitly. Tameness and lukewarmness are simply insipid. It is a heart-trust that God asks for, not a mere head-trust. This was the old complaint urged by the prophet long ago: "And there is none that calleth upon thy name, that stirreth up himself to take hold of thee." A maiden may be told by her enthusiastic lover that it is as easy to trust him for ever with her life as it is to take a flower he offers; she knows better. It is easy to receive facts, perhaps, but not so easy to understand experiences which lie deeper than any mere outward acts. Historic faith is not necessarily saving faith.

4. Yet again: we are to cultivate confidence in the slowly reached answers to our prayers for divine grace. Why is it that so many Christians are like the waves of the sea, continually rising and falling, falling that they may rise, rising that they may fall again, and never getting still at all? Some of us have been brought up in a chronic and constitutional ferment. When one finds it difficult to rest in implicit faith, he is taunted with making God a liar; when he says he has reached assurance, it is insinuated that he should be on his guard against

self-deception. I know the name of a boy, who has grown to be a man in these years since; when he was making his home with an aged relative, one of the very salt-of-the-earth sort of people, he was unable to get the bonds of his burden unloosed, though he lived in daily and hourly struggle for peace. An inveterate investigation of motive and purpose and emotion kept him in turmoil. One day this godly woman quoted the text about casting all sins into the depths of the sea (Mic. 7:19). That expression riveted his attention; he came home from a long walk of meditation, joyous and peaceful in Christ; his sins had been cast away for ever: unfortunately he told of it. "Oh! I am rejoiced with you," said the aged Christian; "now make it thorough; pray with David, 'Search me, O God, and know my heart; see if there be any wicked way in me.'" That set him all afloat again. For weeks he had been urged to stop this endless searching, and just trust; now he was told to stop trusting and just search. For many a solemn year since then that man has thanked God that at times, when it seemed to him that father and mother had forsaken him, the Lord took him up.

5. Yet again: we must distinguish between emotions and religious states. The one may vary, the other is fixed. Faith is a very different thing from the result of faith; and confidence of faith is even a different thing from faith itself; and yet the safety of a soul depends on faith, and on nothing else. We are justified by faith—not by joy or peace or love or hope or zeal. These last are the results of faith,

generally, and will depend largely upon temperament and education. Sometimes one demands that he shall feel that his sins are forgiven; this he can believe, but not feel. Christians are not called knowers or feelers or actors, but believers; for it is the believing that makes them Christians. Christ says: "Him that cometh unto me I will in no wise cast out." Now one believes that to be true, and the moment he comes, and he knows he comes, that moment he believes he is not cast out; and after that he should say, "I am a Christian; the Lord help me to grow in grace." Think how beautiful is this verse: "When thou saidst, Seek ye my face; my heart said unto thee, Thy face, Lord, will I seek." Maclaren compares it to the swift response of the alert and obedient sailor who says over the command of the captain to be sure he obeys it. "Port," cries the captain. "Ay, ay, sir; port it is," says the steersman.

6. Finally, this unbroken courage is a condition of rest. David said that he came near fainting, and should have done it, only he kept on believing to see the goodness of the Lord in the land of the living. We must not think everything is lost when we happen to have become beclouded. That faith is the best which has been tried and tested. In my study lies a little flower. It came to me long ago, by the hand of one who plucked it upon the highest ridge ever reached in the Rocky Mountains. It is of a rich purple color, light and graceful in form, and retains yet, I imagine, a faint and delicate perfume. The lesson which it teaches me is one of

endurance and patience. Away up there, where the snow lies late and the storms come early, it has held its own. The bleak solitudes had no charm for it; nay, I think that this flower was created to give a charm to a solitude which would have been the bleaker without it. To me it is the symbol of trust —absolute and implicit trust in God. It is a living thing that knows how to keep its warmth in despite of ice, and its beauty in despite of desolation all around it.

There was a famous divine who happened once to see from the pulpit one of his friends sitting in the pew—an old and dear comrade in the ministry. He went down immediately to invite him to come up and preach. "Oh, I cannot do that," the man said; "I have no sermon, not even a subject upon which to speak off-hand so!" And the pastor replied: "That is all right; preach to them about *trust in the Lord;* it is an excellent theme; the people always want to hear more about it, and it helps them much. I preached on it myself *twice last Sabbath;* it did good, I know it did; and this was my text:

"Who is among you that feareth the Lord, that obeyeth the voice of his servant, that walketh in darkness, and hath no light? Let him trust in the name of the Lord, and stay upon his God. For the Lord God will help me; therefore shall I not be confounded: therefore have I set my face like a flint, and I know that I shall not be ashamed."

XXV.

THE CORONATION OF A LIFE.

"BE THOU STRONG THEREFORE, AND SHOW THYSELF A MAN."—
1 *Kings* 2:2.

FORTY years now had King David ruled over the children of Israel. His days of strength were mostly ended. He was quietly dwelling in his capital city, infirm in body, weary in heart, and bitterly feeling the results of his domestic mistakes. For his polygamous marriages had brought him only misfortune and increase of care. His children began to wrestle for power and openly plot for the succession. It is curious to notice that in these latest troubles the women come into conspicuousness, each conspiring to defeat the other's plans for the advancement of a favorite son. Haggith put forward Adonijah, but Bathsheba grew formidable from the fact that Solomon was the one chosen by God. It was this consideration which settled David's mind, and which, when the insurrection demanded decision, constrained his action: "Howbeit the Lord God of Israel chose me before all the house of my father to be king over Israel for ever: for he hath chosen Judah to be the ruler; and of the house of Judah, the house of my father; and among the sons of my father he liked me to make me king over all Israel; and of all my sons (for the Lord hath given me many sons), he hath chosen Solomon my son to sit upon the throne of the kingdom of the Lord over Israel."

It will be necessary, in our exposition of the verse that we have selected, for us to consider the somewhat sudden coronation forth to which David summoned his son: afterwards we shall be better able to appreciate the paternal counsel with which he crowned his career as a religious man, and also as a monarch.

I. Most Scripture readers will recall the story of the abrupt summons which brought Solomon to the throne and made him the king of God's people at the early age of nineteen years.

The promise had been given him, under direction of the inspired prophet of the Lord, that, eventually, he should succeed his father in the sovereignty; but David had seemed in no hurry to surrender the position. At this point Adonijah, an indulged and pampered son, made the hazardous attempt to usurp the royal sceptre. Most righteous judgment was this new rebellion upon a parent whose weakness with his children had been notorious; for we are told somewhat suggestively concerning David's lax family government that he had never displeased this unruly boy at any time, even to the extent of asking him, "Why hast thou done so?"

Taking advantage, now, of the old age of his royal father, this ingrate began to stir up a party in his own behalf, and at last made a great feast at the well En-rogel with the intention of having himself immediately proclaimed monarch of the kingdom by the adherents he had tangled into becoming conspirators. He gathered horses and chariots and fifty men to run before him. Of popularity or of shrewdness he had enough to pervert to his cause the warrior Joab and the priest Abiathar. And upon a set day the excited throngs, down at the foot of the valley, began their eating and drinking, ever and anon making the welkin ring with the absurd shouts of "God save the King Adonijah!"

News was brought at once by the faithful Nathan to the ears of the feeble sovereign. The fire of his prompter years awoke in David, and for a moment he seemed to act like himself. Instinctively he apprehended that it would avail nothing for an infirm man like him, now in these last years of his decrepitude, to attempt in his own name to put down so formidable a rising; so, with admirable decision, he sent for Zadok, who remained as usual loyal, and Benaiah, and Nathan, to bring forth Solomon.

These faithful men hastened to obey him, and the youthful prince was put on the king's own mule, and surrounded with the insignia of regal rank, in order that he might be proclaimed at once and invested with the supreme authority as monarch of the realm. Equal to the emergency, these commissioned servants led the train out to Gihon. There they anointed Solomon as David's successor, with the sound of the trumpet in due form.

Gladly was the new sovereign welcomed. The enthusiastic people came up the road after him, piping with pipes and shouting with great joy, "so that the earth rent with the sound of them." This clamor of rejoicing was heard by Adonijah and most of his insurrectionary guests; fear and consternation put a sudden end to their feasting and filled their hearts with unutterable alarm. Each traitor fled his own way. Adonijah rushed up the vale of Jehoshaphat, hid himself in the sanctuary, and finally was reported to be clinging to the very "horns of the altar." There Solomon found him, pitied and pardoned him, magnanimously dismissing him uninjured to his own house, promising him forgetfulness and favor in the future, if he should behave himself.

When our party last visited Jerusalem, our tent was pitched out on the edge of a beautiful declivity, from which the eye easily ran down through a deep valley to a distant, yet quite perceptible, ruin of a fountain. Imagine yourselves there only for a moment. Before you—indeed, at your very feet—lies an excavation lined with masonry, once a reservoir from which were conducted streams of supply into the city close by at your left. And now, with this fragment of history familiarly in mind, come and stand with us where our outlook begins. The great edifices just behind us (modern entirely) are those of the Greek convent, erected by some Russians. That slope to the left is Mt. Zion. The almost dry tank close in front is Upper Gihon. The chasmal cleft between hills, down which your eye ranges, is Hinnom, and the Potter's Field is on the side of it over across. The dilapidated well in the distance is all there is left of the ancient En-rogel. And you are at this moment upon the exact spot where the most splendid monarch of human history received his investiture and first wore his crown. These are the hills around you that rang when the loyal multitude shouted, "God save King Solomon!" Is it possible for any common pulses to keep quiet under the pressure of such associations? Can any mind be tame while the morning sun is unfolding the scene of such stories as these?

II. Thus much for the coronation; now we come to the counsel with which David graced it. We shall see that this was the coronation of a life as well as of a reign. For the words spoken by this father to this son, in whose favor he had abdicated supreme power, are only an exhortation to religious experience: "Now the days of David drew nigh that he should die; and he charged Solomon his son, saying, I go the way of all the earth: be thou strong therefore, and show thyself a man; and keep the charge of the Lord thy God, to walk in his ways, to keep his statutes, and his commandments, and his judgments, and his testimonies, as it is written in the law of Moses, that thou mayest prosper in all that thou doest and whithersoever thou turnest thyself: that the Lord may continue his word which he spake concerning me, saying, If thy children take heed to their way, to walk before me in truth, with all their heart, and with all their soul, there shall not fail thee (said he) a man on the throne of Israel."

But it now appears wisest to add to this general rehearsal a new verse, taken from the more compact annals of the Chronicles, and embodying in its succinct utterance an analysis of doctrine very remarkable for the Old Testament; it really defines piety, and answers the question we labor so often to settle, What is it to be a genuine Christian? In such a verse, therefore, it might be expected we could find help for three classes of persons: for true believers, who always give a welcome to any rehearsal of the steps in salvation; for parents and teachers, who desire information to communicate in detailed particulars to others; and for inquirers, who really wish to be told their way into the peace of the gospel, and so to be saved.

1. What is religious experience? The reply is found here. Let us read over carefully the counsel given, clause by clause: "And thou, Solomon my son, know thou the God of thy father, and serve him with a perfect heart, and with a willing mind, for the Lord searcheth all hearts, and understandeth all the imaginations of the thoughts. If thou seek him, he will be found of thee; but if thou forsake him, he will cast thee off for ever." Religion consists in a form of knowledge, a form of conduct, a form of feeling; and feeling includes affection and submission.

Knowledge stands first in these steps: "And thou, Solomon my son, know thou the God of thy father." It would seem that it must be impossible for any one to become a Christian without some intelligent understanding of the principles of the gospel. A man may not need to consider himself much of a theologian, but evidently he must know that the Saviour died for him. He must be sufficiently advanced to explain and appreciate, for example, such a chapter as the fifty-third of Isaiah or the eleventh of Matthew; or else he would not have knowledge to discern the Lord's body, or to come, weary and heavy laden, to Christ to find rest.

Next to this comes *conduct:* "and serve him." Activity is a sign of life; behavior is the outflow of sentiment: "as a man thinketh in his heart, so is he." When one prays, "Thy will be done," surely he must suppose somebody is going to "do" it. For a petition like this is not to be exhausted in mere resignation. Faith without works is dead. Soldiers of the cross enlist, not simply for camp *fetes*, or for easy quiet of hospital treatment, but for some sort of valiant actual service in the field.

Then there will be *feeling*, likewise: "and serve him with a perfect heart and a willing mind." There must be some eagerness and zest, some emotion, some sensibility, in all true experience of religion; otherwise it cannot have "a perfect heart" in it, in any proper sense. And besides this affection for the Saviour, for his person, his cause, his friends, and his service, a full submission is required. Christ is our Master; and we always are implicitly to obey him, or we cannot have the "willing mind" which King David here urges. In all genuine religion, under gospel invitation and command, there should be penitence of deepest sorrow for sin, zeal of longing for the conversion of others, solicitude of carefulness lest possible injury should be done by any chance forgetfulness in our life, humility of disposition, docile to every suggestion of the Holy Ghost. If such elements be wanting, the experience will certainly be tame, harsh, unenthusiastic, and ungrateful in the sight of our patient God.

2. But how is such a religious experience to be obtained? Once more we must come back to this verse we are studying. The closing clauses of it answer every remaining question: "For the Lord searcheth all hearts, and understandeth all the imaginations of the thoughts; if thou seek him, he will be found of thee; but if thou forsake him, he will cast thee off for ever."

How shall one obtain that knowledge he needs? It is likely that most persons in Christian communities have already gained information enough to be saved; if not, the whole Bible is open; let them "seek" it by study and by prayer. Solomon had only a part of the Old Testament; we have now all that Solomon under inspiration added to it, and all that David did also, and a host of others: and then we have all the New Testament besides.

How shall one attain the conduct he needs? Let him begin anywhere, at the point of weakness in his behavior, whatever it may be. Let him strive to control a wild temper, check a hasty habit of speech; let him seek to become gentle and kind and amiable. Watchfulness and prayer are the means of grace for every lofty attainment. Let each one resist the devil and interdict the flesh and separate himself utterly from the world. One of the converted Chinamen, when he visited America, was somewhat amazed at the fashionableness of some professing Christians whom he met. On one occasion he said, with a most extensive gesture of his arm: "In my country, when Jesus' disciples come out from the world, they come *clear out.*" Compromises are perilous. Satan always watches to attack undecided and irresolute people.

How shall one secure the feeling he needs? This is among the questions perhaps the hardest, because all sincere and profitable sensibility has to be sought indirectly. Our hearts are not under our personal direction. No man ever got an affection by trying to get it. The fact is, religious emotion is spiritually the gift of God. But it sometimes comes graciously to men through the study of the truth; more often it comes through the exercise of obedience. Strike right in anywhere, doing good as best the way opens. Lift those who are down, teach those whose ignorance is worse than your own, search for and urge souls far away from God to come to the cross for pardon. We love the persons we work for, the things that cost us effort. We become interested in the ends we strive after. That is to say, one's very earliest duty is this: submit yourself to God as your Father and Maker; start out with the unconditional and penitent surrender of all you have, and all you are, and all you hope to be, unto Christ as your Saviour; then prayerfully ask, and expect the Holy Ghost to become an indweller and do all the rest for you.

This is the true coronation of a soul, for it is the coronation of a life. We read that when King

George of England was passing out from the ceremonies of investiture to the sacrament of the Lord's Supper, even while the old abbey was ringing with plaudits, he laid aside the royal diadem with which he had just been crowned, and drew near the symbolic feast with his head uncovered and sank down on his bended knees. That coronation of a soul in the presence of its God is the highest of the two; to be a child of grace is more than to be the founder of a dynasty.

And now our story ends, as David glides away out of sight and his equally brilliant son advances into history in his room. We cannot help applauding the grand endeavors of this young monarch to commit himself, more and more fully and publicly before his people, as a servant of the Lord who had elevated him so remarkably to the throne. But just here has been lifted one note of warning. Some of these verses become fairly pathetic as we recall the subsequent history of Solomon. He did not walk obediently in the ways of God unto the end; he left the statutes in which his father walked; he disobeyed the commandments which David kept in uprightness of heart. So at the last his career became unhappy; he wandered away into sin. We shall have to go over this again by-and-by; a merciful obscurity covers his later life. Let us never forget that this was the son to whom his father said, "If thou forsake God, he will cast thee off for ever."

If a magnet should say to the blade of iron, "Cling to me, and I will never let you fall," and then the iron should become wilful and leave its hold, would the magnet be to blame? If a tree should promise a branch that if it would remain in the living graft it should be kept alive; and then the branch, growing perverse, should leave its hold, would the tree be to blame? If Christ says to you and me, "Abide in me, and I in you," can the engagement he makes possibly be misunderstood or misused?

It would be a pity for us to stand in admiration looking at this youthful king advancing now into power, or in consternation wondering at his downfall, so as to lose all the admonition his life gives to ourselves. It is the custom in these times for young men nineteen years old to talk much about chances in life. That is not the earliest nor even the real question. None of us will ever have Solomon's chances, and so none of us will make his failures. The great question is, What shall we do with the chances we have, better or worse?

It is wiser to strike out independently. Some one has said, I do not remember who, that "there are many echoes in the world, but few voices." Are the days of chivalry all gone? Is there nothing knightly or noble to be found now on the earth? Who is on the Lord's side? Who will choose to-day the heavenly Wisdom for his guide, and so crown his life with a glory which patient prayer will perpetuate?

XXVI.

THE FIRST THING TO DO.

"IN GIBEON THE LORD APPEARED TO SOLOMON IN A DREAM BY NIGHT: AND GOD SAID, ASK WHAT I SHALL GIVE THEE."— 1 *Kings* 3: 5.

WHEN into any Old Testament incident there can be pressed the whole significance of a New Testament precept, the study of both becomes a still more eager pursuit. Thus we know that God is the same in character, and the gospel is the same in purpose, through all the ages. Solomon's choice is a plain illustration of the entire meaning of the Lord's command: "Seek ye first the kingdom of God and his righteousness; and all these things shall be added unto you." With this familiar counsel in our thoughts let us take up the story before us, verse by verse, that we may draw from it its evangelical lessons for our own instruction.

1. It will be well now if in the very beginning we learn a fact which not only covers this incident and furnishes a key for its explanation, but covers every Christian's entire religious life, namely this: *every revelation of divine grace is definitely conditioned upon prayer as the instrument of its attainment:* "In Gibeon the Lord appeared to Solomon in a dream by night: and God said, Ask what I shall give thee." Here are Solomon's slumbers interrupted by a call out of heaven. Evidently God is purposing

to do him a great favor; but all that the voice says is that he is to "ask" before anything is to be granted. The grand decree of omnipotence waits upon this exercise of human free-will. And what the Almighty here claims, Christ insists upon in the Sermon on the Mount. God says "ask," and Jesus says "seek." Only we ought to remember that we in an age of blessedness and light, we in these latter times of clearer revelation, have one supreme advantage over those who sought their help under the teaching of that former dispensation; this is no longer a dream-voice that we hear from heaven, but the intelligible living message from the lips of God's Son. And such messages demand the immediate surrender of one's heart and life. "The prophet that hath a dream, let him tell a dream; and he that hath my word, let him speak my word faithfully. What is the chaff to the wheat? saith the Lord. Is not my word like as a fire? saith the Lord; and like a hammer that breaketh the rock in pieces?"

2. Let us pause just here for a moment, before we come to the choice Solomon made, and catch a lesson of general interest like the other: *reminiscences of previous help are an excellent advantage in preparation for present petition.* When we find so young a king referring to former histories in the household and the realm, it becomes clear that he kept his eyes open and his mind thoughtful while the story of Absalom and Mephibosheth in the old times was working itself out, and while the predictions concerning himself were making their impress

on the nation. We can contrast with very favorable comment this unbroken trust of Solomon with the frequent forgetfulnesses of his father and the consequent discouragement he felt. David never seemed to lay to heart those engagements which Samuel had sealed when he anointed him to be king in Israel; so he was always afraid he should one day perish by the hand of Saul. But Solomon stood up bravely against all menaces or mysteries, relying patiently on the covenant God had already made. The great promises would certainly be kept, and on this settled foundation he felt encouraged to open his lips and heart for further requests.

Note his first words: "And Solomon said, Thou hast showed unto thy servant David my father great mercy, according as he walked before thee in truth, and in righteousness, and in uprightness of heart with thee; and thou hast kept for him this great kindness, that thou hast given him a son to sit on his throne, as it is this day." He stirs himself up to a strong faith of devotion by a kind of rehearsal before the Lord of what he had engaged to do for such as trusted him. Now this must be what Matthew Henry means when he makes his often-quoted remark: "Whatsoever God sends down to us in a promise, we are to send back to him in our prayer."

3. Here is another lesson applicable to all experiences alike: *the consciousness of real need in carrying out the Lord's purposes is a forcible argument for importunity in supplication:* "And now, O Lord my God, thou hast made thy servant king instead of David my father: and I am but a little child; I

know not how to go out or come in." Very pathetic is such an acknowledgment on Solomon's part. Most commentators seem to reckon that he was about nineteen years of age; and that is not the period, in modern times at least, when we are apt to find young men calling themselves children. Moreover, we must remember that thus far this newly-crowned king of Israel had been seeking to live a life of mixed motive and undecided allegiance. The record is made of him in the earlier verses of this chapter; his separateness unto God was questionable: "And Solomon loved the Lord, walking in the statutes of David his father: only he sacrificed and burnt incense in high places. And the king went to Gibeon to sacrifice there; for that was the great high place: a thousand burnt offerings did Solomon offer upon that altar."

He loved the Lord with a sort of love, and he walked in the acknowledged statutes of his father with a sort of devotion; but he still kept up a connection with respectable idolatry, as perhaps he deemed necessary for a prince of the blood, and he also burnt incense in high places. But he now felt that he must positively take his stand for the Lord, and for the Lord only. He was pressed with a deep sense of his weakness; he said he could not find out how to go out or come in. What he wanted was, precisely as Christ said in the New Testament, "the kingdom of God and his righteousness" in himself; then he could be a true king. It is worth knowing, this fact: whenever any young man is under the conviction that a responsibility has been laid on him harder than he can bear, he can make out of his pressure a plea for help; for no one in all the world's history was ever put into a place of perilous exposure, for the Lord's sake, without having been surrounded with helps, to be reached by pleading for them.

4. To this argument, moreover, Solomon joins a fresh one: "And thy servant is in the midst of thy people which thou hast chosen, a great people, that cannot be numbered nor counted for multitude."

A weighty responsibility in duties constitutes a motive for asking God to interpose with his benediction of help. Any man who is genuinely religious has an inalienable conviction that the almighty Lord of heaven and earth will never leave him unaided if He has summoned him to the lead in a tremendous undertaking. A burden of care is his reason for seeking audience with his King. He knows he may go straight to him, and may claim, "Thine honor is at stake now in me; aid me, therefore, lest I bring reproach upon thy name by failing when thou hast promised to hold me up."

A bright instance of this precise experience is given in the biography of Martin Luther. In 1532 there was a great drought, and this bold reformer, after quoting the eighteenth and nineteenth verses of the hundred and forty-fifth Psalm, broke out into prayer: "Why wilt thou not give us rain now, for which so long we have cried and prayed? We have prayed so much, prayed so often; and our prayers not being granted, dear Father, the wicked will say that Christ, thy beloved Son, hath told a falsehood in saying, Whatsoever ye shall ask the Father in my name, he will give it you: thus they will give both thee and thy Son the lie. I know we sincerely cry unto thee, and with yearning; why, then, dost thou not hear us?" That same night there fell refreshing rain.

5. At last, here in the story, we come to the exact reply which Solomon made to this invitation brought him in his dream: "Give therefore thy servant an understanding heart to judge thy people, that I may discern between good and bad: for who is able to judge this thy so great a people?" *The first thing to be asked for in God's grace is a new and "understanding heart."* The idea here is a heart of discrimination, a power to discern conscientiously between right and wrong, and to pronounce unerringly for the right. There can be no doubt about the fact of Solomon's religious sentiments in this request. It was not mere intellectual prudence and sharpness that he was seeking. He chose, as Moses did in the long years before, that the Lord should be his God; he was beginning a life of devotion.

As Solomon grew older he would need continual increase in spiritual life. In the order of divine succor to human need, it is the kingdom of God and his righteousness which is to be sought earliest; other advances might be gained afterward. Once, when the pious Bishop Latimer was trying to tell the way in which he, as a yeoman's son, had been trained by his father to shoot at a target, he said, "I used to have my bows bought me according to my age and my strength; as I increased in these so my bows were made bigger and bigger." I suppose this was precisely what the patriarch meant, likewise, when he said, "My glory was fresh in me, and my bow was renewed in my hand." What Solomon needed in the beginning was wisdom as the principal thing; then afterward God would see to it that he had other graces, grace upon grace.

6. Now what was the result of such a choice? There is in the story a revelation from God: "And the speech pleased the Lord, that Solomon had asked this thing." And the lesson for us to learn is this: *he will quickly succeed in life who has the testimony that he pleases God.* From these words any one could predict the future of this young king; for the Lord announced himself his friend.

Think what a history is recorded of Solomon's splendor; what a chance he found for fame and usefulness, what a shining line he drew across the pages of his country's annals. He wrote a thousand songs and uttered a score of thousands of proverbs: he told of the cedar on the top of the mountains and of the hyssop creeping along the wall; he sat in a throne of ivory, and received kings and queens that only came to wonder at his glory and went away dazed. There was no spirit left in them, and yet the half had not been told.

7. We may learn, once more, that *a new heart, wise and understanding, is a better benediction than any other which human wishes could desire:* "And God said unto him, Because thou hast asked this thing, and hast not asked for thyself long life; neither hast

asked riches for thyself, nor hast asked the life of thine enemies: but hast asked for thyself understanding to discern judgment; behold, I have done according to thy word: lo, I have given thee a wise and an understanding heart; so that there was none like thee before thee, neither after thee shall any arise like unto thee." There is something mysterious in this educating force of religious life within one's soul: "the entrance of God's words giveth light." Truth of one kind swiftly affiliates with truth of every kind. The mind grows in power and genuine acuteness under the presence of the Holy Spirit. Solomon passed at once into possession of his vast and imperial acquisition; for in this very chapter is related the story of his wise and ingenious decision concerning the two women and the dead infant which was disputed between them. And the record reads so as to set doubt to rest; it was God who gave him his discretion: "And all Israel heard of the judgment which the king had judged; and they feared the king: for they saw that the wisdom of God was in him, to do judgment."

8. We shall not adequately appreciate the singularity and excellence of Solomon's request unless we take account of such blessings as he might have been, in those times, more likely to seek. The voice from heaven enumerates several of these; kings like this young man would be supposed to wish for long life and many years to reign, for revenge upon their enemies and triumph over their military foes, for riches and renown and conspicuous splendor: these Solomon passed by, and sought the more valuable

though less showy acquisition of wisdom. Now we observe that a reward came to him as welcome as it was wonderful: for God said: "And I have also given thee that which thou hast not asked, both riches and honor; so that there shall not be any among the kings like unto thee all thy days."

It is always so in the ministrations of divine grace. Our lesson here is, perhaps, the very best of all we shall learn to-day: *with this chief blessing of a new heart sought and gained, God grants everything else that is needed.* Solomon took occasion a long time afterwards to put this thought in among his proverbs: "Happy is the man that findeth wisdom, and the man that getteth understanding. For the merchandise of it is better than the merchandise of silver, and the gain thereof than fine gold. She is more precious than rubies: and all the things thou canst desire are not to be compared unto her. Length of days is in her right hand; and in her left hand riches and honor. Her ways are ways of pleasantness, and all her paths are peace."

And certainly this is the familiar promise of the New Testament; to such as seek first the kingdom of God and his righteousness it is engaged that all things shall be added unto them. Riches and honor will come in due order of time so far as shall be for one's good and God's glory. If God delivered up his Son for us, shall he not with him also freely give us all things? Our Heavenly Father is always pleased when any one comes to him in love and trust, seeking to know his duty and pledging his heart to obedience. Just this approach to him, this surrender to him, appears to open, all at once, the treasures of his infinite grace.

Some may possibly have heard of that curious piece of mechanism, constructed so as to give its novel welcome and surprise to the prince who was to open one of our modern expositions. In appearance it was not unlike a clock, but so delicately balanced were its wheels, and so dexterously arranged were its works, that only a breath delivered in the front of it was needed to start it into going. The prince was told that, when he stood in the presence of the vast structure, he must make obeisance and speak to the likeness of his kingly father just beneath the dial: all on a sudden therefore, under impulse of that single word in the air, those hands began to move, the weights began to pull, the signs of mysterious life ran over all its arched face, while a beautiful strain of music came forth as a greeting for the king's son. Something like this, for a memory or a figure, may have been in the imagination of the noted French preacher when he exclaimed, "Prayer it is which sets in motion all the power of God!"

9. The story draws near its end. But there still remains another promise, one act of grace more, which the voice offers: "And if thou wilt walk in my ways, to keep my statutes and my commandments, as thy father David did walk, then I will lengthen thy days. And Solomon awoke; and behold, it was a dream. And he came to Jerusalem, and stood before the ark of the covenant of the Lord, and offered up burnt offerings, and offered

peace offerings, and made a feast to all his servants." *With present answers to prayer always come assurances of continued love and grace to the faithful for the future.*

While these proffers of help are still in our hearing it is wise for every one of the children of God to keep urging his importunate solicitations. Weak desires defeat our ends with a mere mock modesty. The great Augustine was right when once he exclaimed, "We must hold our empty vessel to the mouth of so large a fountain." And indeed, if God's covenant engagements have so fine an indorsement that they will circulate as petitions, it would be well to use them literally and often. It was the lamented Humphrey who was said to have had the power of weaving together the Scripture promises so appropriately into his prayers that his exercises of devotion seemed like cloth of gold.

The great thing is to start right in all our purposes and move straight on in modest dependence upon the faithfulness of our covenant-keeping God; then we shall be certain of success.

> "That low man seeks a little thing to do,
>   Sees it and does it;
> This high man, with a great thing to pursue,
>   Dies ere he knows it.
> That has the world here—should he need the next!—
>   Yet the world mind him!
> This throws himself on God, and, unperplexed,
>   Seeking, shall find him."

XXVII.

THE DEDICATION OF THE TEMPLE.

"BUT WILL GOD INDEED DWELL ON THE EARTH? BEHOLD THE HEAVEN AND HEAVEN OF HEAVENS CANNOT CONTAIN THEE; HOW MUCH LESS THIS HOUSE THAT I HAVE BUILDED!"—1 *Kings* 8:27.

IT is easy for us to picture one of those old Jews going up in after years to the solemn feasts with his tribe, and pausing upon the summit of the Mount of Olives to refresh his sight with the view of that wonderful house which Solomon erected for the worship of God. Worn and weary with the long travel, possibly he had lingered on his staff at the brow of the declivity.

The morning cloud may have still been covering the valley, and through it only a glimpse of an indistinct outline of architectural beauty may have been discerned; and, perhaps, the aged man's mind may have sought to fashion even that into life. But as he intensely gazed, the mist may have parted; then, all on a sudden, the vapors may have folded themselves up into pavilions of splendor to surround the exquisite vision which burst on his sight. We can almost see the spectacle so fully displayed.

Over the clear white walls the sunshine was gleaming, the rays thrown flashingly back from the rich roofing of gold. Simple in its pure loveliness, yet majestic in its grandeur as the habitation of God, "strength and beauty" were in that sanctuary in their highest embodiment of perfection. Its magnificent columns in long line, its stupendous porch and concentric courts around the central fabric, its two guardian pillars of burnished brass at the door, its gates glittering with the metal of Ophir: these would earliest attract his attention; and perhaps (if his position chanced to be near enough) his eye would see the forms of the white-robed servitors going in and out as they ministered at the morning sacrifice within the sacred precincts.

We can soon begin to understand and appreciate the enthusiasm of the "songs of degrees" on the lips of such a pilgrim, as he might sing: "Beautiful for situation is Mt. Zion, the city of the great King, the joy of the whole earth! Peace be within thy walls, and prosperity within thy palaces!"

It is through the medium of such long ranges of subsequent history, so crowded with marks of popular admiration and loving approval, that we best imagine how this new edifice appeared on that day when Solomon came forth to dedicate it to the services of divine worship. Oh, it was a fair, fine offering, the entire surrender of which he now bore freely upon his royal hands!

The stately ceremonies on this occasion are all on permanent record in two books of the Old Testament. The pageant must undoubtedly have been the grandest which the children of Israel ever saw. The inspired narrative grows fairly bewildering with its detailed groups of golden vessels carried in state into the building, so that the act of consecration should embrace actually everything at once.

The reader's mind is dazzled when he appears to see such a glittering procession going into the temple in the Levites' hands. There are the bowls and the golden nets to cover them; four hundred pomegranates of beaten gold; brazen pots, shovels, and basins; the laver, the sea, the altars, with the table for the show-bread; the ten candlesticks, the flowers, the lamps, and the tongs of gold; the snuffers, the spoons, and the censers. All these seem trooping in, during those hours of preparation, like the vast procession of living creatures which once entered the ark of Noah, bidden by the command of heaven. "So was ended all the work that King Solomon made for the house of the Lord. And Solomon brought in the things which David his father had dedicated: even the silver, and the gold, and the vessels, did he put among the treasures of the house of the Lord."

At last the supreme moment arrived, and all the wonderful work of these thirteen years was to be dedicated to the God who would hereafter be worshipped by the whole nation. What fashion of service might now be used in the formula of transfer?

All great things are simple. Solomon was the wisest king that ever lived. He knew just what was fittest. He came forth in person, although he was not an ordained priest; he was royally the servant of Jehovah, and properly representing the people, he was the one to pass over the temple to the tribe chosen long before to manage their ecclesiastical affairs. So he took boldly the whole pageant into his own hands. The liturgy he employed he probably composed himself, and perhaps committed to writing: certainly it has been handed down to the ages with its general form unimpaired. There are several particulars in its literary structure which we might do well to examine in turn.

To begin with, he gave a full expression to the overpowering sense he felt of the greatness of Jehovah, with whom he had to do: then he added the affectionate recognition of divine mercy and grace in the long and illustrious past: he also made his humble acknowledgment of God's wonderful condescension in every part of his work during these seasons of preparation : then mingled with this, he thankfully and trustfully accepted the Lord's invitation to continue to hold communication with him in the future history of the building: and he closed with the suggestion, most extensive and detailed, of his life-long need of God's companionship, praying with all his heart for himself and his people.

Now there can be no doubt that any earnest preacher would be very glad to occupy himself with the prolonged study of this incident as a mere matter of history. The description of these entire services would be picturesque, and the theme would be as full of interest as it would be of instruction to us all. But if one can only link with the development of the story some modern lessons, of spiritual and practical application, concerning truth and conduct, there might be lost nothing in the vividness, and there might be gained much in the vigor. We are reminded anew of some passages in the epistle of Paul where each believer is explicitly declared to be "the temple of the Holy Ghost:" "What! know ye not that your body is the temple of the Holy Ghost which is in you, which ye have of God, and ye are not your own? Know ye not that ye are the temple of God, and that the Spirit of God dwelleth in you? If any man defile the temple of God, him shall God destroy; for the temple of God is holy, which temple ye are."

It becomes a serious question whether it is expected that this individual temple should be formally dedicated as was that of Solomon. And if it be true —as manifestly it has been held in all ages of the church—that each Christian is to bring himself in an act of solemn consecration unto God before even the Holy Spirit will consent to become an indweller in his soul, it is also a question how such an act shall be fittingly performed. May it not be that just here, in the procedure of Israel's king now under our observation, there might be found counsels and directions of the highest value as to the discharge of one's duty? Indeed, I do not hesitate to assert that each of these five particulars in the public formula of this wise and serious monarch offers itself as a step to be taken by every converted man when he makes the ultimate dedication of his whole being to the sovereignty and the service of the God who created him, the Saviour who brought him redemption, and the Holy Spirit who, having given him his new heart, enters into it as its permanent resident.

1. For example, Solomon begins with the expression of his *sober sense of the divine greatness.* He exclaims, "Lord God of Israel, there is no God like thee, in heaven above, or on earth beneath." Now

it will be of no use whatsoever for any human being, who is intelligently proposing to consecrate himself fully to God's service, to attempt to covenant with the Almighty without realizing that he has entered upon the most awfully serious moment of his life: for he is dealing with the one supreme Head of the universe. Even Abraham, who reached the highest stand a creature ever stood upon, and was called the Friend of God, was awe-struck and hushed as he tried to utter his prayers of intercession for the wicked in Sodom: "Behold now, I have taken upon me to speak unto the Lord, which am but dust and ashes."

2. Then, next to this as an experimental step in the dedication of one's self as a temple of the Holy Ghost, comes *an affecting remembrance of the divine grace.* Solomon openly admits that he is now in the immediate presence of that God who was accustomed to keep covenant and mercy with his servants that walk before him with all their heart. He recalls the promises pledged to his father David, and comforts himself with rehearsing ancient engagements, each one of which had been faithfully performed. It is likely that no man who has formerly been a sinner in the sight of heaven could ever have the face to offer himself again to God, unless he felt deeply that his Maker had been kind and forbearing all along, and is yet merciful and gracious, and unwilling that any soul should be lost, speaking with his mouth words of gentle encouragement to all that would trust him, each of which he would in inexhaustible love fulfil with his hands.

3. In the third place, Solomon makes a *humble acknowledgment of the divine condescension.* He has prepared for God this palace; for years he has felt a sort of pride in so magnificent an undertaking. But now in this moment of his highest satisfaction he appears surprised by a fresh revelation of the glory of God. He sees how utterly insufficient after all is anything human heart can offer, or human mind can conceive, for the use of that omnipresent Being who fills the universe and inhabits eternity. No sentence in all this extraordinary address is more pathetic in its disclosure of experience than that we find here: "But will God indeed dwell on the earth? behold, the heaven and heaven of heavens cannot contain thee; how much less this house that I have builded!"

It is the grand simplicity of such an exclamation that fixes an unusual character upon it. The candor of the confession shows a heart penetrated with the consciousness that its very best gift must be sanctified by the altar of God it lies upon before the infinite holiness of Jehovah can accept it. It is this honesty of public admission which shows us that the king bends his heart and will as surely as he does his knees. Oh, how much of mockery there is in our modern consecrations! Just now it is heralded across the world that the king of Cambodia has suffered his head to be shaved in order that a broom of royal hair may be used to sweep the stones before the shrine of the Buddhist college at Colombo. Such forms of melodramatic humiliation have in them some wretched vices of pride. One who brings his whole being to God has not brought much after all. He might well remember that he who cannot be contained even by the heaven of heavens is not highly honored by any gift which it is condescension for him to touch.

4. Then, next, we notice in this story that Solomon trustfully accepts the *fulness of the divine invitation* to continue to hold communication with him in the building he was offering. The record here is so significant that we shall do well to look at its terms; the king quotes to the Lord his special promises: "Yet have thou respect unto the prayer of thy servant, and to his supplication, O Lord my God, to hearken unto the cry and to the prayer, which thy servant prayeth before thee to-day: that thine eyes may be open toward this house night and day, even toward the place of which thou hast said, My name shall be there: that thou mayest hearken unto the prayer which thy servant shall make toward this place. And hearken thou to the supplication of thy servant, and of thy people Israel, when they shall pray toward this place: and hear thou in heaven thy dwelling-place: and when thou hearest, forgive."

Attention was long ago called to the fact that the disciples going to Emmaus were not enlightened so as to recognize Jesus all along the way where they conversed with him; not until they fulfilled his commands in the exercise of hospitality did they suddenly discover how their hearts had burned with the thoughts he had given them. "Not by hearing his precepts," says Gregory in one of his homilies, "but by doing them, did they receive illumination."

The souls that only freely receive, it is not at all certain will be those who will understand. It is when souls freely give, they begin to grow intelligent. Solomon's mind was enlarged as soon as his heart became warm. Then he recalled that the Lord had once said that he would keep his name in the temple so as to be specially there the Hearer of prayer. This it is that appears to have given him a fresh estimate of the vast benediction which Jehovah had lodged in this right of petition at the mercy-seat on which the light shone between the cherubim. He asks as he gives; he holds out his hand as he drops his benefaction out of his fingers. When any one soberly sets about dedicating his being unto God, the very act of giving himself away under a covenant opens his mind to appreciate the value of such divine communications in return.

Mystery then ceases, mysticism ends, and reality begins. There was a mission girl in Africa, educated in a Christian school, who advanced so far in religious enthusiasm that she regarded the Bible with an almost superstitious reverence: at great labor she obtained an entire copy of the New Testament and nightly secreted it as a talisman or charm under her pillow, saying when she was detected that she expected the "spirit of the book" would enter into her, and she would awake some bright morning as good and happy as some of those she knew around her. Surely this is not the way to profit by a gift of celestial charity. One of the loftiest steps of Christian consecration is reached when a man is beginning to realize fully that God has invited him to pray for all he needs, in that very moment in which he has given away all he has in this world. Thereafter prayer is not a charm, but a blessed business transaction. Just as Matthew Henry acutely remarks, it is "the key of the morning, and the bolt of the evening:" provision and protection.

5. So we reach the last step of all in this dedication of a soul to be a temple of the Holy Ghost: Solomon suggests his *sense of a life-long need for the divine companionship and favor.* This lengthy prayer he offered on the present occasion ought to have an extensive study by itself. Seven petitions are found in it, making one think of the seven divisions found in the Lord's Prayer. The astonishing thing to be observed over everything else in this eloquent liturgy, is the commonplaceness of the requests. Solomon talks about trespasses and enemies, about rain and famine, about strangers and battles, about sins, *sins*, last and most of all, as if he felt the supreme peril there must be in the one abominable thing which God hates. It is this final reach of a supereminent trust in committing all one's ways, daily, prosaic, habitual, unto the sole guidance and care of the Almighty, that constitutes the highest act of Christian consecration. Then the soul cries out: "Now therefore arise, O Lord God, into thy resting place, thou, and the ark of thy strength: let thy priests, O Lord God, be clothed with salvation, and let thy saints rejoice in goodness."

As might be expected, this narrative closes with a manifestation of the divine presence. We can seem to see the splendor of the celestial flame; we can almost hear the great volumes of excited voices as those people unite in their chorus with a multitude of psalteries and harps, with the mingled ringing of the cymbals and the blast of the trumpets: "Now when Solomon had made an end of praying, the fire came down from heaven, and consumed the burnt offering and the sacrifices; and the glory of the Lord filled the house. And the priests could not enter into the house of the Lord, because the glory of the Lord had filled the Lord's house. And when all the children of Israel saw how the fire came down, and the glory of the Lord upon the house, they bowed themselves with their faces to the ground upon the pavement, and worshipped, and praised the Lord, saying, For he is good; for his mercy endureth for ever."

It remains for us at the conclusion of this slender, but perhaps quite sufficient analysis, to return to the practical question raised at the beginning of the discourse: How can we most fittingly discharge the duty of dedicating ourselves to God? How can any one begin in the open surrender of himself to the new life which is by Christ?

Let him reflect in the outset that in all such matters he must at once become deeply, desperately serious, for the Almighty God never trifles or admits caprice. Let him recollect that his Maker is his Father: God is merciful and always keeps his covenant. Let him divest himself of all conceit and spiritual vanity, and humble himself before his Supreme Judge. Let him establish open and instant communion in an obedient way with the Hearer of prayer at the foot of his throne. And then let him pass over his whole life and being—body, soul and spirit—without reserve into the keeping of his God. So will he find the Holy Ghost coming down into the temple of his heart as the divine glory came into the house that Solomon builded; so will he find the grand vision of old repeated; so will God's shining love flood the whole being of his chosen child with peace and hope, with joy and song for ever.

> "On some evening soft and golden,
>   In the times far back and olden,
> One who lived amid the lowlands, and within the fading lights,
>   Felt an impulse, a desire,
>   To attain unto the higher,
> And the mountains of Jerusalem allured him to their heights.
>
> "But the climbing was a sign
>   Of a longing more divine,
> Of an ascent leading higher than the feet of man had trod.
>   'I will lift mine eyes desiring
>   To the hills of help aspiring,'
> And his soul was carried upward to the very feet of God.
>
> "And we come to learn, though slowly,
>   That we gain the highest solely
> When we leave the lower things of earth, and stand at last with Him;
>   That the God who dwells above us,
>   Who will ever bless and love us,
> Has the power to draw us upward to the life that is not dim.
>
> "Our eyes are fixed on heaven,
>   And we pray that strength be given
> Unflinchingly to press through the upward, onward way,
>   And that Christ may go beside us,
>   To help us and to guide us
> Till we reach the Home above us, and dwell in perfect day."

XXVIII.

THE QUEEN OF SHEBA'S VISIT.

"AND WHEN THE QUEEN OF SHEBA HEARD OF THE FAME OF SOLOMON CONCERNING THE NAME OF THE LORD, SHE CAME TO PROVE HIM WITH HARD QUESTIONS."—1 *Kings* 10:1.

THE strange history to which this familiar verse refers sounds like a fragment of Oriental romance. If we were not certain that the entire story is inspired, the picture of King Solomon's glory would appear extravagant and florid in its details. Higher in wealth, wisdom, and power no human being has ever ascended than he had reached at the moment when the kings and the queens of that entire continent came to visit him in his palace at Jerusalem, and all the known world rang with his praise.

For we are to bear in mind that this reception of a queen from the lower part of Arabia was not a strange thing, standing alone as an extraordinary event. It became a habit for the conspicuous sovereigns everywhere to go to see this wonderful king on his throne of ivory and hear him discourse. Monarchs could not content themselves with sending deputations to bear him compliments and do him homage. They wanted to behold him as a veritable person, and hear him speak as he was reputed to speak, with proverbs dropping off his tongue and songs falling from a voice that appeared inspired, as indeed it really was. His actual renown as a prince was less than his reputation as a sage: "And God gave Solomon wisdom and understanding exceeding much, and largeness of heart, even as the sand that is on the sea-shore. And Solomon's wisdom excelled the wisdom of all the children of the east country, and all the wisdom of Egypt. For he was wiser than all men: than Ethan the Ezrahite, and Heman, and Chalcol, and Darda, the sons of Mahol: and his fame was in all nations round about. And he spake three thousand proverbs: and his songs were a thousand and five. And he spake of trees, from the cedar-tree that is in Lebanon even unto the hyssop that springeth out of the wall: he spake also of beasts and of fowl and of creeping things and of fishes. And there came of all people to hear the wisdom of Solomon, from all kings of the earth, which had heard of his wisdom."

It will be wise for us now just to take up this Old Testament story into detailed consideration. It is crowded with suggestions of spiritual instruction which will reward our study.

I. We may as well begin with this observation: Christianity challenges the greatest of the world to investigate its bold claims for supremacy as the one religion for the human soul.

It was not mere curiosity which brought this queen of the south to see Solomon. No doubt he was the most conspicuous monarch in what was then known as the world. But there was, everywhere, put forth in his behalf the claim that he was the wisest man in celestial information who had ever lived. Such an astonishing announcement was a direct defiance and demand, whenever a curious ear heard it floating on the wings of popular publication. It must be true, or not true. A question was raised; it could be settled by nothing except rigid experiment. This Jerusalem monarch must be looked up, his assumption put to the test: "And when the queen of Sheba heard of the fame of Solomon, concerning the name of the Lord, she came to prove him with hard questions. And she came to Jerusalem with a very great train, with camels that bare spices and very much gold and precious stones: and when she was come to Solomon, she communed with him of all that was in her heart. And Solomon told her all her questions: there was not anything hid from the king, which he told her not."

Two somewhat unusual forms of expression need to be noticed here. The queen had heard of Solomon's fame "concerning the name of the Lord." We must remember she was a heathen from Arabia; she lived away fifteen hundred miles from the land of Israel. Nearly three months she must have been journeying under a blazing sun and across a burning desert of sand. We shall surely mistake greatly if we imagine she had undertaken so serious a transit because she was merely curious to look upon Solomon's wealth or prowess, his trading in apes and peacocks, his parade of royalty in the entertainment of princes, or listen to his repartees of intellectual sharpness and wit under the riddles and enigmas of Eastern ingenuity. This Jewish sovereign was a worshipper of Jehovah: for that is what the word employed here explicitly means. Solomon's wisdom was not simple scholarship; it was inspiration. He had received it as a gift from heaven; she came to be taught.

The other expression is equally suggestive: "she communed with him of all that was in her heart." There cannot be less in such a statement than the implication that this woman felt some stirrings of conscience, some convictions of need. She may not have been acquainted with God's revelation of his covenant; but had had, most likely, some questions that had agitated her soul. These must have been spiritual and experimental; and her fatiguing endurance in such a stress of travel was a pilgrim's lonely patience. She was on a religious errand, resembling that which in after years took the Ethiopian eunuch over much the same weary path to the same city. When she heard of the wisdom which a beneficent heaven had bestowed on Solomon, she believed that a counsellor so gifted would be worth seeking, and she longed without doubt to test his power in bringing rest to her soul.

So we press the point: this "queen of the south came from the uttermost parts of the earth to hear the wisdom of Solomon: and behold, a greater than Solomon is here." Christ has represented himself in Christianity; he is to be tested in the system of faith he came to proclaim. And what we insist upon is, that every thinking soul is bound to seek, search, sift, and examine what this Son of God, who was the Son of man, has to say. This revelation from heaven for men's salvation is either everything or nothing to each immortal being going to God's judgment. For it claims to be all that any one needs for the final redemption of his soul. Its one invitation is that which it gave at the opening of the parley between God and man—"Come and see." Off from a hilltop in any Christian land the eye sees a hundred of its steeples, every spire of which is either an index-finger to point heavenward with a trusty direction, or is an impudent and intolerable lie: and he who will not set himself to investigate its assumptions is a peril to himself and a shame to the race.

II. We are ready now to move onward to another observation: skeptics might as well pause in uttering their decisons of personal rejection of Christ till they have fully understood him.

It is not every one that is competent even to disbelieve. It requires much thought to dispose of Christianity thoroughly. It is a system that stands very determinately upon conduct; and it insists that, before any intelligent investigator shall come to a fixed conclusion, he shall follow up what he already knows by working it into his life. And then he will, quite possibly, be surprised by further disclosures which he did not previously suspect. There is a great pertinence just here in the splendid figure of the traveller Humboldt; he says: "At the limits of exact knowledge, as from a lofty island shore, one's eye loves to glance towards the distant regions. The images that it sees may be illusive; but, like the illusive images that people imagined they had seen from the Canaries, or the Azores, long before the time of Columbus, these may also lead to the discovery of a new world." There is no field of study of which this remark is truer than that which religious investigation offers. For Christianity, especially, holds out suggestions and inspirations, sometimes highly picturesque or imaginative, for a vivid and venturesome faith to use as hints and lures for further advances. And not till one has followed up his clews to the end is he in condition to pronounce on what he has learned of himself or of God.

This account of the queen's visit gives us her experience after she had met Solomon and had opened her whole soul to him: "And when the queen of Sheba had seen all Solomon's wisdom, and the house that he had built, and the meat of his table, and the sitting of his servants, and the attendance of his ministers, and their apparel, and his cup-bearers, and his ascent by which he went up unto the house of the Lord; there was no more spirit in her." Evidently she was subdued to the last degree of astonishment or humiliation: "there was no more spirit in her." Adam Clarke is willing to go so far in his comment as to say, "She fainted."

It may be advantageous for us now to consider the skeptical reply to these inferences we are seeking to draw from such a confusion as this she manifests. We are intimating that her defeat was on a religious ground: and we are met by the rehearsal of an ancient Jewish legend concerning the errand she came upon, which, it is insisted, gives an entirely different phase to her conduct. The rabbinical story relates that this woman had a previous correspondence with the king. In answer to one of his regal summons to her, to submit to his sceptre, she determined to send him an embassage, and propitiate him with gifts. She called five hundred boys, whom she dressed like girls, and the same number of girls, whom she arrayed in the clothes of boys. Then she gathered a thousand carpets of gold and silver tissue, with a great quantity of expensive perfumes, and added a crown which glittered with pearls and brilliants. In a curious box she also placed a pearl, beautiful and solid, a diamond, pierced in a tangling line, and a crystal goblet. These strange messengers bore with them an epistle to Solomon, telling him that, if such a king was likewise a prophet, he would be able to describe the contents of the casket: that he must string the diamond, perforate the pearl, and fill the goblet with water that neither fell from heaven nor bubbled from the earth. When the embassy arrived, Solomon easily guessed all there was concealed; he drew out of his treasures a mysterious amulet, with which he drilled in a moment an orifice in the pearl; examining the diamond, and detecting that the hole in it was crooked and winding in zig-zags, he took a fibre of silk, summoned a worm, placed one end of his thread in its mouth, and passed it inside the stone, so that it should crawl through to the other face; and, all this time, one of his negro slaves, at his command, had been riding a wild animal from the desert till it reeked and dripped with sweat, with which the chalice was soon filled from neither earth nor heaven. When these exploits had delighted his court, he bade his slaves bring silver ewers, in which the messengers of the queen should wash. Solomon watched, and saw that the boys only dipped their hands, but the girls rolled their sleeves up to their shoulders; and so he knew them all at once; and the witnesses applauded.

From this it is inferred that the "questions" which Solomon answered were only the perplexing and quibbling puzzles usually bandied between the wits who claimed to be sages. It cannot satisfy the needs of the story thus to interpret the visit. This old foolish legend has no shadow of authority or of wisdom. We are not able to believe that our Saviour would condescend to put himself on such a low level of comparison. It could not be that he only claimed to be a greater riddle-reader than Solomon. He was not summoning those lawyers, who thronged him, to ask him a mass of enigmatical questions; he had enough of that, as it was. Jesus was not solemnly and pathetically reproaching his hearers for not coming forward to test his gifts as a guesser or a seer. And we return to our conviction, that this woman was anxious as to things in her heart, which only one skilled in religious matters could explain to her soul's rest. We do not believe —however violently strong-minded or conceitedly smart such a woman may be conceived to be—that she would cross a continent to adjust a match of wits with Israel's king, and then, dumbfounded

and dashed, would thank the Lord his God, who
delighted in him, for having put him on the throne,
because he loved Israel for ever. No: we say
again that her experience was honestly a wise and
worthy suggestion for cavillers to ponder; she was
left with no spirit in her, because Solomon spoke
with divine inspiration. We read the Proverbs of
this man, we study the sermons of Ecclesiastes, this
royal preacher, we even sing the Song of Songs in
its wonderful pictures of the Messiah; and we nowhere find that he wasted his heavenly gifts in
threading diamonds or piercing pearls. On the
contrary, we insist on saying of him in the Old
Testament, as we say of Jesus in the New, "Never
man spake like this man." And whoever goes
meekly and humbly to Christ may be sure he will
find he has no spirit of cavil left in him.

III. We learn, therefore, a fresh lesson: religious
inquirers should not hesitate in coming to Jesus
Christ for a satisfying answer to all the soul perplexities which beset them.

If there were only the revelations of God in nature for a direction and a comfort, there would be no
small gain over what the heathen have in their
poems and dreams; for what would come to us
would be at least trustworthy, because it would be
true. The best minds have often found solace in
the mute world around them. Chaucer used to say
that walking in the meadows, at dawn of day, to see
the blossoms spread against the sun, was a blissful
sight which softened all his sorrows. Henry Mar-
tyn, lonely and sad, in his far-away mission-field,

exclaimed, "Even a leaf is good company." And Ruskin writes in his essay: "What a fine thought that was, when God Almighty earliest thought of a tree!" Even with this for our Bible, our Lord would excel Ecclesiastes: "Consider the lilies how they grow: they toil not, they spin not; and yet I say unto you, that Solomon in all his glory was not arrayed like one of these. If then God so clothe the grass, which is to-day in the field, and to-morrow is cast into the oven; how much more will he clothe you, O ye of little faith?"

But the living Word and the written Word are better for a man, immortal and sensitively intelligent, than all this friendly communing with nature only, for he is pondering questions in his heart. Nature does not discuss sin; nature lives by law of its Creator; and by law man is crushed and cursed, and lies for ever bleeding, and is going to be slain. A new revelation must come for his help from outside of nature and outside of himself. And Law stood grandly and gladly pointing towards the Gospel as John the Baptist lifted his finger towards Jesus, and exclaimed, "Behold the Lamb of God, which taketh away the sin of the world!"

Here, then, we find all we want in Jesus Christ; and this Helper is close at hand, to be reached in the Bible and at the mercy-seat in prayer. So the counsel of the great Augustine as to spiritual perplexities is clear: "I cannot see these things, you say: believe, and you will see: perchance your eye is wounded and obscured and disturbed, by anger, by avarice, by desire, by insane lust; your eye is troubled, it cannot behold the light; believe, in order to see: then you will be cured, you will see."

"For Christ is the end of the law for righteousness to every one that believeth. For Moses describeth the righteousness which is of the law, That the man which doeth these things shall live by them. But the righteousness which is of faith speaketh on this wise, Say not in thy heart, Who shall ascend into heaven? (that is, to bring Christ down from above:) or, Who shall descend into the deep? (that is, to bring up Christ again from the dead.) But what saith it? The word is nigh thee, even in thy mouth, and in thy heart: that is, the word of faith, which we preach: That if thou shalt confess with thy mouth the Lord Jesus, and shalt believe in thy heart that God hath raised him from the dead, thou shalt be saved. For with the heart man believeth unto righteousness; and with the mouth confession is made unto salvation."

XXIX.

SOLOMON'S FALL.

"AND SOLOMON DID EVIL IN THE SIGHT OF THE LORD, AND WENT NOT FULLY AFTER THE LORD, AS DID DAVID HIS FATHER."— 1 *Kings* 11:6.

ON the whole, most thoughtful Christians would pronounce this one of the saddest chapters in the Bible. We had been led to have so much hope of Solomon's career that it breaks our human confidence in any prediction of success. This bright young monarch began with fairest expectations, all conditioned on his fidelity to Jehovah, his father's God; and yet here we discover that his conduct stoops to lowest wickedness, and his religious profession has degenerated into the worship of the worst of promiscuous gods. Nay, more: our very "Preacher" has become one of the preachers of evil; he has denied his own proverbs, he is rejecting his own songs, he has left the temple he built.

I. Thus our first lesson to learn is, that *neither age nor experience brings any release to a man from his exposure to sin:* "For it came to pass, when Solomon was old, that his wives turned away his heart after other gods: and his heart was not perfect with the Lord his God, as was the heart of David his father."

"When Solomon was old:" certainly he was mature; for most commentators calculate that he was at least fifty-five years of age; he had reigned thirty-five years as king in Jerusalem. If any one grows curious enough to ask for the reason of the disappointment, the answer is found in a single verse of the record: "And he had seven hundred wives, princesses, and three hundred concubines: and his wives turned away his heart." In addition to the daughter of Pharaoh, who might perhaps be considered his queen, he gathered to himself a harem of a thousand women at once; and many of these were heathen, and were married contrary to the law of Moses and of God. We may as well conjecture that Solomon had no use for a thousand and one of such creatures; it is likely that he did not share the acquaintance of a large number of them; but his vanity was extreme, and perhaps a splendid harem is to be reckoned among his indulgences of it.

But this does not need discussion; the lesson we learn is, that mere time does not always render men safe; calmness and repose are not in every instance the fruits of experience; even a long public life, with the dignities of office included, is not to be relied upon for keeping one pure and true; a preacher may write the solemn warnings to young men, which seem so weighty among the Proverbs, and yet have three hundred concubines in his showy seraglio. There is no fool worse than an old fool. Wise man it was who said, "Count no one safe or happy till he dies."

II. Then we learn, likewise, that *it is possible for even a devout man to become a practical idolater in his secret heart:* "For Solomon went after Ashtoreth the goddess of the Zidonians, and after Milcom the abomination of the Ammonites. And Solomon did evil in the sight of the Lord, and went not fully after the Lord, as did David his father." Ashtoreth was a goddess whose worship was indescribably obscene, and Milcom was Moloch with but a new title. All this while, remember, there stood the temple of Jehovah, which this man had so enthusiastically builded in the name of the nation: but no longer did Solomon keep himself true to its worship. One by one, in his wandering hours of sensuality, did his old religious principles give way: and at last we find him actually hunting up alliances with foreigners and foes who enticed him into deeper sin.

Let us understand; it is unwise to reject the admonitions offered us here, on the ground that there is no likelihood of a modern believer's committing Solomon's crime; for it is not habitual in our day for intelligent people to kneel at the shrines of false goddesses. The spirit of idolatry is what constitutes its abomination. Many of those who profess to be followers of the Lord Jesus Christ, even in this Christian land, are in mortal peril of putting some favorite idol in the throne of Jehovah. Twice in the very language of the New Testament epistles are we told that "covetousness is idolatry." Worshippers can easily be found in most walks of life around us who kneel before fashion and wealth, before avarice and pride, before rank and political preferment. We are solemnly warned against idols in our hearts, three times in one chapter, by a prophet. Idolatry is still a possible sin to dread.

III. Now let us seek another lesson: *progress by steps of persistent advance into deeper sin may always be expected when one has taken quick start away from the right and towards wrong:* "Then did Solomon build a high place for Chemosh, the abomination of Moab, in the hill that is before Jerusalem, and for Molech, the abomination of the children of Ammon. And likewise did he for all his strange wives, which burnt incense and sacrificed unto their gods." How strangely these verses follow on with disclosures of new defection! Solomon began with weakness and dullness in Jehovah's service; then he "went after" heathen gods; then he "built high places" for them; then he took "his strange wives" with him, instead of teaching them better things; then he "burnt incense" openly to baser deities, and "sacrificed" publicly on the altars. Led, he ends by leading. Turned away by his wives at the first, he finishes his surrender by rushing his vast family into ruin.

It is just this subtle power of the adversary which overthrows the good in our world. There is nothing more to be feared than the unperceived inroad of what might be termed a little sin. The old parable relates that the trees of the forest once held a solemn parliament, wherein they consulted concerning the innumerable wrongs which the axe, first and last, had done unto them and their neighbors. They insisted that this dangerous implement of steel had no power of its own; and they therefore instantly passed an enactment that no tree should hereafter be allowed to furnish any blade with a helve on pain of being itself cut down to the root. So the axe journeyed through the forests, begging but a bit of wood from the oak, from the ash, from the cedar, from the elm, from even the willow and the poplar; but a stern denial met it at each turn; not one would lend it so much as a splinter from its branches. At last, it desired just this small indulgence: give it but a chip—a mere handle with which it could trim away useless boughs, or cut off briers and bushes, for such suckers, as was well known, only used up the juices of the ground; they always hindered the growth of any thrifty tree and obscured its fairness and beauty. The forest was impressed with such moderation in the argument; it agreed that the axe in this instance might be supplied with one fragment which a storm had riven from an unfortunate sapling—a mere little stick, lying there, which no one prized and no one dreaded. But the instant that keen edge of steel was fitted with any sort of a handle, it struck off the branch of a sturdy oak at a stroke, then hewed itself a new helve at its will; and down went the elms, over toppled the cedars, and the hills grew bare as never before. The time for all defence was passed when the forest surrendered.

IV. We learn, further, that *the guilt of all transgression is in the sight of a holy God aggravated by past warnings given:* "And the Lord was angry with Solomon, because his heart was turned from the Lord God of Israel, which had appeared unto him twice, and had commanded him concerning this thing, that he should not go after other gods:

but he kept not that which the Lord commanded."

In the New Testament we are told that Simon Peter's denials had all been predicted some time before; but he forgot the warnings until the crowing of the cock brought him to his senses; then a sad recollection filled him with remorse, and "he went out and wept bitterly." Here we read that Solomon's wickedness became inexcusable, and indeed received deeper condemnation, because a gracious appearance of the Lord had been vouchsafed unto him on two remarkable occasions, and he had been "commanded concerning this thing." And what awakes our supreme surprise is the fact that this great reprobate king is the very one who wrote, "Surely in vain the net is spread in the sight of any bird." He sinned with his eyes wide open. And he it is who has written for the ages the most appalling threat found in the inspired word: "Because I have called, and ye refused; I have stretched out my hand, and no man regarded: but ye have set at naught all my counsel, and would none of my reproof: I also will laugh at your calamity; I will mock when your fear cometh: when your fear cometh as desolation, and your destruction cometh as a whirlwind; when distress and anguish cometh upon you. Then shall they call upon me, but I will not answer; they shall seek me early, but they shall not find me: for that they hated knowledge, and did not choose the fear of the Lord: they would none of my counsel: they despised all my reproof."

It is a vast privilege to be openly rebuked by God, to be checked and disciplined, to be hindered and hedged, to be admonished and commanded. Such things may fret a proud spirit: they will sometimes, however, deliver an imperilled soul. Better, by far better, is it that one's right arm be cut off, or his right eye plucked out, than that the whole soul and body be cast into hell-fire. And he who neglects his privileges is sure to have them reacting upon him by-and-by, and hurrying him down faster into wrong. Sadder eyes this pitying world never beholds below than those of such men as look wistfully back over the years of gracious opportunity, with only the knowledge left to them then that the days *have been* in which they could have been prospered and pardoned. Once having put their bright chances behind them, they laughed at the helps they would give worlds to bring back!

V. We reach another lesson: *retribution gathers up the entire history of the sinner, even if it is discharged in one act:* "Wherefore the Lord said unto Solomon, Forasmuch as this is done of thee, and thou hast not kept my covenant and my statutes which I have commanded thee, I will surely rend the kingdom from thee, and will give it to thy servant." Henceforward it would do no good for this rejected monarch to awake himself to paternal zeal, and try to build up the fortunes of his shattered realm for his children. The kingdom would certainly go to wreck soon, anyway, and nothing he could do would avail to stay the advance of its doom. The son must suffer for the father's guilt, the throne would be troubled because of the king's transgression. People and ruler were going to drag each other down with reciprocal plotting. There was no opening left now even for some patriot's fidelity; retrieval was impossible.

It is often worth while to attempt to avert a great catastrophe; but one of the punishments sometimes inflicted for sin is the denial to the sinners of all success in after usefulness. A little child in Holland was once trudging home in the night along the pathway skirting a dyke. It was near the full of the moon, and he noticed that the water was trickling, like a white thread, through a small crevice in one of the wide canals close by the sea. He was wise enough to know that this opening would be spreading every moment, and would soon let in the wash of awful waves over all the flat regions behind. At once he started to run, hoping to summon help. But then, he thought to himself, he could stop the stream with his own hand now, but before workmen could be found it might be too large to control. So he, a humble patriot, sat down on the bank, and thrust his small palm with a mere sod of grass into the leak. And the stars came out, and the hours sped slowly, and the ocean air chilled him to the bone. Still, that heroic young watcher kept his post until the gray morning dawned. The village clergyman, out upon his early pastoral errands, was the first one to find the small pale creature, shivering there under the quiet stars. "What are you trying to do?" he asked. "I am saving the dear country from being drowned," replied the child. To his surprise, the good man suddenly burst into tears. "O my child," he exclaimed, "it is not of the least avail now! *no use, no use;* for the dykes are to be torn away to-morrow: the enemy is coming: our homes are to sink under the billows; our men fail; the whole army surrenders!"

Thus, often in God's retributive providence, one who has committed sin has forfeited his hope for the future. He feels it as his punishment that no power of his can retrieve the injury; no fidelity of friends, lofty or lowly, no patience, no further self-sacrifice, will avail to stay the sure ruin just on ahead. No use! no use! the day of opportunity is ended, and the night of judgment comes with its gloom. And what makes it all seem so fatally hopeless is the understanding at last, in this swift sweep of the soul over the whole position, that the cause of the abrupt outbreak of retribution is not to be looked for alone in some single sin, which may have served as a final grain of dust to sway the balance of justice, but in the whole gathered mass of iniquity, that has been growing, perhaps, for years. Here, again, we clinch the admonition with Solomon's own words: "All this have I seen, and applied my heart unto every work that is done under the sun: there is a time wherein one man ruleth over another to his own hurt. And so I saw the wicked buried, who had come and gone from the place of the holy, and they were forgotten in the city where they had so done: this is also vanity. Because sentence against an evil work is not executed speedily, therefore the heart of the sons of men is fully set in them to do evil. Though a sinner do evil a hundred times, and his days be prolonged, yet surely I know that it shall be well with them that fear God, which fear before him: but it shall not be well with the wicked, neither shall he prolong his days, which are as a shadow; because he feareth not before God."

VI. Finally, we learn *it may be possible to misunderstand and even pervert God's forbearance into excuse for further sin:* "Notwithstanding, in thy days I will not do it for David thy father's sake: but I will rend it out of the hand of thy son. Howbeit, I will not rend away all the kingdom; but will give one tribe to thy son, for David my servant's sake, and for Jerusalem's sake which I have chosen."

Here, twice in succession, are men told that the almighty God was bearing all this provocation, and patiently withholding his hand from an infliction of judgment, not for Solomon's sake in the least, but for the sake of David, and for the sake of Jerusalem, which he had chosen. But the king took advantage of a delay so kind for fresh sin. Such conduct was a daring perversion of divine long-suffering almost incredible. Solomon plunged forward into new wickedness, and stayed not to consider. On the shore of eternal history stands this beacon-light for human warning. The wisest man in the world lived to behave like a fool!

Strange it is that the strongest comment with which we retire from the study of this chapter was made by Solomon himself: "He that deviseth to do evil shall be called a mischievous person. The thought of foolishness is sin: and the scorner is an abomination to men. If thou faint in the day of adversity, thy strength is small. If thou forbear to deliver them that are drawn unto death, and those that are ready to be slain; if thou sayest, Behold, we knew it not; doth not he that pondereth the heart consider it? and he that keepeth thy soul, doth not he know it? and shall not he render to every man according to his works?"

It does not seem worth while to discuss hastily the question which has been raised by some concerning Solomon's future retribution. We have no right to invade the reserve of the Almighty. If only we had the dates certainly, we could say perhaps that he repented at the last, was graciously forgiven, and died leaving behind him the book of Ecclesiastes as his testimony for holiness and his protest against sin. The Greek Church divided irreconcilably from the Latin in the utterance of dogmatic opinion. We cannot reason from silence. Does it appear possible that one who had once shown himself so truly religious and prayerful, who had assuredly been inspired to write several books of the Bible, could have been left at the last to be a castaway? One passage there is in Nehemiah's history which says, even while recounting his crimes, that this king was "beloved of his God." There we can afford to leave his name, his fame, his soul.

BRIGHT AND SUGGESTIVE BOOKS

BY REV. CHARLES S. ROBINSON, D. D., LL. D.

STUDIES IN MARK'S GOSPEL. 12mo. 300 pp. Cloth, $1 25. Stout paper with cloth back, 50 cents. Covering week by week the Sunday-school lessons for the first half of 1889.

"A very helpful volume. Few men can write so usefully and so well."—CHRISTIAN INQUIRER.

FROM SAMUEL TO SOLOMON. (In press.) 12mo. 310 pp. Cl., $1 25; stout paper, 50 cts. A fresh and thoughtful book for Sunday-school teachers for the last half of 1889.

STUDIES IN THE NEW TESTAMENT. 12mo. 316 pp. Cl., $1 25. 27 interesting and instructive chapters.

STUDIES OF NEGLECTED TEXTS. 12mo. 329 pp. Cloth, $1 25.

"Will be read and relished, and leave lasting impressions."—NATIONAL BAPTIST.

"Marked by evangelical fervor, doctrinal soundness, and felicity of illustration, and that, above everything else, they are popularly readable."—S. S. TIMES.

SABBATH EVENING SERMONS. 12mo. 306 pp. Cloth, $1 25. Quiet and meditative; suited to a Sabbath evening at home.

SERMONS IN SONGS. 12mo. 322 pp. $1 25. Written *con amore* by one specially fond of sacred song.

CHURCH WORK. 12mo. 319 pp. $1 25. 26 Sermons: "The Common Humanity," Prov. 22:2; "Division of Labor," John 4:37; "Faith and Failure," Num. 14:48, etc., etc.

BETHEL AND PENUEL. 12mo. 317 pp. $1 25. 26 Sermons: "A Man Asleep," Gen. 28:11; "The Ladder of Life," Gen. 28:12; "Wrestling Jacob," Gen. 32:24, etc., etc.

American Tract Society,

150 Nassau St., New York; Boston, 54 Bromfield St.; Philadelphia, 1512 Chestnut St.; Rochester, 93 State St.; Chicago, 122 Wabash Ave.; Cincinnati, 176 Elm St.; San Francisco, 735 Market St.

INSTRUCTIVE VOLUMES.

By that eminent author

REV. E. F. BURR, D. D., LL. D.

ECCE CŒLUM. 12mo. 198 pp. $1.

"I have gotten a better idea of Astronomy, as a whole, from it than I ever got before from all other sources."—HORACE BUSHNELL.

PATER MUNDI; or Modern Science Testifying to the Heavenly Father. First Series. 12mo. 307 pp. $1 25.

"It discusses with masterly ability the testimonies of Modern Science to the being of a God."—PRESBYTERIAN REVIEW.

PATER MUNDI; or The Doctrine of Evolution. Second Series. 12mo. 370 pp. $1 25.

"A complete and unanswerable reply to Evolutionism."—LUTHERAN QUARTERLY REVIEW.

AD FIDEM. 12mo. 388 pp. $1 50.

"One of the finest defences of the Christian religion that has been made in this country."—CHRISTIAN QUARTERLY.

TEMPTED TO UNBELIEF. 12mo. 224 pp. $1.

"We should like to see it circulating actively from house to house in every community."—CONGREGATIONALIST.

CELESTIAL EMPIRES. 12mo. 302 pp. $1 50.

"A very grand view of the revelations of science."—Prof. JAMES DANA.

UNIVERSAL BELIEFS. 12mo. 312 pp. $1 25.

"An able and opportune volume, forcibly setting forth essential truths."—President MARK HOPKINS.

LONG AGO: as Interpreted by the Nineteenth Century. 12mo. 388 pp. Cloth, $1 50.

"We cannot too strongly recommend this book. We have been greatly impressed by it, and would consider we had done our readers a great service if we could induce them every one to buy and read it."—CHRISTIAN NATION.

"The author has placed Bible readers under obligations to him for the graphic and life-like pictures he has given them."—REF. CHURCH MESSENGER.

American Tract Society,

150 Nassau St., New York; Boston, 54 Bromfield St.; Philadelphia, 1512 Chestnut St.; Rochester, 93 State St.; Chicago, 122 Wabash Ave.; Cincinnati, 176 Elm St.; San Francisco, 735 Market St.

www.ingramcontent.com/pod-product-compliance
Lightning Source LLC
Chambersburg PA
CBHW022048230426
43672CB00008B/1109